THE COMPLETE
VEGETARIAN
COOKBOOK

THE COMPLETE
VEGETARIAN
COOKBOOK

THUNDER BAY
P·R·E·S·S

Vegetable and Watercress Soup, page 50

Lentil Rissoles, page 172

Asparagus and Pistachio Risotto, page 171

Contents

Asparagus and Mushroom Salad, page 111

You will find the following cookery ratings on the recipes in this book:

A single pot symbol indicates a recipe that is simple and generally straightforward to make—perfect for beginners.

Two symbols indicate the need for just a little more care and a little more time.

Three symbols indicate special recipes that need more investment in time, care and patience—but the results are worth it.

Vegetable Casserole with Herb Dumplings, page 201

Vegetable Shapes with Crème Fraîche and Fried Leek, page 219

Spinach and Feta Triangles, page 65

Pumpkin and Basil Lasagne, page 90

The Vegetarian Choice

People can be drawn to a vegetarian diet for a variety of reasons. Some have ethical or health concerns, for others it is a matter of religious belief. But for many the decision to stop eating meat could just as easily be an aesthetic or gastronomic one. The variety of fresh seasonal ingredients, abundance of possible dishes and scope that vegetarian cuisine offers for creative cooking and eating are often dismissed or not recognised by confirmed meat-eaters.

For many in the developed world, meat has always been the easy option. Certainly meat dishes have appeared through the ages as the centrepiece of most meals. This tradition has led to a diet often lacking in variety and, consequently, in a beneficial balance of nutrients, as well as to the health consequences of eating too many saturated fats. A diet that over-emphasises meat is a product of affluence, and not necessarily a good one.

Many people have recognised an imbalance in their way of eating and are modifying the amount of flesh foods included in their diets. The discovery of vegetarian food often begins in this way. As people gain confidence, experiment more and discover the pleasures of cooking vegetarian foods they often welcome increased vitality and say goodbye to weight problems. Other benefits might be clearer skin and a more regular and comfortable bowel. Many choose to abandon eating meat altogether.

The term 'vegetarian' is used quite loosely. Some people call themselves vegetarian or 'semi-vegetarian' while still eating a little fish or chicken and no red meat. Many just exclude all meat and fish from their diets. Vegans, on the other hand, exclude all other animal products such as milk, cheese and eggs as well. Most vegetarians, however, are lacto-ovo vegetarians who still eat eggs and dairy products.

This book features no flesh foods, or products from them such as fish sauce or shrimp paste. It is not specifically a vegan cookbook, in that dairy foods such as eggs, butter, cheese and cream are used liberally. However, there are plenty of recipes that are suitable for vegans, particularly in the grains, pulses and tofu chapter. Nor is this a book of vegetarian substitutes for a meat-centred diet, offering recipes for pale imitations of meatloaf or burgers, or fake meat flavourings. The recipes are for anyone who loves preparing, serving and eating good food. It is neither a diet nor a health-food book, but is designed to expand the menu of possibilities, to show that one can be a connoisseur of good food, a fine cook and a vegetarian.

THE VEGETARIAN HEALTHY FOOD PYRAMID

If you were raised a vegetarian (and children thrive on a vegetarian diet), you are probably already in the habit of making sure all your nutritional needs are met. But for those just making the transition, there are a few things to bear in mind. It is just as possible to have a poor diet eating exclusively vegetarian foods as it is eating excessive amounts of animal products. The vegetarian healthy food pyramid is a good starting point if you want to check whether your diet is adequate. Its principles are simple:

EAT MOST
GRAINS: wheat, rice, barley, corn, oats, rye, millet, buckwheat
FOODS MADE FROM GRAINS: pasta, bread, wholegrain breakfast cereals
FRUIT AND VEGETABLES

EAT MODERATELY
DAIRY: milk, yoghurt, cheese
PULSES: peas, beans of all kinds, lentils
NUTS
EGGS

EAT LEAST
SUGARS: sugar, honey
FATS: butter, cream, margarine, oils, coconut milk
STIMULANTS: alcohol, tea, coffee

Meal-planning becomes easier if you make a habit of glancing at the food pyramid as a guide. There should be in each day a majority of foods from the 'Eat Most' group: fruit, cereals and toast for breakfast, bread or bread rolls, salads or cooked vegetable dishes and fruit for lunch or dinner; and pasta or rice-based main course for your largest meal (whether that's at lunchtime or in the evening) with fresh bread or rolls, and more fruit for dessert or snacks.

Small amounts of dairy foods from the 'Eat Moderately' group should form part of the day's meals (unless, or course, you are a vegan): yoghurt with breakfast or lunch, a little cheese with lunch or dinner. Being a vegetarian certainly doesn't mean going hungry: your main meal should include plenty of carbohydrate and protein—dishes and hearty soups made from beans or lentils, as well as egg dishes. Nuts are great for snacking.

The 'Eat Least' category means exactly that—a little butter or margarine on your breakfast toast, a drizzle of virgin olive oil with the salad

EAT LEAST

EAT MODERATELY

EAT MOST

The vegetarian pyramid

or to stir-fry the evening meal, a glass of wine with dinner. Like most things in life, sugary treats are fine, as long as they are enjoyed in moderation. You can balance the nutritional content of the day's meals so that the overall pattern easily satisfies the food pyramid guidelines. Compensate for an unavoidably fatty lunch, for example, with an evening meal made up of vegetables, grains and fruit.

THE MAJOR FOOD GROUPS
Over the following pages you will find more information about the different nutritional groups that make up the foods in the vegetarian healthy eating pyramid (protein, carbohydrates, dietary fibre and fat), including their value to our bodies, their importance in the vegetarian diet and the best sources for finding them. So that you can be a creative cook *and* a well-informed vegetarian.

Protein

Nobody needs huge amounts of protein from any source, but everybody needs some. Growing children and pregnant women need a little more than other people. Protein provides the basic structure for the human body—it is the main source of building material for our cells, tissues, muscles, nails, hair, skin, bones, blood and internal organs. We need protein to make and repair cells and tissues and to create hormones, enzymes, antibodies and other immune-system molecules. It is also needed for the regulation of the body's internal environment, including acid and alkaline balance, water balance, and the proper elimination of wastes. However, although it performs all these important tasks, our daily requirements are actually quite small.

AND WHAT IS IT?
Protein is made up of small compounds known as amino acids, which are arranged in chains of varying combinations. There are 23 amino acids, most of which are termed 'non-essential' as they can be made in the body.

But not all amino acids can be manufactured in the body—some must be derived from the diet, and these are termed the 'essential' amino acids. There are eight essential amino acids for adults—isoleucine, leucine, lysine, phenylalanine, methionine, threonine, tryptophan, valine—and an extra one, histidine, for infants.

Sources of these essential amino acids are animal products: meat, poultry, fish and dairy foods. This is why some people worry that a vegetarian diet will be lacking in essential nutrients. But there is no need for concern as there are many good vegetarian and vegan sources of protein: nuts and legumes (beans, peas, lentils, soya beans and products such as soy flour, soy milk, tofu and tempeh). However, these foods don't contain *all* the essential amino acids in the one food source like animal proteins do.

Plant proteins do have an advantage over animal proteins, as they contain fibre and carbohydrates, which makes them easy to digest as well as being high in vitamins and minerals and low in saturated fats and kilojoules.

IS FOOD-COMBINING REALLY NECESSARY?
In the past it was thought that because no one vegetarian source of protein contains *all* the essential amino acids, it was necessary to carefully combine vegetarian proteins with other foods, such as wholegrains, to provide all the essential amino acids in their correct proportions. This was known as 'food-combining' and, although it sound complicated, it's really very simple… baked beans on toast, or dhal with pitta bread are both ideal examples of food-combining which have evolved into our everyday diet.

However, recent research suggests that as long as there is a healthy mix of legumes, nuts, seeds, wholegrains and vegetables in the diet overall, the body will obtain enough protein for its needs. So, once again, the basic message is to have a balanced diet.

DAILY INTAKE
Our daily requirement of protein is approximately 12–20 per cent of our total kilojoule intake, varying according to an individual's size, weight, health and levels of stress and activity. Extra protein is needed during periods of growth: childhood, adolescence, pregnancy and lactation.

PROTEIN DEFICIENCY
It must be noted that Western vegetarians have very little chance of suffering from a protein deficiency. Insufficient protein in the diet can result in physical symptoms such as anaemia, lethargy, muscle weakness and wasting, dry and dull hair, dry skin and poor wound healing.

PROTEIN IN EXCESS
In most Western diets, in fact, there is a much greater chance of consuming an excess of protein than there is of not consuming enough. It is easy to get concerned about protein—this is probably a legacy of the meat-rich diets of the past—but the truth is that most people eat far more protein than they need and if there is too much protein in the diet it is simply converted to body fat.

BEST LEGUMES for protein

Black beans	Lentils
Black-eyed beans	Mung beans
Broad beans	Navy beans
Chickpeas	Peas
Kidney beans	Soya beans

SAMPLE MEALS — one of these will provide your daily protein.

BREAKFAST
- Muesli with soy milk (top with ground nuts/seeds and banana)
- Porridge with soy milk
- Baked beans on wholemeal toast
- Boiled egg with wholemeal toast
- Nut butter (e.g. almond, brazil, cashew or peanut) on toast

LUNCH
- Lentil/bean/pea curry with rice
- Lentil and spinach soup (page 48)
- Beetroot hummus (page 233) and salad in wholemeal pitta bread
- Felafel with tomato salsa (page 227)
- Bean nachos (page 226) with avocado
- Miso soup with tofu, rice and vegetables
- Soya bean/tofu burger

DINNER
- Dhal and rice
- Tofu with rice and vegetables
- Mushroom risotto (page 179)
- Barbecue vegetable and tofu kebabs (page 182) with tomato sauce
- Mushroom nut roast with tomato sauce (page 194)

SNACKS
- Seeds (sesame or sunflower)
- Tamari nut mix (page 220)
- Tahini/hummus on wholewheat/rye/rice crackers

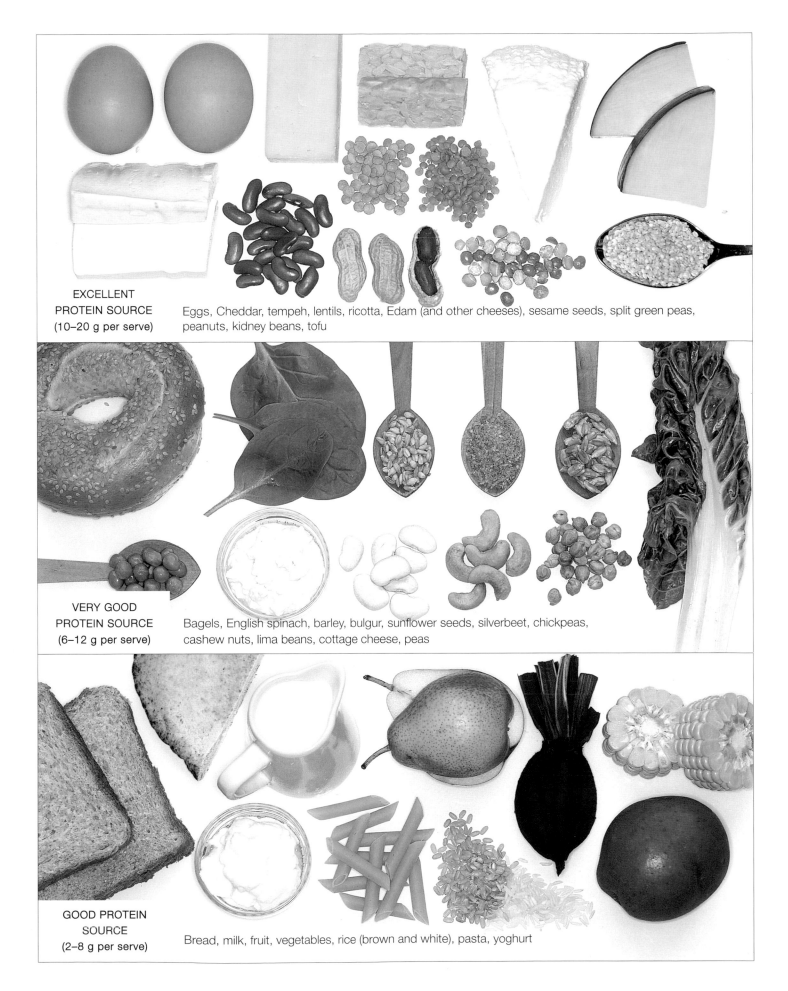

EXCELLENT PROTEIN SOURCE
(10–20 g per serve)

Eggs, Cheddar, tempeh, lentils, ricotta, Edam (and other cheeses), sesame seeds, split green peas, peanuts, kidney beans, tofu

VERY GOOD PROTEIN SOURCE
(6–12 g per serve)

Bagels, English spinach, barley, bulgur, sunflower seeds, silverbeet, chickpeas, cashew nuts, lima beans, cottage cheese, peas

GOOD PROTEIN SOURCE
(2–8 g per serve)

Bread, milk, fruit, vegetables, rice (brown and white), pasta, yoghurt

Carbohydrates

The principal energy source in the diet is carbohydrate. The vital role carbohydrates play cannot be underestimated as they provide fuel for both the muscles and the brain. Carbohydrates occur in the form of starches and sugars from grains and their products (e.g. flour, bread, pasta) as well as potatoes, legumes, fruits and, to a lesser degree, nuts.

WHAT DO THEY DO?

Carbohydrates break down in the body into glucose and glycogen, both of which are used for energy. The body uses up glucose first and if there is a shortage (for example, during exercise) it converts glycogen, which is stored in the liver, to glucose.

Carbohydrates are generally divided into two categories: simple and complex. A simple carbohydrate is consumed in a form closest to sugar, which takes little breaking down by the body, giving a quick rush of energy, then usually a drop which makes you feel tired or down.

Complex carbohydrates take longer to break down in the body, giving a slower release of sugar and more sustained energy. You probably recognise this phenomenon—you may need a boost, and grab a snack bar or soft drink. Initially you feel better, but soon you will feel worse than you did to start with. Snacking on a complex carbohydrate, such as bread, will give you longer-lasting energy.

FAT OR FICTION?

Carbohydrates have gained a bad reputation in the past and have been labelled fattening, mainly because of their bulk. But we now know that this is why they are so valuable—they are filling yet usually contain little or no fat. All carbohydrates have less than half the amount of kilojoules per gram than dietary fat and the body converts dietary fat into body fat more efficiently than it does carbohydrates. When you eat carbohydrates, your chance of storing their calories as fat is 20 per cent lower than if you eat fat.

Some people argue that fresh or dried fruits are sweet and are therefore high in sugar. This may be so, but fruit also contains valuable nutrients and fibre that the body needs. It is processed cane sugar—found in so many snack foods—that should be avoided. It provides no nutritional value and is often accompanied by large quantities of fat.

DAILY INTAKE

It is recommended that about 60 per cent of your daily kilojoules should come from carbohydrates. (See the table below for further information.)

VALUE FOR VEGETARIANS

In a vegetarian diet, complex carbohydrates give substance to a meal by filling you up and giving a feeling of satisfaction and repleteness. However, take care what you eat with your carbohydrates. It is easy enough to load a jacket potato with butter or sour cream, or dish up a bowl of pasta with a rich creamy sauce. So, in fact, it is the toppings that can make carbohydrates fatty, and not the carbohydrates themselves.

Wherever possible, choose carbohydrates that are the least refined. For instance, use brown rice rather than white, go for wholemeal instead of white bread, and rolled oats in the form of porridge or muesli at breakfast rather than processed (and often high in added sugar) cereals. These wholegrain products are broken down slowly by the body and therefore give a more sustained release of energy.

Complex carbohydrates are particularly important at breakfast to keep you alert and productive throughout the day, which is why breakfast is traditionally cereal and/or toast. Research has shown that by skipping breakfast, students are less attentive and workers less productive. A hidden danger in missing breakfast is that you'll find you have a craving for sugary snacks later on in the day.

SAMPLE MEALS—one of these will provide your daily carbohydrates

BREAKFAST
- Puffed corn cereal (page 19)
- Porridge
- Mixed berry couscous (page 18)

LUNCH
- Any pasta dish
- Wholegrain muffin with tomato

DINNER
- Udon noodle stir-fry (page 140)
- Couscous vegetable loaf (page 170)
- Chunky chickpea and herb dumpling soup (page 38)

SNACKS
- Vietnamese spring rolls (page 231)
- Nuts and dried fruit

HOW MUCH CARBOHYDRATE DO I NEED?

The amount of carbohydrate you need depends on your weight and the amount and level of activity you do. Use this guide to estimate the carbohydrate you should eat each day.

Activity level	Continuous exercise	Carbohydrate x kg body weight per day
Light	< 1 hour/day	4.0–4.5 g
Light–moderate	1 hour/day	4.5–5.5 g
Moderate	1–2 hours/day	5.5–6.5 g
Moderate–heavy	2–4 hours/day	6.5–7.5 g
Heavy	4–5 hours/day	7.5–8.5 g

Example: A man who weighs 90 kg and does less than 1 hour's continuous light exercise each day needs 360–405 grams of carbohydrate per day.

EXCELLENT CARBOHYDRATE SOURCE (20–50 g per serve)   Bread, honey, muesli, dried fruit, flour (wholemeal and white), Lebanese bread, fruit loaf, polenta, couscous

VERY GOOD CARBOHYDRATE SOURCE (10–30 g per serve)   Pasta, baked beans, berries, breakfast wheat biscuit, banana, pumpkin, potato, rice, noodles

GOOD CARBOHYDRATE SOURCE (2–20 g per serve)   Tofu, tomatoes, milk, fruit, oats, lentils, nuts, yoghurt

Dietary fibre

Dietary fibre consists of the cellulose and gums found in fruits, vegetables, grains and legumes—there is no fibre at all in any animal products. Fibre is not a nutrient, but rather a substance that ensures proper digestive functioning. It is a group of food components that is digested (i.e. passes through the stomach and small intestine) but is largely unabsorbed in the process and reaches the large intestine virtually unchanged.

SOLUBLE AND INSOLUBLE
Dietary fibre may be classified as soluble or insoluble. Soluble fibre is abundant in legumes, oats, barley and most fruits and vegetables. It has the consistency of a gel and tends to slow digestion time, which has the effect of regulating blood sugar—this is particularly important for diabetics.

Insoluble fibre ('roughage') is found in fruit and vegetable skins and the bran coating around grain kernels. Wholegrains (especially wheat, rice and maize), vegetables and nuts are good sources. Insoluble fibre passes through the digestive tract largely unchanged and speeds up the passage of material through the bowel.

It is important to have a variety of both soluble and insoluble fibre in the diet as each type has a different function: foods that provide both are apples, dried fruits and wholegrains.

GETTING ENOUGH FIBRE

- Leave the skin on fruit and vegetables, such as apples and potatoes.
- Eat whole pieces of fruit and vegetables rather than consuming them as juices.
- Choose wholegrain products such as breads, breakfast cereals, wholemeal pasta and brown rice.
- Drink plenty of water during the day to help digest fibre (6–8 glasses is recommended).
- Snack on fresh or dried fruit rather than biscuits or cakes.

SOLUBLE AND INSOLUBLE FIBRE FOODS

Good sources of insoluble fibre

- Cellulose   plant foods, wholegrains, bran, dried fruit, cabbage family
- Lignin   grains, vegetables, fruit
- Hemicellulose   wheat bran, bran cereal

Good sources of soluble fibre

- Pectins   slippery elm, agar, okra, psyllium
- Gums/mucilages apples, citrus fruit, sugar beet

BENEFITS
There are many benefits to a high-fibre diet. Both soluble and insoluble fibre readily absorb water, increasing stool bulk and making it softer and easier to expel. However, dietary fibre is not just important for efficient bodily functions and for comfort; it can also help in the prevention of bowel cancer and other bowel disorders, reduce the risk of diabetes, lower cholesterol (which helps prevent heart disease) and reduce the incidence of constipation and haemorrhoids. And, the more unrefined the source of fibre, the more effective it is for improved gastrointestinal health.

FIBRE DEFICIENCY
Diets that lack fresh, whole high-fibre foods and instead contain an abundance of refined foods together with animal products (which contain no fibre) have a much higher incidence of diabetes, cardiovascular disease, diverticulitis and bowel and rectal cancer.

FIBRE IS NOT BORING
There are many misconceptions surrounding the consumption and benefits of fibre. As people turned to 'health foods' in the last few decades, it was thought that large amounts of roughage, such as bran, were needed in the diet. Things were taken to excess and some of the roughage that was consumed was fairly unpalatable—this is probably where health foods and vegetarian diets earned a reputation for being wholesome but boring and unappetising, the worthy fare of the 'the brown rice and lentil brigade'.

With the greater knowledge of the last few years, we now realise just how wrong this perception is. Fibre is present in different forms and in many different foods that we probably already consume on a daily basis. So the addition of 'roughage', such as bran, to other foods is not really necessary, and in fact can be detrimental as it can inhibit the metabolism of other nutrients (for example, iron). Eating a variety of sources of fibre is essential as excessive fibre from a single rather than varied source can inhibit the absorption of other nutrients.

BONUS FOR VEGETARIANS
Vegetarians have the edge over meat eaters when it comes to fibre intake, as the bulk of a vegetarian diet, such as cereals and beans, along with fruit and vegetables, is generally rich in fibre. The main thing to remember is to eat a wide variety of foods, ensuring that a range of fibre is consumed—both soluble and insoluble.

DAILY INTAKE
Nutritionists recommend an intake of 30 grams of fibre per day. A typical serving of grains, fruits or vegetables contains between 1–3 grams of dietary fibre. To get the recommended levels of dietary fibre, you need to consume at least 10 or more servings of fibre-containing foods daily. This should be an easy task for most vegetarians.

EXCELLENT DIETARY FIBRE SOURCE (5–15 g per serve) Split peas, kidney beans, fruit (e.g. kiwi fruit), vegetables (e.g. pumpkin, capsicum and asparagus), wholewheat pasta, haricot beans, garlic, wheat bran

VERY GOOD DIETARY FIBRE SOURCE (3–8 g per serve) Wholemeal bread, dried fruit, peanuts (and other nuts), baked beans, pasta, lentils, chickpeas, raspberries, corn

GOOD DIETARY FIBRE SOURCE (1–3 g per serve) Apples, tempeh, Brussels sprouts, mushrooms, carrots, wholegrain bread, tomatoes, bananas, brown rice, strawberries

Fat

Fats are our most concentrated dietary energy source. At 37 kilojoules per gram, they contain more than double the kilojoules of carbohydrates and protein. This is probably what gives this nutrient group its bad reputation, but, of course, no food group is without a specific use to our body and fat is a vital part of our diet.

THE GOOD NEWS

Everyone needs a certain amount of fat in their body to help with growth and development. Fats supply and help absorb the fat-soluble vitamins A, D, E and K, and they are involved in the conversion of beta-carotene to vitamin A. It is not fat itself that is the problem, rather the quantity and type of fat that we eat.

BAD FATS

The fats most commonly linked to health problems are saturated fats. These are usually solid at room temperature and are derived primarily from animal sources—meat and dairy foods—but they are also found in coconut and palm oils.

The body uses saturated fats mainly for storage, insulation and body heat or energy. An excessive consumption of saturated fats in the diet tends to raise blood cholesterol levels and cause fatty deposits in the arteries and blood vessels. This can lead to hardening of the arteries, elevated blood pressure and the formation of blood clots—greatly increasing the risk of heart disease and stroke.

GOOD FATS

The 'good' fats are unsaturated fats, which are usually liquid at room temperature and are derived from vegetable, nut or seed sources. There are two different types of unsaturated fats—monounsaturated fats and polyunsaturated fats.

Monounsaturated fats are generally considered to be 'good' fats, as they do not increase cholesterol levels. They

are found in significant amounts in most nuts, olives and olive oil. Other good vegetarian sources are avocados, chickpeas, eggs and sesame seeds.

Polyunsaturated fats are also considered to be 'good'. They are found in nuts, grains and seeds and are usually soft or liquid at room temperature. These fats are the most important group of fats as they are the only source of the two essential fatty acids—omega-3 and omega-6 fats.

It is very important to get an adequate intake of omega-3 and omega-6 because they protect against cardiovascular disease, promote healthy skin and are necessary for normal functioning of the nervous and immune systems. Good vegetarian sources of omega-3 are walnuts and some vegetable oils such as soya, canola, mustard seed and flaxseed. Omega-6 can also be found in vegetable oils such as safflower, sunflower, sesame and soya bean, as well as in evening primrose oil.

CHOLESTEROL

Cholesterol is yet another type of fat. It is a wax-like substance present in all animals but not in plants. It is an essential element for good health and is part of every living cell of the human body. It is not necessary to obtain cholesterol from dietary sources as it is manufactured by the liver and adrenal glands to make stress and sex hormones. It is also required for the

nervous system and is essential for the breakdown and elimination of fats. Vegetarian foods that are high in cholesterol include egg yolks and dairy foods. Cholesterol intake should be monitored, but research has shown that it is more important to reduce saturated fat intake, which raises cholesterol, than it is to reduce dietary cholesterol itself.

DAILY INTAKE

It is recommended that you try to have no more than 30–40 g of fat per day (30 g for women and small men, 40 g for men and tall women). Nutritionists estimate that most people living on a Western diet consume twice the amount of fat that they actually need. And vegetarians cannot assume that all vegetarian meals are low in fat, particularly if dairy foods are eaten.

TIPS FOR REDUCING FAT INTAKE

- Make your meals as filling as possible by choosing foods which take longer to chew and swallow (e.g. whole fruit not fruit juice, whole potatoes, not mashed).
- Don't skip meals or you'll snack later. If you do snack, choose fruits and raw vegetables.
- Spread your food intake over the day to keep you calm and full of energy.
- Become aware of times when you are likely to overeat (stressed, bored, lots of food around) and check your real hunger level before eating.
- Use low-fat plain or skim-milk yoghurt in sauces instead of cream.
- Be careful of hidden fats in snack and processed foods—cakes, biscuits, french fries, potato chips, corn chips, crackers and fast foods. The vegetable oils used in processed foods are the saturated coconut and palm oils.
- Choose polyunsaturated or monounsaturated oils and margarines.

DON'T GO HUNGRY

LOW-FAT SNACK IDEAS

- Fresh fruit and vegetables (but go easy on the avocado)
- Fresh fruit and vegetable juices
- Skim milk and low-fat milk drinks; low-fat yoghurt
- Pasta with tomato-based sauces
- Steamed rice with vegetables
- Baked jacket potato with low-fat yoghurt and cheese
- Wholegrain bread and bread rolls
- Rice cakes

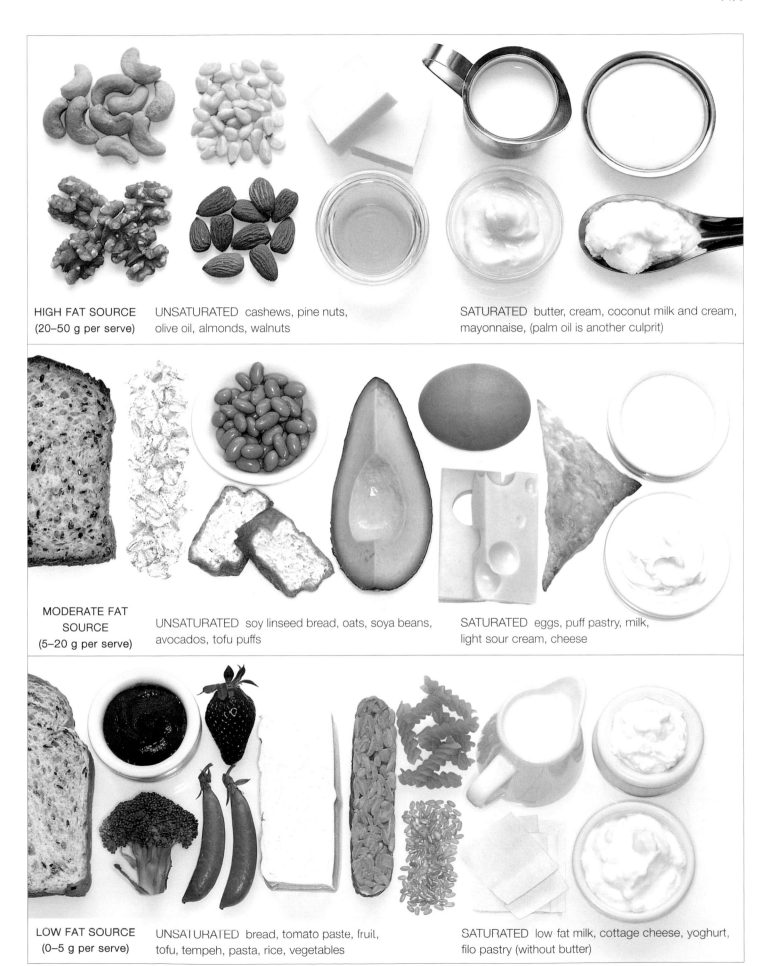

HIGH FAT SOURCE (20–50 g per serve)

UNSATURATED cashews, pine nuts, olive oil, almonds, walnuts

SATURATED butter, cream, coconut milk and cream, mayonnaise, (palm oil is another culprit)

MODERATE FAT SOURCE (5–20 g per serve)

UNSATURATED soy linseed bread, oats, soya beans, avocados, tofu puffs

SATURATED eggs, puff pastry, milk, light sour cream, cheese

LOW FAT SOURCE (0–5 g per serve)

UNSATURATED bread, tomato paste, fruit, tofu, tempeh, pasta, rice, vegetables

SATURATED low fat milk, cottage cheese, yoghurt, filo pastry (without butter)

Breakfasts & Brunches

POACHED EGGS WITH GARLIC YOGHURT DRESSING AND SPINACH

Preparation time: 10 minutes
Total cooking time: 15 minutes
Serves 4

DRESSING
1/2 cup (125 g/4 oz) sheep's milk
    yoghurt
1 small clove garlic, crushed
1 tablespoon snipped fresh chives

300 g (10 oz) baby English spinach
    leaves
30 g (1 oz) butter, chopped
herbed salt
4 tomatoes, halved
1 tablespoon white vinegar
8 eggs
1 round loaf light rye bread,
    cut into 8 thick slices

1 To make the dressing, mix together the yoghurt, garlic and chives.

2 Wash the spinach and place it in a large saucepan with just the little water that is left clinging to the leaves. Cover the pan and cook over low heat for 3–4 minutes, or until the spinach has wilted. Add the butter. Season with herbed salt. Set aside and keep warm. Cook the tomatoes under a hot grill for 3–5 minutes.
3 Fill a frying pan three-quarters full with cold water and add the vinegar and some salt to stop the egg whites spreading. Bring to a gentle simmer. Gently break the eggs one by one into a small bowl, then carefully slide each one into the water. Reduce the heat so that the water barely moves. Cook for 1–2 minutes, or until the eggs are just set. Remove with an egg flip. Drain.
4 Toast the bread. Top each slice of toast with spinach, an egg and some dressing. Serve with tomato halves.

NUTRITION PER SERVE
Protein 25 g; Fat 20 g; Carbohydrate 45 g;
Dietary Fibre 7.5 g; Cholesterol 384 mg;
1895 kJ (453 cal)

Cook the spinach leaves until they are wilted, then stir in the butter.

Cook the eggs until they are just set, then remove with an egg flip.

MIXED BERRY COUSCOUS

Preparation time: 15 minutes
Total cooking time: 5 minutes
Serves 4

1 cup (185 g/6 oz) instant couscous
2 cups (500 ml/16 fl oz) apple and
    cranberry juice
1 cinnamon stick
2 teaspoons orange zest
250 g (8 oz) fresh raspberries
250 g (8 oz) fresh blueberries
250 g (8 oz) strawberries, halved

200 g (6¹/₂ oz) Greek yoghurt
2 tablespoons golden syrup
fresh mint leaves, to garnish

1 Place the couscous in a bowl. Pour the apple and cranberry juice into a saucepan and add the cinnamon stick. Cover and bring to the boil, then remove from the heat and pour over the couscous. Cover the couscous with plastic wrap and leave for about 5 minutes, or until all the liquid has been absorbed. Remove the cinnamon stick from the bowl.
2 Separate the grains of couscous

with a fork, then gently fold in the orange zest and most of the raspberries, blueberries and strawberries. Spoon the couscous mixture into four serving bowls and sprinkle with the remaining berries. Serve with a generous dollop of the yoghurt, then drizzle with the golden syrup. Garnish with fresh mint leaves and serve immediately.

NUTRITION PER SERVE
Protein 8.5 g; Fat 3 g; Carbohydrate 70 g;
Dietary Fibre 7 g; Cholesterol 8 mg;
1448 kJ (345 cal)

Pour the hot apple and cranberry juice over the instant couscous.

Separate the grains of couscous with a fork to ensure they are fluffy.

Gently fold in most of the raspberries, blueberries and strawberries.

PUFFED CORN CEREAL

Preparation time: 10 minutes
Total cooking time: 15 minutes
Serves 20 (makes about 1.5 kg)

85 g (3 oz) puffed corn
85 g (3 oz) puffed millet
2 x 200 g (6½ oz) packets dried fruit and nut mix
180 g (6 oz) unprocessed natural bran

60 g (2 oz) flaked coconut
⅓ cup (60 g/2 oz) pepitas
¾ cup (185 ml/6 fl oz) maple syrup
1 cup (70 g/2¼ oz) processed bran cereal
2 x 200 g (6½ oz) packets dried fruit salad mix, cut into small pieces

1 Preheat the oven to moderate 180°C (350°F/Gas 4). Spread out the corn, millet, fruit and nut mix, bran, coconut and pepitas in a large roasting tin.

2 Pour the maple syrup over the puffed corn mixture and stir until the dry ingredients are well coated.
3 Stir in the bran cereal and fruit salad mix and bake for 15 minutes, or until golden, turning the cereal several times during cooking. Cool completely before storing in an airtight container.

NUTRITION PER SERVE
Protein 5 g; Fat 4 g; Carbohydrate 47 g; Dietary Fibre 9 g; Cholesterol 0 mg; 965 kJ (231 cal)

Using kitchen scissors, cut the dried fruit salad mixture into small pieces.

Spread out the puffed corn mixture in a large roasting tin.

Pour the maple syrup evenly over the dry ingredients in the roasting tin.

RICOTTA PANCAKES WITH GOAT'S MILK YOGHURT AND PEARS

Preparation time: 15 minutes
Total cooking time: 50 minutes
Serves 4

1¹/₂ cups (185 g/6 oz) plain flour
2 teaspoons baking powder
2 teaspoons ground ginger
2 tablespoons caster sugar
4 eggs, separated
350 g (11 oz) low-fat ricotta
1 pear, peeled, cored and grated
1¹/₄ cups (315 ml/10 fl oz) milk
40 g (1¹/₄ oz) butter
3 beurre bosc pears, unpeeled

40 g (1¹/₄ oz) butter
1 tablespoon soft brown sugar
1 teaspoon ground cinnamon
200 g (6¹/₂ oz) goat's milk yoghurt

1 Sift the flour, baking powder, ginger and sugar into a bowl and make a well in the centre. Pour the combined egg yolks, ricotta, grated pear and milk into the well and mix until smooth.
2 Beat the egg whites until soft peaks form, then fold into the mixture.
3 Heat a frying pan over medium heat and melt some of the butter. Pour ¹/₄ cup (60 ml) of the batter into the pan and swirl gently to create an even pancake. Cook for 1–1¹/₂ minutes, or until bubbles form on the surface, then turn and cook the other side

for 1 minute, or until golden. Repeat with the remaining butter and mixture to make 11 more pancakes. Keep warm.
4 Cut the pears into thick slices lengthways. Melt the butter in a frying pan and add the sugar and cinnamon, then stir until the sugar dissolves. Add the pears and cook in batches, turning once, until golden and tender. Serve stacks of pancakes with the pears and yoghurt.

NUTRITION PER SERVE
Protein 26 g; Fat 41 g; Carbohydrate 85 g; Dietary Fibre 5.5 g; Cholesterol 266 mg; 3341 kJ (799 cal)

Stir the combined egg yolks, ricotta, grated pear and milk into the flour.

Cook the pancake until bubbles form on the surface, then turn over.

Cook the pears in batches in the buttery sauce, turning to coat in the mixture.

FRUIT SALAD IN VANILLA, GINGER AND LEMON GRASS SYRUP

Preparation time: 20 minutes +
  chilling time
Total cooking time: 15 minutes
Serves 4

500 g (1 lb) watermelon, cubed
260 g (8 oz) honeydew melon,
  cubed
1/2 small pineapple, chopped
1 mango, diced
250 g (8 oz) strawberries, halved
1/4 cup (5 g/1/4 oz) small mint sprigs

LEMON GRASS SYRUP
1/2 cup (125 ml/4 fl oz) lime juice
1/4 cup (45 g/11/2 oz) soft brown sugar
1 stem lemon grass, finely sliced
2 tablespoons grated fresh ginger
1 vanilla bean, split

1 Place the fruit and mint in a bowl and mix gently.
2 To make the syrup, place the lime juice, sugar and 1/2 cup (125 ml) water in a small saucepan and stir over low heat until the sugar dissolves, then add the lemon grass, ginger and vanilla bean. Bring to the boil, reduce the heat and simmer for 10 minutes, or until reduced and slightly thickened. Remove the vanilla bean, pour the syrup over the fruit and refrigerate until cold.

NUTRITION PER SERVE
Protein 3.5 g; Fat 0.5 g; Carbohydrate 40 g;
Dietary Fibre 6 g; Cholesterol 0 mg;
797 kJ (190 cal)

NOTE: If you prefer your syrup without the lemon grass pieces but like the flavour, bruise the white part of the lemon grass with a rolling pin, place in the syrup, cook and remove along with the vanilla bean.

Remove the skin from the mango and cut the flesh into small cubes.

Simmer the lemon grass syrup until it is reduced and slightly thickened.

BAKED RICOTTA WITH PRESERVED LEMON AND SEMI-DRIED TOMATOES

Preparation time: 15 minutes +
    10 minutes standing
Total cooking time: 30 minutes
Serves 8–10

2 kg (4 lb) round ricotta cheese
olive oil
2 cloves garlic, crushed
1 preserved lemon, rinsed, pith and
    flesh removed, cut into thin strips
150 g (5 oz) semi-dried tomatoes,
    roughly chopped
1 cup (30 g/1 oz) finely chopped fresh
    flat-leaf parsley
1 cup (50 g/1¾ oz) chopped fresh
    coriander leaves
⅓ cup (80 ml/2¾ fl oz) extra virgin
    olive oil
3 tablespoons lemon juice

1 Preheat the oven to very hot 250°C (500°F/Gas 10). Place the ricotta on a baking tray lined with baking paper, brush lightly with the olive oil and bake for 20–30 minutes, or until golden brown. Leave for 10 minutes then, using egg flips, transfer to a large platter. (If possible, have someone help you move the ricotta.)
2 Meanwhile, place the garlic, preserved lemon, semi-dried tomato, parsley, coriander, oil and lemon juice in a bowl and mix together well.
3 Spoon the dressing over the baked ricotta and serve with crusty bread. It is delicious hot or cold.

NUTRITION PER SERVE (10)
Protein 20 g; Fat 30 g; Carbohydrate 3 g;
Dietary Fibre 0.5 g; Cholesterol 95 mg;
1542 kJ (368 cal)

Remove the flesh from the lemon and cut the rind into thin strips.

Put all the dressing ingredients in a bowl and mix together thoroughly.

Spoon the dressing evenly over the baked ricotta and serve hot or cold.

FRIED TOMATOES WITH MARINATED HALOUMI

Preparation time: 15 minutes +
overnight marinating
Total cooking time: 10 minutes
Serves 4

400 g (13 oz) haloumi cheese, cut into
eight 1 cm (1/2 inch) slices
250 g (8 oz) cherry tomatoes, halved
250 g (8 oz) teardrop tomatoes,
halved
1 clove garlic, crushed
2 tablespoons lemon juice
1 tablespoon balsamic vinegar
2 teaspoons fresh lemon thyme
1/4 cup (60 ml) extra virgin olive oil
2 tablespoons olive oil
1 small loaf wholegrain bread, cut into
8 thick slices

1 Place the haloumi and tomatoes in a
non-metallic dish. Whisk together the
garlic, lemon juice, balsamic vinegar,
thyme and extra virgin olive oil in a
jug and pour over the haloumi and
tomatoes. Cover and marinate for
3 hours or overnight. Drain well,
reserving the marinade.
2 Heat the olive oil in a large frying
pan. Add the haloumi and cook in
batches over medium heat for
1 minute each side, or until golden
brown. Transfer to a plate and keep
warm. Add the tomatoes and cook
over medium heat for 5 minutes, or
until their skins begin to burst.
Transfer to a plate and keep warm.
3 Toast the bread until it is golden
brown. Serve the fried haloumi on
top of the toasted bread, piled high
with the tomatoes and drizzled
with the reserved marinade. Best
served immediately.

NUTRITION PER SERVE
Protein 30 g; Fat 40 g; Carbohydrate 34 g;
Dietary Fibre 7 g; Cholesterol 53 mg;
2690 kJ (645 cal)

Pour the marinade over the haloumi and the
mixed tomatoes.

Cook the haloumi until it is golden brown on
both sides.

Cook the tomatoes for 5 minutes, or until their
skins start to burst.

23

CORN AND POLENTA PANCAKES WITH TOMATO SALSA

Preparation time: 15 minutes
Total cooking time: 10 minutes
Serves 4

TOMATO SALSA
2 ripe tomatoes
1 cup (150 g/5 oz) frozen broad beans
2 tablespoons chopped fresh basil
1 small Lebanese cucumber, diced
2 small cloves garlic, crushed
1¹/₂ tablespoons balsamic vinegar
1 tablespoon extra virgin olive oil

CORN AND POLENTA PANCAKES
³/₄ cup (90 g/3 oz) self-raising flour
³/₄ cup (110 g/3¹/₂ oz) fine polenta
1 cup (250 ml/8 fl oz) milk
310 g (10 oz) can corn kernels
olive oil, for frying

1 To make the salsa, score a cross in the base of each tomato, then place in a bowl of boiling water for 30 seconds. Plunge into cold water and peel the skin away from the cross. Dice. Pour boiling water over the broad beans and leave for 2–3 minutes. Drain and rinse under cold water. Remove the skins. Put the beans in a bowl and stir in the tomato, basil, cucumber, garlic, vinegar and extra virgin olive oil.

2 To make the pancakes, sift the flour into a bowl and stir in the polenta. Add the milk and corn and stir until just combined, adding more milk if the batter is too dry. Season.
3 Heat the oil in a large frying pan and spoon half the batter into the pan, making four 9 cm (3¹/₂ inch) pancakes. Cook for 2 minutes each side, or until golden and cooked through. Repeat with the remaining batter, adding more oil if necessary. Drain well and serve with the salsa.

NUTRITION PER SERVE
Protein 11 g; Fat 18.5 g; Carbohydrate 56 g; Dietary Fibre 8.5 g; Cholesterol 8.5 mg; 1809 kJ (432 cal)

After blanching, it will be easy to peel the skin off the broad beans.

Stir the milk and corn kernels into the flour and polenta mixture.

Cook the pancakes for 2 minutes each side, or until golden and cooked through.

MIXED MUSHROOMS IN BRIOCHE

Preparation time: 15 minutes
Total cooking time: 20 minutes
Serves 6

750 g (1¹/₂ lb) mixed mushrooms
   (Swiss brown, shiitake, button,
   field, oyster)
75 g (2¹/₂ oz) butter
4 spring onions, chopped
2 cloves garlic, crushed
¹/₂ cup (125 ml/4 fl oz) dry white wine
300 ml (10 fl oz) cream
2 tablespoons chopped fresh thyme
6 small brioche (see NOTE)

1 Preheat the oven to moderate 180°C (350°F/Gas 4). Wipe the mushrooms with a clean damp cloth to remove any dirt. Cut the larger mushrooms into thick slices but leave the smaller ones whole.
2 Heat the butter in a large frying pan over medium heat. Add the spring onion and garlic and cook for 2 minutes. Increase the heat, add the mushrooms and cook, stirring frequently, for 5 minutes, or until the mushrooms are soft and all the liquid has evaporated. Pour in the wine and boil for 2 minutes to reduce slightly.
3 Stir in the cream and boil for a further 5 minutes to reduce and slightly thicken the sauce. Season to taste with salt and cracked black pepper. Stir in the thyme and set aside for 5 minutes.
4 Slice the top off the brioche and, using your fingers, pull out a quarter of the bread. Place the brioche and their tops on a baking tray and warm in the oven for 5 minutes.
5 Place each brioche on an individual serving plate. Spoon the mushroom sauce into each brioche, allowing it to spill over one side. Replace the top and serve warm.

NUTRITION PER SERVE
Protein 7.5 g; Fat 33 g; Carbohydrate 15 g;
Dietary Fibre 4 g; Cholesterol 100 mg;
1587 kJ (380 cal)

NOTE: You can use bread rolls, but the flavour won't be as good.

Cut the large mushrooms into thick slices, but leave the smaller ones whole.

Cook the mushrooms, stirring frequently, until they are soft.

Add the cream to the sauce and cook until it has thickened slightly.

Slice off the top of each brioche and pull out a quarter of the bread.

WARM ASPARAGUS AND EGG SALAD WITH HOLLANDAISE

Preparation time: 5 minutes
Total cooking time: 15 minutes
Serves 4

HOLLANDAISE SAUCE
175 g (6 oz) butter
4 egg yolks
1 tablespoon lemon juice

4 eggs, at room temperature
310 g (10 oz) asparagus spears,
   trimmed
Parmesan shavings, to serve

1 To make the hollandaise, melt the butter in a small saucepan and skim off any froth. Remove from the heat and cool. Mix the egg yolks and 2 tablespoons water in another small saucepan for 30 seconds, or until pale and foamy. Place the saucepan over very low heat and whisk for 2–3 minutes, or until thick and foamy—do not overheat or it will scramble. Remove from the heat. Gradually add the butter, whisking well after each addition (avoid using the whey at the bottom). Stir in the lemon juice and season. If the sauce is runny, return to the heat and whisk until thick—do not scramble.
2 Place the eggs in a saucepan half

filled with water. Bring to the boil and cook for 6–7 minutes, stirring occasionally to centre the yolks. Drain and cover with cold water until cooled a little, then peel off the shells.
3 Plunge the asparagus into a large saucepan of boiling water and cook for 3 minutes, or until just tender. Drain and pat dry. Divide among four plates. Spoon on the hollandaise. Cut the eggs in half and arrange two halves on each plate. Sprinkle with Parmesan shavings to serve.

NUTRITION PER SERVE
Protein 13 g; Fat 47 g; Carbohydrate 1.5 g;
Dietary Fibre 1 g; Cholesterol 475 mg;
1995 kJ (477 cal)

Whisk the yolks over very low heat until they are thick and foamy and the whisk leaves a trail.

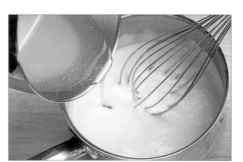

Gradually add the cooled butter, whisking well after each addition.

Cook the asparagus in a large saucepan of boiling water until just tender.

CORN MUFFINS

Preparation time: 20 minutes
Total cooking time: 25 minutes
Makes 12

2¹/₂ cups (310 g/10 oz) self-raising
    flour
¹/₂ cup (75 g/2¹/₂ oz) cornmeal
1 cup (250 ml/8 fl oz) milk
125 g (4 oz) butter, melted
2 eggs, lightly beaten
130 g (4¹/₂ oz) can corn kernels,
    drained
2 spring onions, finely chopped
¹/₂ cup (60 g/2 oz) grated Cheddar

1 Preheat the oven to hot 210°C
(415°F/Gas 6–7). Grease two trays
of six ¹/₂-cup (125 ml/4 fl oz) muffin
holes with butter. Sift the flour and
cornmeal into a large bowl and make a
well in the centre.
2 Whisk together the milk, butter,
eggs, corn, spring onion, Cheddar and
salt and pepper in a separate bowl and
pour into the well. Fold gently with a
metal spoon until all the ingredients
are just combined. Do not overmix—
the mixture should still be very lumpy.
3 Spoon the mixture into the tin and
bake for 20–25 minutes, or until lightly
golden. Leave for 5 minutes before
removing from the tin. Serve split in
half and spread with butter or cream
cheese. Delicious either hot or at
room temperature.

NUTRITION PER MUFFIN
Protein 6 g; Fat 12 g; Carbohydrate 27 g;
Dietary Fibre 1.5 g; Cholesterol 65 mg;
1009 kJ (240 cal)

VARIATION: Muffins are so versatile,
you can virtually add whatever you
have in the cupboard. Try adding
2 tablespoons chopped chives, ¹/₄ cup
(40 g/1¹/₄ oz) chopped, drained
sun-dried tomatoes or capsicum in oil,
2 finely chopped red chillies or
¹/₂ finely chopped red or green
capsicum into the mixture with the
milk and Cheddar.

STORAGE TIME: Store the muffins in
an airtight container for up to 2 days.

Trim the tops and tails from the spring onions and
then chop finely.

Sift the flour and cornmeal into a large bowl and
make a well in the centre.

Pour the milk mixture into the well in the dry
ingredients and fold gently until just combined.

Spoon the dough into the muffin holes and bake
until lightly golden.

27

CHEESE SOUFFLE

Preparation time: 10 minutes
Total cooking time: 35 minutes
Serves 4

60 g (2 oz) butter
45 g (1½ oz) plain flour
1¼ cups (315 ml/10 fl oz) milk, warmed
1½ cups (185 g/6 oz) grated Cheddar, firmly packed
1 teaspoon Dijon mustard
4 eggs, separated
1 tablespoon freshly grated Parmesan

1 Preheat the oven to moderately hot 200°C (400°F/Gas 6). Brush a 1.5 litre soufflé dish with melted butter or oil.

Melt the butter in a large pan then add the flour. Stir over low heat for 2 minutes, or until the flour is lightly golden and bubbling. Remove from the heat and gradually add the milk, stirring until the mixture is smooth. Return the pan to the heat and stir constantly over low heat until the mixture boils and thickens. Simmer for 1 minute, then remove from the heat.
2 Add the grated Cheddar, Dijon mustard and egg yolks, and stir until the cheese has melted. Season to taste with salt and cracked black pepper. Cover the surface with plastic wrap to prevent a skin forming and leave the sauce to cool slightly.
3 Put the egg whites in a clean dry bowl and whisk until stiff peaks form. Using a metal spoon, fold one third of the egg whites into the sauce, then gently fold in the remaining egg whites, being careful not to lose any volume. Gently pour the mixture into the prepared dish. Run your thumb or a knife around the edge of the dish to push the soufflé mixture slightly away from the edge—this will help the soufflé to rise evenly.
4 Sprinkle with the Parmesan and bake the soufflé for 25–30 minutes, or until well risen and cooked through (cover it if it appears to be over-browning). Serve immediately.

NUTRITION PER SERVE
Protein 30 g; Fat 50 g; Carbohydrate 15 g; Dietary Fibre 0.5 g; Cholesterol 365 mg; 2655 kJ (635 cal)

Lightly brush the soufflé dish with a little melted butter or oil.

Gently fold the egg whites into the sauce with a metal spoon.

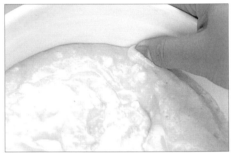

Run your thumb around the top of the soufflé to help it rise evenly.

BUBBLE AND SQUEAK

Preparation time: 15 minutes
Total cooking time: 30 minutes
Serves 4

750 g (1½ lb) floury potatoes
½ cup (125 ml/4 fl oz) milk
90 g (3 oz) butter
450 g (14 oz) green vegetables (such as cabbage, leek, Brussels sprouts, spinach), finely sliced

1 Cut the potatoes into even-sized pieces and put them in a pan of cold water. Bring to the boil, then lower the heat and simmer until tender—do not boil or the potatoes may break up and absorb water before they cook through. Drain thoroughly.
2 Heat the milk in the pan. Add the potatoes and half of the butter, then mash with a potato masher or a fork until the mixture is smooth and creamy.
3 Melt half of the remaining butter in a large heavy-based frying pan with a handle suitable for using under a grill, and cook the green vegetables until they are tender and cooked through. Add them to the potato and mix together. Season to taste with salt and cracked black pepper.
4 Melt the remaining butter in the frying pan and spoon in the potato mixture, smoothing off the top. Cook until the bottom is browned and crispy. Remove the pan from the heat and place it under a preheated grill until the top of the bubble and squeak is browned and golden. If you prefer, you can turn the bubble and squeak over in the pan and cook it on the other side, but grilling is easier. Delicious as a main meal by itself or an accompaniment to poached eggs.

NUTRITION PER SERVE
Protein 7 g; Fat 18 g; Carbohydrate 30 g; Dietary Fibre 5.5 g; Cholesterol 55 mg; 1280 kJ (305 cal)

HINT: If you don't have a frying pan with a cast iron handle suitable for flashing under the grill, cover a wooden or plastic handle with tin foil.

Add the green vegetables to the pan and cook until tender.

MINI FRITTATAS

Preparation time: 30 minutes
Total cooking time: 45 minutes
Makes 12

1 kg (2 lb) orange sweet potato
1 tablespoon oil
30 g (1 oz) butter
4 leeks, white part only,
    finely sliced
2 cloves garlic, crushed
250 g (8 oz) feta cheese, crumbled
8 eggs
1/2 cup (125 ml/4 fl oz) cream

1 Preheat the oven to moderate 180°C (350°F/Gas 4). Grease or brush twelve 1 cup (250 ml/8 fl oz) muffin holes with oil or melted butter. Cut small rounds of baking paper and place into the base of each hole. Cut the sweet potato into small cubes and boil, steam or microwave until tender. Drain well and set aside.
2 Heat the oil and butter in a frying pan and cook the leek for 10 minutes, stirring occasionally, or until very soft and lightly golden. Add the garlic and cook for a further 1 minute. Cool, then stir in the feta and sweet potato. Divide among the muffin holes.

3 Whisk the eggs and cream together and season with salt and cracked black pepper. Pour the egg mixture into each hole until three-quarters filled, then press the vegetables down gently. Bake for 25–30 minutes, or until golden and set. Leave in the tins for 5 minutes, then ease out with a knife. Delicious either served hot or at room temperature.

NUTRITION PER FRITTATA
Protein 10 g; Fat 15 g; Carbohydrate 13 g; Dietary Fibre 2.5 g; Cholesterol 155 mg; 1000 kJ (240 cal)

Cut small rounds of baking paper and put one in the base of each muffin hole.

Spoon the vegetable mixture evenly into the muffin holes.

Whisk the eggs and cream together, season and pour into the muffin holes.

SCRAMBLED EGGS

Preparation time: 5 minutes
Total cooking time: 5 minutes
Serves 2

6 eggs
1 tablespoon milk or cream
50 g butter
2 slices toast

1 Crack the eggs into a bowl, add the milk or cream and season well. Whisk gently with a fork until well combined.
2 Melt half the butter in a small pan or frying pan over low heat. Add the eggs, and stir constantly with a wooden spoon. Do not turn up the heat—scrambling must be done slowly and gently. When most of the egg has set, add the remaining butter and remove the pan from the heat. There should be enough heat left in the pan to finish cooking the eggs and melt the butter. Scrambled eggs should be creamy, not dry or rubbery. Serve immediately on toast—they will not sit even for a minute.

NUTRITION PER SERVE
Protein 20 g; Fat 35 g; Carbohydrate 15 g; Dietary Fibre 1 g; Cholesterol 605 mg; 1935 kJ (460 cal)

NOTE: It is very important to use fresh eggs when scrambling. To check whether an egg is fresh put it in a bowl of cold water. If it sinks on its side it is fresh, and if it floats on its end it is stale. If it is somewhere between the two it is not perfectly fresh but still good enough to use.

VARIATIONS: Scrambled eggs are also delicious with cheese such as Gruyère stirred through them, or a handful of chopped fresh herbs. You can also add roasted vegetables such as capsicum, tomato, onion and a few basil leaves to make Piperade.

Break up the eggs with a fork and stir gently until well combined.

Pour in the eggs and stir constantly with a wooden spoon.

When the eggs are nearly set, add the butter and remove from the heat.

LIGHT AND FLUFFY OMELETTES

Preparation time: 5 minutes
Total cooking time: 5 minutes
Serves 1 (see NOTE)

3 eggs
10 g (1/4 oz) butter
1/2 teaspoon oil

1 Crack the eggs into a small bowl and add a teaspoon of water. Break them up with a fork but do not overbeat them—the yolks and whites should be just combined. Season well.
2 Melt the butter and oil in a non-stick or well-seasoned frying pan (15 cm/6 inches diameter is about the right size for 3 eggs). When the butter has melted, swirl it around the pan, turn up the heat and pour in the egg.
3 Tilt the pan to cover the base with egg and leave it for a few seconds. Using a spatula or egg flip, draw the sides of the omelette into the centre and let any extra liquid egg run to the outside. As soon as the egg is almost set, tip the pan on a 45-degree angle and flip one half of the omelette into the middle and then over again so you have a flat roll. Slide the omelette onto a plate and eat immediately. The egg will continue cooking inside the omelette.

NUTRITION PER SERVE
Protein 18 g; Fat 28 g; Carbohydrate 0.5 g; Dietary Fibre 0 g; Cholesterol 565 mg; 1345 kJ (320 cal)

NOTE: If you are making omelettes for more than one person make each one separately. For the best results, use very fresh eggs.

VARIATION: Add 30 g grated strong-tasting cheese, such as Gruyère. Alternatively, add 4 quartered cherry tomatoes when you melt the butter and oil, and cook until warmed through and slightly softened. Add 1 teaspoon chopped fresh chives to the beaten egg, then cook as above.

Gently break up the eggs with a fork so that the whites and yolks are just combined.

Draw the sides of the omelette into the centre so any liquid egg flows to the outside.

When the egg is almost set, flip half of the omelette into the middle.

INDIVIDUAL OVEN-BAKED ROSTI

Preparation time: 20–25 minutes
Total cooking time: 55 minutes
Makes 12

500 g (1 lb) waxy potatoes (Desiree, Pontiac), peeled
1 onion
30 g (1 oz) butter, melted

1 Preheat the oven to hot 220°C (425°F/Gas 7). Cook the potatoes in a pan of boiling salted water for 7 minutes, or until just tender. Drain.
2 Prepare a 12-hole muffin tin, with holes measuring 6 cm ($2^{1}/_{2}$ inches) at the top and 4.5 cm ($1^{3}/_{4}$ inches) at the base, by brushing with a little of the butter. Grate the potatoes and onion, mix together in a bowl and pour the melted butter over the mixture. Season with salt and mix together well. Using

two forks, divide the mixture among the muffin holes, gently pressing it in. Cook the rosti in the oven for 45 minutes, or until golden.
3 Using a small palette knife, loosen each rosti around the edge and lift out. Serve on a warm serving dish.

NUTRITION PER ROSTI
Protein 1 g; Fat 2 g; Carbohydrate 6 g; Dietary Fibre 1 g; Cholesterol 6 mg; 200 kJ (50 cal)

Lightly brush the muffin tin with some of the melted butter.

Use two forks to put some mixture into each hole of the muffin tin.

Before lifting the rosti out, loosen around the edge with a small palette knife.

HASH BROWNS

Preparation time: 30 minutes
Total cooking time: 15–20 minutes
Serves 4

800 g (1 lb 10 oz) waxy potatoes
   (Desiree, Pontiac), peeled
120 g (4 oz) butter

1 Boil or steam the potatoes until just tender. Drain, cool, chop coarsely and season with salt and pepper.

2 Heat half the butter in a large heavy-based frying pan and put four lightly greased egg rings into the pan. Spoon the potato evenly into the egg rings, filling the rings to the top and pressing the potato down lightly to form flat cakes. Cook over medium-low heat for 5–7 minutes, or until a crust forms on the bottom. Be careful not to burn. Shake the pan gently to prevent sticking.
3 Turn the hash browns with a large spatula. Gently loosen the egg rings and remove with tongs. Cook for

another 4–5 minutes, or until browned and crisp. Remove from the pan and drain on paper towels. Add a little more butter to the pan, if necessary, and cook the remaining potato in the same way. Serve immediately.

NUTRITION PER SERVE
Protein 3 g; Fat 25 g; Carbohydrate 35 g;
Dietary Fibre 4 g; Cholesterol 75 mg;
1535 kJ (365 cal)

NOTE: If you don't have egg rings, cook as one large cake.

Fill the egg rings with the chopped potato and press the mixture down lightly.

Cook until a crust forms on the bottom. Be careful to prevent burning or sticking.

Use a large spatula to turn the hash brown over once a crust has formed on the bottom.

EGG AND VEGETABLE TORTILLAS

Preparation time: 1 hour 30 minutes
Total cooking time: 1 hour
Serves 4–6

1 tablespoon extra virgin olive oil
2 red onions, finely sliced
1 clove garlic, crushed
90 g (3 oz) English spinach, roughly
    chopped
2 red capsicums
1 kg (2 lb) potatoes, cut into
    shoestring chips
vegetable oil, for deep-frying
6 eggs, beaten
3 tablespoons of combined fresh
    chopped herbs (basil, parsley
    and oregano)

1 Heat the oil in a heavy–based pan and stir the onions over high heat for 2–3 minutes. Reduce the heat and cook for 30–40 minutes, until the onion starts to caramelize and break down. Increase the heat slightly, add the garlic and stir for 1 minute. Add the spinach, toss through and cook for another minute.
2 Cut the capsicums into quarters and remove the seeds and membrane. Grill, skin-side-up, until the skin is blackened and blistered. Cover with a damp tea towel until cooled. Peel and slice the flesh into fine strips.
3 Heat the oil to 160°C/315°F (a cube of bread will brown in 30 seconds) and deep-fry the chips until cooked but not brown. Remove and drain on paper towels. In a bowl, mix the onion, spinach, capsicum and chips.
4 Combine the eggs and herbs, add to the vegetables and toss through. Lightly grease a small 20 cm (8 inch) frying pan and add enough of the tortilla mixture to cover the base of the pan. Cook over medium heat for 2–3 minutes, until the underside is golden. Flip and cook the other side. Keep warm while cooking the remaining tortilla mixture.

NUTRITION PER SERVE (6)
Protein 15 g; Fat 20 g; Carbohydrate 25 g; Dietary Fibre 5 g; Cholesterol 180 mg; 1350 kJ (325 cal)

Cook the onion over low heat, very slowly so that it caramelizes.

Cut the capsicums into quarters and grill until blackened and blistered.

Deep-fry the chips in hot oil, until they are cooked but not browned.

Cook the tortilla until the underside is golden, then flip over.

Soups & Starters

ROAST PUMPKIN SOUP

Preparation time: 20 minutes
Total cooking time: 55 minutes
Serves 6

1.25 kg (2¹/₂ lb) pumpkin, peeled
    and cut into chunks
2 tablespoons olive oil
1 large onion, chopped
2 teaspoons ground cumin
1 large carrot, chopped
1 celery stick, chopped
1 litre (32 fl oz) vegetable stock
sour cream, to serve
finely chopped fresh parsley, to serve
ground nutmeg, to serve

1 Preheat the oven to moderate 180°C (350°F/Gas 4). Put the pumpkin on a greased baking tray and lightly brush with half the olive oil. Bake for 25 minutes, or until softened and slightly browned around the edges.
2 Heat the remaining oil in a large pan. Cook the onion and cumin for 2 minutes, then add the carrot and celery and cook for 3 minutes more, stirring frequently. Add the roasted pumpkin and stock. Bring to the boil, then reduce the heat and simmer for 20 minutes.
3 Allow to cool a little then purée in batches in a blender or food processor. Return the soup to the pan and gently reheat without boiling. Season to taste with salt and cracked black pepper. Top with sour cream and sprinkle with chopped parsley and ground nutmeg before serving.

NUTRITION PER SERVE
Protein 5 g; Fat 8.5 g; Carbohydrate 15 g;
Dietary Fibre 3.5 g; Cholesterol 4.5 mg;
665 kJ (160 cal)

NOTE: Butternut pumpkin is often used in soups as it has a sweeter flavour than other varieties.

HINT: If the soup is too thick, thin it down with a little more stock.

Lightly brush the pumpkin chunks with oil and bake until softened.

Transfer the cooled mixture to a blender or food processor and purée in batches.

CHUNKY CHICKPEA AND HERB DUMPLING SOUP

Preparation time: 30 minutes
Total cooking time: 35 minutes
Serves 4

1 tablespoon oil
1 onion, chopped
2 cloves garlic, crushed
2 teaspoons ground cumin
1 teaspoon ground coriander
1/4 teaspoon chilli powder
2 x 300 g (10 oz) cans chickpeas
3 1/2 cups (875 ml/28 fl oz) vegetable stock
2 x 425 g (14 oz) cans chopped tomatoes

1 tablespoon chopped fresh coriander leaves
1 cup (125 g/4 oz) self-raising flour
25 g (3/4 oz) butter, chopped
2 tablespoons grated Parmesan
2 tablespoons mixed chopped fresh herbs (chives, parsley, coriander)
3 tablespoons milk

1 Heat the oil in a large saucepan, and cook the onion over medium heat for 2–3 minutes, or until soft. Add the garlic, cumin, ground coriander and chilli and cook for 1 minute, or until fragrant. Add the chickpeas, stock and tomato. Bring to the boil, then reduce the heat and simmer, covered, for 10 minutes. Stir in the coriander.
2 To make the dumplings, sift the flour into a bowl and add the chopped butter. Rub together with your fingertips until the mixture resembles fine breadcrumbs. Stir in the cheese and herbs. Make a well in the centre, add the milk and mix with a flat-bladed knife until just combined. Bring together into a rough ball, divide into eight portions and roll into small balls.
3 Add the dumplings to the soup, cover and simmer for 20 minutes, or until a skewer comes out clean when inserted in the centre of a dumpling.

NUTRITION PER SERVE
Protein 17 g; Fat 16 g; Carbohydrate 50 g;
Dietary Fibre 12 g; Cholesterol 23 mg;
1767 kJ (422 cal)

Stir the chopped coriander into the simmering chickpea mixture.

Add the milk to the dumpling mixture and mix with a flat-bladed knife.

Pierce the dumplings with a skewer to test if they are cooked.

SPINACH AND RICOTTA GNOCCHI

Preparation time: 45 minutes +
  1 hour refrigeration
Total cooking time: 15 minutes
Serves 6 as a starter

4 slices white bread
1/2 cup (125 ml/4 fl oz) milk
500 g (1 lb) frozen spinach, thawed
250 g (8 oz) ricotta cheese
2 eggs
60 g (2 oz) Parmesan, grated
1/4 cup (30 g/1 oz) plain flour
Parmesan shavings, to serve

GARLIC BUTTER SAUCE
100 g (3 1/2 oz) butter
2 cloves garlic, crushed
3 tablespoons chopped fresh basil
1 ripe tomato, diced

1 Remove the crusts from the bread and soak in milk in a shallow dish for 10 minutes. Squeeze out any excess milk from the bread. Squeeze out any excess liquid from the spinach.
2 Place the bread, spinach, ricotta, eggs and Parmesan in a bowl and mix thoroughly. Refrigerate, covered, for 1 hour. Fold the flour in well.
3 Lightly dust your hands in flour and roll heaped teaspoons of the mixture into dumplings. Lower batches of the gnocchi into a large saucepan of boiling salted water. Cook for about 2 minutes, or until the gnocchi rise to the surface. Transfer to a serving plate and keep warm.
4 To make the sauce, combine all the ingredients in a small saucepan and cook over medium heat for 3 minutes, or until the butter is nutty brown. Drizzle over the gnocchi and sprinkle with the shaved Parmesan.

NUTRITION PER SERVE (6)
Protein 17 g; Fat 26 g; Carbohydrate 16 g;
Dietary Fibre 5 g; Cholesterol 137 mg;
1504 kJ (360 cal)

Gently squeeze out any excess milk from the soaked bread.

With floured hands, roll teaspoons of the mixture into dumplings.

Cook the gnocchi in batches until they rise to the surface of the water.

CHILLI, CORN AND RED CAPSICUM SOUP

Preparation time: 20 minutes
Total cooking time: 45 minutes
Serves 4

1 coriander sprig
4 corn cobs
30 g (1 oz) butter
2 red capsicums, diced
1 small onion, finely chopped
1 small red chilli, finely chopped
1 tablespoon plain flour
2 cups (500 ml/16 fl oz)
   vegetable stock
1/2 cup (125 ml/4 fl oz) cream

1 Trim the leaves off the coriander and finely chop the root and stems. Cut the kernels off the corn cobs.
2 Heat the butter in a large saucepan over medium heat. Add the corn kernels, capsicum, onion and chilli and stir to coat the vegetables in the butter. Cook, covered, over low heat, stirring occasionally, for 10 minutes, or until the vegetables are soft. Increase the heat to medium and add the coriander root and stem. Cook, stirring, for 30 seconds, or until fragrant. Sprinkle with the flour and stir for a further minute. Remove from the heat and gradually add the vegetable stock, stirring together. Add 2 cups (500 ml/16 fl oz) water and

return to the heat. Bring to the boil, reduce the heat to low and simmer, covered, for 30 minutes, or until the vegetables are tender. Cool slightly.
3 Ladle about 2 cups (500 ml/16 fl oz) of the soup into a blender and purée until smooth. Return the purée to the soup in the saucepan, pour in the cream and gently heat until warmed through. Season to taste with salt. Sprinkle with the coriander leaves to serve. Delicious with grilled cheese on pitta bread.

NUTRITION PER SERVE
Protein 5.5 g; Fat 20 g; Carbohydrate 24 g;
Dietary Fibre 4 g; Cholesterol 62 mg;
1269 kJ (303 cal)

Using a sharp knife, cut all the kernels from the corn cob.

Trim the leaves and finely chop the root and stems of the coriander.

Simmer for 30 minutes, or until the vegetables are tender.

CARROT TIMBALES WITH CREAMY SAFFRON AND LEEK SAUCE

Preparation time: 25 minutes
Total cooking time: 1 hour
Serves 6 as a starter

60 g (2 oz) butter
2 leeks, sliced
2 cloves garlic, crushed
1 kg (2 lb) carrots, sliced
1¹/₂ cups (375 ml/12 fl oz) vegetable
    stock
1¹/₂ tablespoons finely chopped fresh
    sage
¹/₄ cup (60 ml/2 fl oz) cream
4 eggs, lightly beaten

CREAMY SAFFRON AND
    LEEK SAUCE
40 g (1¹/₄ oz) butter
1 small leek, finely sliced
1 large clove garlic, crushed
¹/₄ cup (60 ml/2 fl oz) white wine
pinch of saffron threads
¹/₃ cup (90 g/3 oz) crème fraîche

1 Preheat the oven to warm 170°C (325°F/Gas 3). Lightly grease six ³/₄ cup (185 ml) timbale moulds. Heat the butter in a saucepan and cook the leek for 3–4 minutes, or until soft. Add the garlic and carrot and cook for a further 2–3 minutes. Pour in the stock and 2 cups (500 ml/16 fl oz) water, bring to the boil, then reduce the heat and simmer, covered, for 5 minutes, or until the carrot is tender. Strain, reserving ³/₄ cup (185 ml/6 fl oz) of the liquid.

2 Blend the carrot mixture, ¹/₂ cup (125 ml/4 fl oz) of the reserved liquid and the sage in a food processor or blender until smooth. Cool the mixture slightly and stir in the cream and egg. Season and pour into the prepared moulds. Place the moulds in a roasting tin filled with enough hot water to come halfway up their sides. Bake for 30–40 minutes, or until just set.

3 To make the sauce, melt the butter in a saucepan and cook the leek for 3–4 minutes without browning. Add the garlic and cook for 30 seconds. Add the wine, remaining reserved liquid and saffron and bring to the boil. Reduce the heat and simmer for 5 minutes, or until reduced. Stir in the crème fraîche.

4 Turn out the timbales onto serving plates and serve with the sauce.

NUTRITION PER SERVE
Protein 7 g; Fat 25 g; Carbohydrate 11 g;
Dietary Fibre 6 g; Cholesterol 187 mg;
1258 kJ (300 cal)

Pour the mixture into the prepared moulds and place in a roasting tin.

Cook the leek, garlic, wine, reserved liquid and saffron on low heat until reduced.

Carefully turn out the carrot timbales onto serving plates.

FRENCH ONION SOUP

Preparation time: 30 minutes
Total cooking time: 1 hour 30 minutes
Serves 4

55 g (2 oz) butter
1 tablespoon olive oil
1 kg (2 lb) onions, thinly sliced into
    rings
840 ml (27 fl oz) well-flavoured
    vegetable stock
1/2 cup (125 ml/4 fl oz) dry sherry
1/2 French bread stick
1/3 cup (35 g/1 oz) grated Parmesan
1 cup (125 g/4 oz) finely grated
    Cheddar or Gruyère
chopped fresh parsley, to serve

1 Heat the butter and oil in a large pan, then add the onion and cook, stirring frequently, over low heat for 45 minutes, or until softened and golden brown. It is important not to rush this stage—cook the onion thoroughly so that it caramelizes and the flavours develop.
2 Add the vegetable stock, sherry and 1 cup (250 ml/8 fl oz) water. Bring to the boil, then reduce the heat and simmer for 30 minutes. Season to taste.
3 Meanwhile, slice the bread into four thick slices and arrange them in a single layer under a hot grill. Toast one side, turn and sprinkle with Parmesan, and toast until crisp and golden and the cheese has melted.
4 Put the bread slices into serving bowls. Ladle in the hot soup, sprinkle with the cheese and parsley and serve.

NUTRITION PER SERVE
Protein 17 g; Fat 27 g; Carbohydrate 19 g; Dietary Fibre 4 g; Cholesterol 65 mg; 1735 kJ (415 cal)

Using a large sharp knife, thinly slice the onions into rings.

Heat the oil and butter in a large pan and then add the onion.

Stir frequently over low heat until the onion is softened and golden brown.

INDIVIDUAL VEGETABLE TERRINES WITH A SPICY TOMATO SAUCE

Preparation time: 40 minutes
Total cooking time: 50 minutes
Serves 4 as a starter

1/2 cup (125 ml/4 fl oz) oil
2 zucchini, sliced on the diagonal
500 g (1 lb) eggplant, sliced
1 small fennel bulb, sliced
1 red onion, sliced
300 g (10 oz) ricotta cheese
60 g (2 oz) Parmesan, grated
1 tablespoon chopped fresh
    flat-leaf parsley
1 tablespoon chopped fresh chives
1 red capsicum, grilled, peeled and
    cut into large pieces
1 yellow capsicum, grilled, peeled and
    cut into large pieces

SPICY TOMATO SAUCE
1 tablespoon oil
1 onion, finely chopped
2 cloves garlic, crushed
1 red chilli, seeded and chopped
425 g (14 oz) can chopped tomatoes
2 tablespoons tomato paste

1 Heat 1 tablespoon of the oil in a large frying pan. Cook the vegetables in separate batches over high heat for 5 minutes, or until golden, adding the remaining oil as needed. Drain each vegetable separately on paper towels.
2 Preheat the oven to moderately hot 200°C (400°F/Gas 6). Place the cheeses and herbs in a small bowl and mix together well. Season to taste.
3 Lightly grease four 1¹/₄ cup (315 ml/10 fl oz) ramekins and line with baking paper. Using half the eggplant, put a layer in the base of each dish. Layer the zucchini, capsicum, cheese mixture, fennel and onion over the eggplant. Cover with the remaining eggplant and press down firmly. Bake for 10–15 minutes, or until hot. Leave for 5 minutes before turning out.
4 To make the sauce, heat the oil in a saucepan and cook the onion and garlic for 2–3 minutes, or until soft. Add the chilli, tomato and tomato paste and simmer for 5 minutes, or until thick and pulpy. Purée in a food processor. Return to the saucepan and keep warm. Spoon over the terrines.

NUTRITION PER SERVE
Protein 18 g; Fat 48 g; Carbohydrate 16 g;
Dietary Fibre 8.5 g; Cholesterol 48 mg;
2346 kJ (560 cal)

Cook the capsicums under a hot grill until blackened. Cool, peel, then cut into pieces.

Layer the fennel over the cheese mixture, then add a layer of onion.

Simmer the tomato sauce for 5 minutes, or until thick and pulpy.

SOBA NOODLE SOUP

Preparation time: 15 minutes +
  5 minutes standing
Total cooking time: 10 minutes
Serves 4

250 g (8 oz) packet soba noodles
2 dried shiitake mushrooms
2 litres (64 fl oz) vegetable stock
120 g (4 oz) snow peas, cut into thin
  strips
2 small carrots, cut into thin strips
2 cloves garlic, finely chopped
6 spring onions, cut into 5 cm (2 inch)
  lengths and sliced lengthways

3 cm (1 inch) piece ginger, cut into
  julienne strips
1/3 cup (80 ml/2 3/4 fl oz) soy sauce
1/4 cup (60 ml/2 fl oz) mirin or sake
1 cup (90 g/3 oz) bean sprouts
fresh coriander, to garnish

1 Cook the noodles according to the packet instructions. Drain.
2 Soak the mushrooms in 1/2 cup (125 ml/4 fl oz) boiling water until soft. Drain, reserving the liquid. Remove the stalks and finely slice the mushrooms.
3 Combine the vegetable stock, mushrooms, reserved liquid, snow peas, carrot, garlic, spring onion and ginger in a large saucepan. Bring slowly to the boil, then reduce the heat to low and simmer for 5 minutes, or until the vegetables are tender. Add the soy sauce, mirin and bean sprouts. Cook for a further 3 minutes.
4 Divide the noodles among four large serving bowls. Ladle the hot liquid and vegetables over the top and garnish with coriander.

NUTRITION PER SERVE
Protein 13 g; Fat 1.5 g; Carbohydrate 30 g;
Dietary Fibre 6 g; Cholesterol 11 mg;
1124 kJ (270 cal)

Cut the ginger into julienne strips (thin strips the size and shape of matchsticks).

After soaking the mushrooms, drain and finely slice them.

Simmer the vegetables for 5 minutes, or until they are tender.

VEGETABLE SOUP

Preparation time: 20 minutes +
    overnight soaking
Total cooking time: 1 hour
Serves 6

1/2 cup (105 g/3 1/2 oz) dried red
    kidney beans or borlotti beans
1 tablespoon olive oil
1 leek, halved lengthways and
    chopped
1 small onion, diced
2 carrots, chopped
2 celery sticks, chopped
1 large zucchini, chopped
1 tablespoon tomato paste
1 litre (32 fl oz) vegetable stock
400 g (13 oz) pumpkin, cubed
2 potatoes, cubed
3 tablespoons chopped fresh flat-leaf
    parsley

1 Put the beans in a large bowl, cover
with cold water and soak overnight.
Rinse, then transfer to a saucepan,
cover with cold water and cook for
45 minutes, or until just tender. Drain.
2 Meanwhile, heat the oil in a large
saucepan. Add the leek and onion and
cook over medium heat for
2–3 minutes without browning, or
until they start to soften. Add the
carrot, celery and zucchini and cook
for 3–4 minutes. Add the tomato paste
and stir for a further 1 minute. Pour in
the stock and 1.25 litres (40 fl oz)
water and bring to the boil. Reduce the
heat to low and leave to simmer for
20 minutes.
3 Add the pumpkin, potato, parsley

and red kidney beans and simmer for
a further 20 minutes, or until the
vegetables are tender and the beans
are cooked. Season to taste. Serve
immediately with crusty wholemeal or
wholegrain bread.

NUTRITION PER SERVE
Protein 7.5 g; Fat 4 g; Carbohydrate 19 g;
Dietary Fibre 7 g; Cholesterol 0 mg;
600 kJ (143 cal)

HINT: To save time, use a 420 g
(14 oz) can of red kidney beans. Rinse
and drain well before use.

Using a sharp knife, cut the flesh of the pumpkin
into small cubes.

Add the vegetables and beans and simmer until
the vegetables are tender.

PARSNIP AND MUSTARD SOUP

Preparation time: 25 minutes
Total cooking time: 30 minutes
Serves 4–6

30 g (1 oz) butter
1 onion, chopped
750 g (1¹/₂ lb) parsnips, chopped
4 cups (1 litre/32 fl oz) vegetable stock
¹/₂ cup (125 ml/4 fl oz) milk
¹/₂ cup (125 ml/4 fl oz) cream
2–3 tablespoons wholegrain mustard
2 tablespoons chopped flat-leaf
    parsley, to serve

1 Melt the butter in a large pan, add the onion and cook over moderate heat, stirring occasionally, until soft but not brown.
2 Add the parsnip and stock and bring to the boil. Simmer, covered, for 25 minutes, or until the parsnip is tender. Set aside to cool slightly.
3 Blend the soup in batches, in a blender or food processor. Return to the pan, add the milk and cream and reheat gently, but do not allow the soup to boil. Stir in the wholegrain mustard and season to taste with salt and freshly ground black pepper. Serve topped with the chopped fresh parsley.

NUTRITION PER SERVE (6)
Protein 4 g; Fat 15 g; Carbohydrate 15 g;
Dietary Fibre 4 g; Cholesterol 45 mg;
850 kJ (200 cal)

Cut the peeled parsnips into strips, then chop into small pieces.

Add the parsnip and vegetable stock to the pan.

Stir in the wholegrain mustard—this will add a delicious texture to the soup.

LEEK AND POTATO SOUP

Preparation time: 15 minutes
Total cooking time: 30 minutes
Serves 4

4 leeks, white part only
30 g (1 oz) butter
3 floury potatoes, chopped
3 cups (750 ml/24 fl oz) vegetable
    stock
1 cup (250 ml/8 fl oz) milk
1/4 teaspoon ground nutmeg
cream and chopped fresh spring
    onions, to garnish

1 Wash the leeks thoroughly before use—slice them down their length but without cutting off the root, so they still hold together. Then rinse under running water to get rid of any grit hidden in the layers. Now chop well. Heat the butter in a large heavy-based pan. Add the leek and cook for 3–4 minutes, stirring frequently, until softened. Add the potato and stock. Bring slowly to the boil, then reduce the heat and simmer for 20 minutes, or until the vegetables are tender.

2 Cool the mixture slightly then transfer to a blender or food processor and purée in batches. Return to the pan, stir in the milk and nutmeg, and season well with salt and cracked black pepper. Reheat gently and serve garnished with a swirl of cream and a scattering of spring onion.

NUTRITION PER SERVE
Protein 4 g; Fat 6.5 g; Carbohydrate 16 g;
Dietary Fibre 4 g; Cholesterol 20 mg;
584 kJ (140 cal)

Slice the leeks along their length, then wash under running water to remove any dirt.

Cook the leek in the butter, stirring frequently, until it has softened.

Transfer the soup to a blender or food processor and purée in batches.

GAZPACHO

Preparation time: 40 minutes
+ 3 hours refrigeration
Total cooking time: Nil
Serves 4–6

750 g (1 1/2 lb) ripe tomatoes
1 Lebanese cucumber, chopped
1 green capsicum, chopped
2–3 cloves garlic, crushed
1–2 tablespoons finely chopped
  black olives
1/3 cup (80 ml/2 3/4 fl oz) red or white
  wine vinegar
1/4 cup (60 ml/2 fl oz) olive oil
1 tablespoon tomato paste

ACCOMPANIMENTS
1 onion, finely chopped
1 red capsicum, finely chopped
2 spring onions, finely chopped
1 Lebanese cucumber, finely chopped
2 hard-boiled eggs, chopped
chopped fresh mint or parsley
croutons

1 To peel the tomatoes, score a cross
in the base of each tomato. Cover with
boiling water for 30 seconds, then
plunge into cold water. Drain and peel
away the tomato skin from the cross.
Chop the flesh so finely that it is
almost a purée.
2 Mix together the tomato, cucumber,
capsicum, garlic, olives, vinegar, oil,

and tomato paste, and season to taste
with salt and freshly ground black
pepper. Cover and refrigerate for
2–3 hours.
3 Use 2–3 cups (750 ml/24 fl oz) of
chilled water to thin the soup to your
taste. Serve chilled, with the chopped
onion, capsicum, spring onion,
cucumber, boiled egg, herbs and
croutons served separately for diners
to add to their own bowls.

NUTRITION PER SERVE (6)
Protein 5 g; Fat 2 g; Carbohydrate 7 g;
Dietary Fibre 4 g; Cholesterol 70 mg;
310 kJ (75 cal)

Halve the cucumber lengthways, cut into strips and chop finely.

Put the tomatoes in a heatproof bowl and cover with boiling water.

Using a sharp knife, chop the tomato flesh very finely to a purée.

LENTIL AND SPINACH SOUP

Preparation time: 25 minutes
Total cooking time: 1 hour
Serves 8

1/2 cup (95 g/3 oz) brown lentils
2 tablespoons vegetable oil
1 leek, chopped
1 onion, chopped
1 stick celery, chopped
600 g (1 1/4 lb) potatoes, chopped

4 cups (1 litre/32 fl oz) vegetable stock
250 g (8 oz) English spinach

1 Put the lentils in a pan. Cover with
water and bring to the boil, reduce the
heat and simmer for 20 minutes, or
until tender; drain.
2 Heat the oil in a large pan. Cook the
leek, onion and celery for 5 minutes,
or until softened. Add the potato
and cook, stirring frequently, for
10 minutes. Add the vegetable stock
and bring to the boil. Reduce the heat
and simmer, covered, for 20 minutes,

or until the potato is tender.
3 Remove the stalks from the spinach,
wash the leaves well, add to the soup
and cook for 1–2 minutes. Let the soup
cool for a couple of minutes, then
purée in a food processor or blender.
Return to the pan, add the lentils and
reheat gently before serving.

NUTRITION PER SERVE
Protein 5 g; Fat 5 g; Carbohydrate 15 g;
Dietary Fibre 4 g; Cholesterol 0 mg;
505 kJ (120 cal)

Place the lentils in a pan and cover with plenty of cold water.

Cook the leek, onion and celery until soft, then add the chopped potato.

Add the cooked and drained lentils to the puréed soup in the pan.

VEGETABLE AND WATERCRESS SOUP

Preparation time: 40 minutes
Total cooking time: 1 hour
Serves 4

VEGETABLE STOCK
1 tablespoon oil
1 onion
2 leeks, chopped
4 carrots, chopped
2 parsnips, chopped
4 sticks celery, with leaves
8 cm (3 inch) piece of ginger, roughly
    chopped

2 carrots, extra
2 sticks celery, extra
2 leeks, extra
200 g (6¹/₂ oz) whole baby corn
1 head broccoli
50 g (1³/₄ oz) baby beans or whole
    beans cut into short lengths
100 g (3¹/₂ oz) sugar snap peas
2–3 tablespoons soy sauce
1–2 tablespoons sesame oil
2 cups (60 g/2 oz) watercress sprigs,
    to serve

1 To make the stock, heat the oil in a large pan and cook the vegetables, covered, for 5 minutes, without colouring. Add the ginger and 8 cups (2 litres) of water and bring to the boil. Reduce the heat to simmer for 1 hour.
2 Cut the extra carrots and celery into matchsticks and the leeks into strips. Cut the corn in half lengthways and trim the broccoli into florets.
3 Strain the stock and discard the vegetables. Strain again, back into the pan and bring the stock to a simmer. Add the carrot, corn and baby beans and cook for 3 minutes. Add the celery, leek, broccoli and sugar snap peas and cook for 3–4 minutes. Do not overcook the vegetables—they should be tender but crisp.
4 Add the soy sauce and sesame oil and season to taste. Stir in the watercress and serve immediately.

NUTRITION PER SERVE
Protein 9 g; Fat 6 g; Carbohydrate 25 g;
Dietary Fibre 10 g; Cholesterol 0 mg;
800 kJ (200 cal)

Trim the coarse stems from the watercress, leaving just the leaves and fine stems.

Cut the carrots and celery into matchsticks, and the leeks into strips.

Using a sharp knife, divide the broccoli into small florets.

Strain the stock a second time, so that any bits of vegetable are removed.

EGGPLANT AND CORIANDER TOSTADAS

Preparation time: 20 minutes
Total cooking time: 30 minutes
Serves 4 as a starter

1 small eggplant, cut into cubes
1/2 red capsicum, cut into cubes
1/2 red onion, cut into thin wedges
2 tablespoons olive oil
1 large clove garlic, crushed
1 small loaf wood-fired bread, cut into
    12 slices
1 small ripe tomato, halved
2 tablespoons chopped fresh mint
2 tablespoons chopped fresh
    coriander roots, stems and leaves
60 g (2 oz) slivered almonds, toasted

1 Preheat the oven to very hot 240°C (475°F/Gas 9). Put the eggplant, capsicum, onion and oil in a large bowl and mix to coat with the oil. Spread out in a single layer in a large roasting tin. Bake for 15 minutes, then turn and bake for a further 10 minutes, or until tender. Transfer to a bowl, add the garlic and season to taste with salt and pepper.
2 Place the bread on a baking tray and bake for 4 minutes, or until crisp. Rub the cut side of the tomato onto one side of each bread slice, squeezing the tomato to get as much liquid as possible, then finely chop the tomato flesh and add to the vegetables with the mint and coriander.
3 Spoon the vegetables onto the tomato side of the bread and sprinkle with the almonds. Serve immediately.

NUTRITION PER SERVE
Protein 10 g; Fat 18 g; Carbohydrate 34 g;
Dietary Fibre 5 g; Cholesterol 0 mg;
1415 kJ (340 cal)

NOTE: You can roast the vegetables and toast the almonds up to a day ahead. Store in an airtight container.

Spread the oil-coated vegetables in a single layer in a large roasting tin.

Tip the roasted vegetables into a bowl and mix with the garlic and seasoning.

Rub the cut side of the tomato onto one side of each slice of bread.

CREAM OF ASPARAGUS SOUP

Preparation time: 20 minutes
Total cooking time: 55 minutes
Serves 4–6

1 kg (2 lb) asparagus spears
30 g (1 oz) butter
1 onion, finely chopped
1 litre (32 fl oz) vegetable stock
1/4 cup (7 g/1/4 oz) basil leaves,
   chopped
1 teaspoon celery salt
1 cup (250 ml/8 fl oz) cream

1 Break off the woody ends from the asparagus (hold both ends of the spear and bend it gently—the woody end will snap off and can be thrown away) and trim off the tips. Blanch the tips in boiling water for 1–2 minutes, refresh in cold water and set aside. Chop the asparagus stems into large pieces.
2 Melt the butter in a large pan and cook the onion for 3–4 minutes over medium-low heat, or until soft and golden. Add the chopped asparagus stems and cook for 1–2 minutes, stirring continuously.
3 Add the stock, basil and celery salt. Bring to the boil, reduce the heat and simmer, covered, for 30 minutes.
4 Check that the asparagus is well cooked and soft. If not, simmer for a further 10 minutes. Set aside and allow to cool slightly.
5 Pour into a processor and process in batches until smooth. Then sieve into a clean pan. Return to the heat, pour in the cream and gently reheat. Do not allow the soup to boil. Season to taste with salt and white pepper. Add the asparagus tips and serve immediately.

NUTRITION PER SERVE (6)
Protein 6 g; Fat 22 g; Carbohydrate 5 g;
Dietary Fibre 3 g; Cholesterol 70 mg;
990 kJ (237 cal)

HINT: If you are not using home-made stock, always taste before adding seasoning to your soup—shop-bought stock can be very salty.

The woody end from the asparagus spear will snap off when you bend the spear.

Test whether the asparagus is well cooked by piercing it with a fork.

CREAM OF MUSHROOM SOUP

Preparation time: 30 minutes
Total cooking time: 15 minutes
Serves 4

500 g (1 lb) large field mushrooms
50 g (1³/4 oz) butter
4 spring onions, finely chopped
3 cloves garlic, finely chopped
1 teaspoon chopped lemon thyme
2 teaspoons plain flour

1 litre (32 fl oz) vegetable stock
1 cup (250 ml/8 fl oz) cream
chives and thyme, to garnish

1 Thinly slice the mushroom caps, discarding the stalks. Melt the butter in a heavy-based pan and cook the spring onion, garlic and lemon thyme, stirring, for 1 minute, or until the garlic is golden. Add the mushroom and a good shake each of salt and white pepper. Cook for 3–4 minutes, or until the mushroom just softens. Add the flour and cook, stirring, for 1 minute.

2 Remove from the heat and add the stock, stirring continuously. Return to the heat and bring to the boil, stirring. Reduce the heat and simmer gently for 2 minutes, stirring occasionally.
3 Whisk the cream into the soup, then reheat gently, stirring. Do not allow the soup to boil. Season to taste and garnish with the chives and thyme.

NUTRITION PER SERVE
Protein 8 g; Fat 50 g; Carbohydrate 6 g;
Dietary Fibre 4 g; Cholesterol 190 mg;
1985 kJ (475 cal)

Pull the lemon thyme leaves from the stems and chop them.

Remove the stalks from the mushrooms and thinly slice the caps.

Whisk in the cream, then reheat the soup gently without boiling.

CREAM OF TOMATO SOUP

Preparation time: 25 minutes
Total cooking time: 30 minutes
Serves 4

1.25 kg (2¹/₂ lb) very ripe tomatoes
1 tablespoon oil
1 onion, chopped
1 clove garlic, chopped
1¹/₂ cups (375 ml/12 fl oz)
   vegetable stock
2 tablespoons tomato paste
1 teaspoon sugar
1 cup (250 ml/8 fl oz) cream

1 Score a cross in the base of each tomato. Cover with boiling water for 30 seconds, then plunge into iced water, drain and peel away the skins. Scoop out the seeds and discard, then roughly chop the flesh.

2 Heat the oil in a large pan and cook the onion for 3 minutes, or until soft. Add the garlic and cook for 1 minute longer. Add the tomato and cook for 5 minutes, stirring occasionally, until very soft. Stir in the stock, bring to the boil, reduce the heat and simmer for 10 minutes.

3 Cool slightly, then transfer to a food processor. Process in batches until smooth, and return to the pan. Add the tomato paste and sugar and bring to

the boil, stirring continuously. Reduce the heat and stir in the cream but do not allow the soup to boil. Season to taste before serving. Serve with a swirl of cream and chopped parsley.

NUTRITION PER SERVE
Protein 5 g; Fat 30 g; Carbohydrate 10 g;
Dietary Fibre 5 g; Cholesterol 85 mg;
1480 kJ (350 cal)

HINT: It is best to use plump, ripe tomatoes for this recipe.

NOTE: If you are not using home-made stock, remember to taste the soup before seasoning. Shop-bought stock can be very salty.

Plunge the tomatoes into iced water, then peel away the skin.

Cook, stirring with a wooden spoon, until the tomato is very soft.

Add the tomato paste and sugar and bring to the boil, stirring until smooth.

BLUE CHEESE GNOCCHI

Preparation time: 20 minutes
Total cooking time: 20 minutes
Serves 8 as a starter

500 g (1 lb) potatoes, quartered
1¼ cups (155 g/5 oz) plain flour

SAUCE
300 ml (10 fl oz) cream
125 g (4 oz) gorgonzola cheese,
    roughly chopped
2 tablespoons chopped fresh chives

1 Cook the potatoes in boiling salted water for 15–20 minutes or in the microwave until tender. Stir through a generous amount of salt. Drain the potatoes, then mash until completely smooth. Transfer to a bowl.

2 Sprinkle the flour into the bowl with one hand while kneading it into the potato mixture with the other hand. Continue kneading until all the flour is worked in and the dough is smooth. This should take a few minutes and will be sticky at first.

3 Divide the dough into three and roll each portion into a sausage that is 2 cm thick. Cut into 2.5 cm lengths and, using floured hands, press each gnocchi against a fork to flatten it and indent one side (the indentation helps the sauce coat the gnocchi).

4 Bring a large pan of water to the boil. Drop in the gnocchi, then reduce the heat and simmer until they rise to the surface. This will take 2–3 minutes. Lift out of the water with a slotted spoon and drain well. Arrange on a warm serving dish and keep warm.

5 Put the cream into a small pan and bring to the boil. Boil rapidly, stirring constantly, for about 5 minutes, or until reduced by one third. Remove from the heat and stir in the cheese. Season with salt and pepper, and pour over the gnocchi. Scatter the chives over the top and serve immediately.

NUTRITION PER SERVE
Protein 10 g; Fat 22 g; Carbohydrate 22 g; Dietary Fibre 1.5 g; Cholesterol 65 mg; 1370 kJ (325 cal)

Add the flour with one hand while kneading it into the potato with the other.

Gently knead the mixture until all the flour is mixed in and the dough is smooth.

Press the gnocchi against a fork to flatten it and indent one side.

Drop the gnocchi into boiling water and simmer until they rise.

Pies & Pastries

MUSHROOM, RICOTTA AND OLIVE PIZZA

Preparation time: 30 minutes + proving
Total cooking time: 1 hour
Serves 6

4 Roma (egg) tomatoes, quartered
3/4 teaspoon caster sugar
7 g (1/4 oz) dry yeast or
    15 g (1/2 oz) fresh yeast
1/2 cup (125 ml/4 fl oz) skim milk
13/4 cups (220 g/7 oz) plain flour
2 teaspoons olive oil
2 cloves garlic, crushed
1 onion, thinly sliced
750 g (11/2 lb) cap mushrooms, sliced
1 cup (250 g/8 oz) ricotta cheese
2 tablespoons sliced black olives
small fresh basil leaves

1 Preheat the oven to hot 210°C (415°F/Gas 6–7). Put the tomatoes on a baking tray covered with baking paper, sprinkle with salt, cracked black pepper and 1/2 teaspoon sugar and bake for 20 minutes, or until the edges are starting to darken.
2 Stir the yeast and remaining sugar with 3 tablespoons warm water until the yeast dissolves. Cover and leave in a warm place until foamy (if the yeast doesn't foam you will have to throw it away and start again). Warm the milk. Sift the flour into a large bowl and stir in the yeast and milk. Mix to a soft dough, then turn onto a lightly floured surface and knead for 5 minutes. Leave, covered, in a lightly oiled bowl in a warm place for 40 minutes, or until doubled in size.
3 Heat the oil in a pan and fry the garlic and onion until soft. Add the mushrooms and stir until they are soft and the liquid has evaporated. Cool.
4 Turn the dough out onto a lightly floured surface and knead lightly. Roll out to a 36 cm (15 inch) circle and transfer to a lightly greased oven or pizza tray. Spread with the ricotta, leaving a border to turn over the filling. Top with the mushrooms, leaving a circle in the centre and arrange the tomato and olives in the circle. Fold the dough edge over onto the mushroom and dust the edge with flour. Bake for 25 minutes, or until the crust is golden. Garnish with basil.

NUTRITION PER SERVE
Protein 15 g; Fat 7.5 g; Carbohydrate 30g;
Dietary Fibre 6 g; Cholesterol 20 mg;
1100 kJ (265 cal)

Leave the yeast in a warm place until it begins to foam and become active.

Spread the ricotta over the pastry, leaving a border to turn over the filling.

VEGETABLE, FETA AND PESTO PARCELS

Preparation time: 40 minutes
Total cooking time: 30 minutes
Serves 4

30 g (1 oz) butter
2 cloves garlic, crushed
150 g (5 oz) asparagus spears,
    trimmed and chopped
1 carrot, cut into julienne strips
1 zucchini, cut into julienne strips
1 red capsicum, cut into julienne strips
6 spring onions, thinly sliced on the
    diagonal
90 g (3 oz) mild feta cheese, crumbled
8 sheets filo pastry
60 g (2 oz) butter, melted
1/3 cup (90 g/3 oz) good-quality ready-
    made pesto
2 teaspoons sesame seeds

1 Preheat the oven to moderately hot
200°C (400°F/Gas 6). Heat the butter in
a large frying pan, then add the garlic
and vegetables. Cook over medium
heat for 3–4 minutes, or until just
tender. Cool completely and fold in
the feta. Divide the mixture into four
equal portions.

2 Work with four sheets of pastry at a
time, keeping the rest covered with a
damp tea towel. Brush each sheet with
melted butter and lay them on top of
one another. Cut in half widthways
and spread 1 tablespoon of the pesto
in the centre of each half, leaving a
2 cm (1 inch) border lengthways. Place
one portion of the vegetable feta
mixture on top of the pesto. Repeat
the process with the remaining pastry,
pesto and filling.

3 Brush the edges of filo with a little
butter, tuck in the sides and fold over
the ends to make four parcels. Place
on a greased baking tray, seam-side-
down, brush with the remaining butter
and sprinkle with sesame seeds. Bake
for 20–25 minutes, or until golden. Cut
in half diagonally and serve hot with
tomato chutney.

NUTRITION PER SERVE
Protein 28 g; Fat 16 g; Carbohydrate 126 g;
Dietary Fibre 6 g; Cholesterol 30 mg;
3205 kJ (766 cal)

Cut the carrot and zucchini into julienne strips
(the size and shape of matchsticks).

Cook the garlic and vegetables over medium
heat until just tender.

Cover the pesto with one portion of the
vegetable feta mixture.

Tuck in the sides and roll up the parcel until it sits
on the unsecured end.

BOREKAS

Preparation time: 30 minutes
Total cooking time: 20 minutes
Makes 24

225 g (7 oz) feta cheese,
    crumbled
200 g (6¹/₂ oz) cream cheese,
    slightly softened
2 eggs, lightly beaten
¹/₄ teaspoon ground nutmeg
20 sheets filo pastry
60 g (2 oz) butter, melted
3 tablespoons sesame seeds

1 Preheat the oven to moderate 180°C (350°F/Gas 4). Place the feta, cream cheese, egg and nutmeg in a bowl and mix until just combined—the mixture will be lumpy.

2 Work with five sheets of pastry at a time, keeping the rest covered with a damp tea towel. Lay each sheet on a work surface, brush with melted butter and lay them on top of each other. Use a ruler as guidance to cut the filo into six equal strips.

3 Place 1 tablespoon of the filling at one end of a strip, leaving a narrow border. Fold the pastry over to enclose the filling and form a triangle.

Continue folding the triangle over until you reach the end of the pastry, tucking any excess pastry under. Repeat with the remaining ingredients to make 24 triangles, and place on a lined baking tray.

4 Lightly brush with the remaining melted butter and sprinkle with sesame seeds. Bake for 15–20 minutes, or until puffed and golden.

NUTRITION PER BOREKA
Protein 4.5 g; Fat 8.5 g; Carbohydrate 6.5 g; Dietary Fibre 0.5 g; Cholesterol 35 mg; 505 kJ (120 cal)

Mix together the feta, cream cheese, egg and nutmeg until just combined.

Using a straight edge for guidance, cut the filo sheets into six even strips.

Fold the pastry over the filling, then continue folding until the end.

TOFU PASTRIES

Preparation time: 30 minutes +
4 hours refrigeration
Total cooking time: 20 minutes
Serves 4

150 g (5 oz) firm tofu
2 spring onions, chopped
3 teaspoons chopped fresh coriander
leaves
1/2 teaspoon grated orange rind
2 teaspoons soy sauce
1 tablespoon sweet chilli sauce
2 teaspoons grated fresh ginger
1 teaspoon cornflour
1/4 cup (60 g/2 oz) sugar
1/2 cup (125 ml/4 fl oz) rice vinegar

1 small Lebanese cucumber,
finely diced
1 small red chilli, thinly sliced
1 spring onion, extra, thinly sliced on
the diagonal
2 sheets ready-rolled puff pastry
1 egg, lightly beaten

1 Drain the tofu, then pat dry and cut into small cubes.
2 Put the spring onion, coriander, rind, soy and chilli sauces, ginger, cornflour and tofu in a bowl and gently mix. Cover, then refrigerate for 3–4 hours.
3 To make the dipping sauce, place the sugar and vinegar in a small saucepan and stir over low heat until the sugar dissolves. Remove from the

heat and add the cucumber, chilli and extra spring onion. Cool completely.
4 Preheat the oven to hot 220°C (425°F/Gas 7). Cut each pastry sheet into four squares. Drain the filling and divide into eight. Place one portion in the centre of each square and brush the edges with egg. Fold into a triangle and seal the edges with a fork.
5 Put the triangles on two lined baking trays, brush with egg and bake for 15 minutes. Serve with the sauce.

NUTRITION PER SERVE
Protein 9 g; Fat 24 g; Carbohydrate 48 g;
Dietary Fibre 2 g; Cholesterol 66 mg;
1946 kJ (464 cal)

Remove the saucepan from the heat and add the spring onion, cucumber and chilli.

Fold the pastry to enclose the filling, then seal the edges with a fork.

Gently mix the tofu and other ingredients together in a bowl.

SWEET POTATO AND LENTIL PASTRY POUCHES

Preparation time: 45 minutes
Total cooking time: 55 minutes
Makes 32

2 tablespoons olive oil
1 large leek, finely chopped
2 cloves garlic, crushed
125 g (4 oz) button mushrooms,
　roughly chopped
2 teaspoons ground cumin
2 teaspoons ground coriander
1/2 cup (95 g/3 oz) brown or green
　lentils
1/2 cup (125 g/4 oz) red lentils
2 cups (500 ml/16 fl oz) vegetable
　stock
300 g (10 oz) sweet potato, diced
4 tablespoons finely chopped fresh
　coriander leaves
8 sheets ready-rolled puff pastry
1 egg, lightly beaten
1/2 leek, extra, cut into thin strips
200 g (6 1/2 oz) plain yoghurt
2 tablespoons grated Lebanese
　cucumber
1/2 teaspoon soft brown sugar

1 Preheat the oven to moderately hot 200°C (400°F/Gas 6). Heat the oil in a saucepan over medium heat and cook the leek for 2–3 minutes, or until soft. Add the garlic, mushrooms, cumin and ground coriander and cook for 1 minute, or until fragrant.
2 Add the combined lentils and stock and bring to the boil. Reduce the heat and simmer for 20–25 minutes, or until the lentils are cooked through, stirring occasionally. Add the sweet potato in the last 5 minutes.
3 Transfer to a bowl and stir in the coriander. Season to taste. Cool.

4 Cut the pastry sheets into four even squares. Place 1 1/2 tablespoons of filling into the centre of each square and bring the edges together to form a pouch. Pinch together, then tie each pouch with string. Lightly brush with egg and place on lined baking trays. Bake for 20–25 minutes, or until the pastry is puffed and golden.
5 Soak the leek strips in boiling water

for 30 seconds. Remove the string and re-tie with a piece of blanched leek. Put the yoghurt, cucumber and sugar in a bowl and mix together well. Serve with the pastry pouches.

NUTRITION PER PASTRY POUCH
Protein 5 g; Fat 11 g; Carbohydrate 20 g;
Dietary Fibre 2 g; Cholesterol 17 mg;
835 kJ (200 cal)

Stir the coriander leaves into the cooked lentils and sweet potato.

Put the filling in the centre of each square, form a pouch and tie with string.

Blanch the long strips of leek by soaking them for 30 seconds in boiling water.

61

VEGETABLE TART WITH SALSA VERDE

Preparation time: 30 minutes +
  30 minutes refrigeration
Total cooking time: 50 minutes
Serves 6

1³/4 cups (215 g/7 oz) plain flour
120 g (4 oz) chilled butter, cubed
¹/4 cup (60 ml/2 fl oz) cream
1–2 tablespoons chilled water
1 large (250 g/8 oz) Desiree potato,
  cut into 2 cm (1 inch) cubes
1 tablespoon olive oil
2 cloves garlic, crushed
1 red capsicum, cut into cubes
1 red onion, sliced into rings
2 zucchini, sliced
2 tablespoons chopped fresh dill
1 tablespoon chopped fresh thyme
1 tablespoon drained baby capers
150 g (5 oz) marinated quartered
  artichoke hearts, drained
²/3 cup (30 g/1 oz) baby English
  spinach leaves

SALSA VERDE
1 clove garlic
2 cups (40 g/1¹/4 oz) fresh flat-leaf
  parsley
¹/3 cup (80 ml/2³/4 fl oz) extra virgin
  olive oil
3 tablespoons chopped fresh dill
1¹/2 tablespoons Dijon mustard
1 tablespoon red wine vinegar
1 tablespoon drained baby capers

1 Sift the flour and ¹/2 teaspoon salt into a large bowl. Add the butter and rub it into the flour with your fingertips until it resembles fine breadcrumbs. Add the cream and water and mix with a flat-bladed knife until the mixture comes together in beads. Gather together and lift onto a lightly floured work surface. Press into a ball, then flatten into a disc, wrap in plastic wrap and refrigerate for 30 minutes.

2 Preheat the oven to moderately hot 200°C (400°F/Gas 6). Grease a 27 cm (11 inch) loose-bottomed flan tin. Roll the dough out between two sheets of baking paper large enough to line the tin. Remove the paper and invert the pastry into the tin. Use a small pastry ball to press the pastry into the tin, allowing any excess to hang over the side. Roll a rolling pin over the tin, cutting off any excess. Cover the pastry with a piece of crumpled baking paper, then add baking beads. Place the tin on a baking tray and bake for 15–20 minutes. Remove the paper and beads, reduce the heat to moderate 180°C (350°F/Gas 4) and bake for 20 minutes, or until golden.

3 To make the salsa verde, combine all the ingredients in a food processor and process until almost smooth.

4 Boil the potato until just tender. Drain. Heat the oil in a large frying pan and cook the garlic, capsicum and onion over medium heat for 3 minutes, stirring frequently. Add the zucchini, dill, thyme and capers and cook for 3 minutes. Reduce the heat to low, add the potato and artichokes, and heat through. Season to taste.

5 To assemble, spread 3 tablespoons of the salsa over the pastry. Spoon the vegetable mixture into the case and drizzle with half the remaining salsa. Pile the spinach in the centre and drizzle with the remaining salsa.

NUTRITION PER SERVE
Protein 7 g; Fat 37 g; Carbohydrate 36 g;
Dietary Fibre 4.5 g; Cholesterol 65 mg;
2110 kJ (505 cal)

Rub the butter into the flour and salt with your fingertips until it resembles fine breadcrumbs.

Mix with a flat-bladed knife until the dough comes together in beads.

Press the pastry gently into the side of the greased flan tin.

Bake the pastry case until it is dry to the touch and golden brown.

Mix together the salsa verde ingredients in a food processor until almost smooth.

Spread salsa verde over the pastry base, then fill with the hot vegetables.

RATATOUILLE TARTE TATIN

Preparation time: 45 minutes +
  20 minutes refrigeration
Total cooking time: 50 minutes
Serves 6

1½ cups (185 g/6 oz) plain flour
90 g (3 oz) butter, chopped
1 egg
1 tablespoon oil
30 g (1 oz) butter, extra
2 zucchini, halved lengthways and
  sliced
250 g (8 oz) eggplant, diced
1 red capsicum, diced
1 green capsicum, diced
1 large red onion, diced
250 g (8 oz) cherry tomatoes, halved
2 tablespoons balsamic vinegar
½ cup (60 g/2 oz) grated Cheddar
300 g (10 oz) sour cream
3 tablespoons good-quality pesto

1 Sift the flour into a bowl and add the butter. Rub the butter into the flour with your fingertips until it resembles fine breadcrumbs. Make a well in the centre and add the egg (and 2 tablespoons water if the mixture is too dry). Mix with a flat-bladed knife, using a cutting action, until the mixture comes together in beads. Gather the dough together and lift onto a floured work surface. Press into a ball, flatten slightly into a disc, then wrap in plastic wrap and refrigerate for 20 minutes.

2 Preheat the oven to moderately hot 200°C (400°F/Gas 6). Grease a 25 cm (12 inch) springform tin and line with baking paper. Heat the oil and extra butter in a large frying pan and cook the zucchini, eggplant, capsicums and

onion over high heat for 8 minutes, or until just soft. Add the tomatoes and vinegar and cook for 3–4 minutes.

3 Place the tin on a baking tray and neatly lay the vegetables in the tin, then sprinkle with cheese. Roll the dough out between two sheets of baking paper to a 28 cm (11 inch) circle. Remove the paper and invert the pastry into the tin over the filling. Use a spoon handle to tuck the edge of the pastry down the side of the tin. Bake for 30–35 minutes (some liquid

will leak out), then leave to stand for 1–2 minutes. Remove from the tin and place on a serving plate, pastry-side-down. Mix the sour cream and pesto together in a small bowl. Serve with the tarte tatin.

NUTRITION PER SERVE
Protein 10 g; Fat 40 g; Carbohydrate 29 g;
Dietary Fibre 4.5 g; Cholesterol 144 mg;
2277 kJ (544 cal)

Mix with a flat-bladed knife until the mixture comes together in beads.

Add the cherry tomatoes and balsamic vinegar and cook for 3–4 minutes.

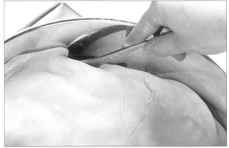
Use a spoon handle to tuck the edge of the pastry down the side of the tin.

SPINACH AND FETA TRIANGLES

Preparation time: 30 minutes
Total cooking time: 40 minutes
Makes 8

1 kg (2 lb) English spinach
1/4 cup (60 ml/2 fl oz) olive oil
1 onion, chopped
10 spring onions, sliced
1/3 cup (20 g/3/4 oz) chopped fresh
    parsley
1 tablespoon chopped fresh dill
large pinch of ground nutmeg
1/3 cup (35 g/1 1/4 oz) freshly grated
    Parmesan
150 g (5 oz) crumbled feta cheese
90 g (3 oz) ricotta cheese
4 eggs, lightly beaten
40 g (1 1/4 oz) butter, melted
1 tablespoon olive oil, extra
12 sheets filo pastry

1 Trim any coarse stems from the spinach. Wash the leaves thoroughly, roughly chop and place in a large pan with just a little water clinging to the leaves. Cover and cook gently over low heat for 5 minutes, or until the leaves have wilted. Drain well and allow to cool slightly before squeezing tightly to remove the excess water.
2 Heat the oil in a heavy-based frying pan. Add the onion and cook over low heat for 10 minutes, or until tender and golden. Add the spring onion and cook for a further 3 minutes. Remove from the heat. Stir in the drained spinach, parsley, dill, nutmeg, Parmesan, feta, ricotta and egg. Season well.
3 Preheat the oven to moderate 180°C (350°F/Gas 4). Grease two baking trays. Combine the melted butter with the extra oil. Work with three sheets of pastry at a time, keeping the rest covered with a damp tea towel. Brush each sheet with butter mixture and lay them on top of each other. Cut in half lengthways.
4 Spoon 4 tablespoons of the filling on an angle at the end of each strip. Fold the pastry over to enclose the filling and form a triangle. Continue folding the triangle over until your reach the end of the pastry. Put the triangles on the baking trays and brush with the remaining butter mixture. Bake for 20–25 minutes, or until the pastry is golden brown.

NUTRITION PER TRIANGLE
Protein 15 g; Fat 25 g; Carbohydrate 10 g; Dietary Fibre 4.5 g; Cholesterol 125 mg; 1325 kJ (315 cal)

NOTE: Feta is a salty Greek cheese that should be stored immersed in lightly salted water in the fridge. Rinse and pat dry before using.

VARIATION: If spinach isn't in season you can use silverbeet instead. Use the same quantity and trim the coarse white stems from the leaves.

Brush each sheet of filo pastry with the mixture of butter and oil.

Spoon the filling onto the end of the pastry at an angle. Fold the pastry over it to make a triangle.

Continue folding the triangle parcel until you reach the end of the pastry sheet.

CHEESE AND CHIVE SOUFFLE TART

Preparation time: 40 minutes
Total cooking time: 55 minutes
Serves 6–8

80 g (2³/₄ oz) butter
¹/₃ cup (40 g/1¹/₄ oz) sifted flour
1 cup (250 ml/8 fl oz) cream
²/₃ cup (170 ml/5¹/₂ fl oz) sour cream
4 eggs, separated
125 g (4 oz) Gruyère cheese, grated
3 tablespoons chopped chives
¹/₄ teaspoon ground nutmeg
pinch of cayenne pepper
12 sheets filo pastry

1 Preheat the oven to moderately hot 190°C (375°F/Gas 5). Grease a deep loose-based fluted flan tin measuring 20 cm (8 inches) across the base. Melt half the butter in a pan. Add the flour and cook, stirring, for 1 minute. Remove from the heat and gradually whisk in the cream and sour cream.
2 Return to the heat and whisk constantly until the mixture boils and thickens. Remove from the heat and whisk in the egg yolks. Then cover with plastic wrap and set aside to cool slightly. Whisk in the cheese, chives, nutmeg and cayenne.
3 Melt the remaining butter and brush some over each sheet of pastry. Fold each one in half and use to line the tin,

allowing the edges to overhang.
4 Beat the egg whites until stiff peaks form, then stir a spoonful into the cheese mixture to loosen it up a little. Gently fold in the rest. Spoon the mixture into the pastry shell and then carefully fold the edges of the filo pastry over the top, trying to keep as much volume in the soufflé as possible. Brush the top with the remaining melted butter and bake for 40–45 minutes, or until puffed and golden. Serve immediately.

NUTRITION PER SERVE (8)
Protein 10 g; Fat 40 g; Carbohydrate 15 g;
Dietary Fibre 1 g; Cholesterol 200 mg;
1895 kJ (450 cal)

Fold each buttered sheet of filo in half, and use to line the flan tin.

Fold a spoonful of the beaten egg white into the cheese mixture.

Carefully fold the filo pastry over the top of the filling, keeping as much volume as possible.

ROASTED TOMATO AND ZUCCHINI TARTLETS

Preparation time: 45 minutes
Total cooking time: 1 hour 20 minutes
Serves 6

3 Roma tomatoes, halved lengthways
1 teaspoon balsamic vinegar
1 teaspoon olive oil
3 small zucchini, sliced
375 g (12 oz) block puff pastry
1 egg yolk, beaten, to glaze
12 small black olives
24 capers, rinsed and drained

PISTACHIO MINT PESTO
1/2 cup (75 g/2 1/2 oz) unsalted shelled
    pistachio nuts
2 cups (40 g/1 1/4 oz) firmly packed
    mint leaves
2 cloves garlic, crushed
1/3 cup (80 ml/2 3/4 fl oz) olive oil
1/2 cup (50 g/1 3/4 oz) freshly grated
    Parmesan

1 Preheat the oven to slow 150°C (300°F/Gas 2). Place the tomatoes, cut-side-up, on a baking tray. Roast for 30 minutes, then brush with the combined vinegar and oil and roast for a further 30 minutes. Increase the oven to hot 210°C (415°F/Gas 6–7).
2 To make the pesto, place the pistachios, mint and garlic in a processor and process for 15 seconds. With the motor running, slowly pour in the olive oil. Add the Parmesan and process briefly.
3 Preheat the grill and line with foil. Place the zucchini in a single layer on the foil and brush with the remaining balsamic vinegar and oil. Grill for about 5 minutes, turning once.
4 Roll the pastry out to 25 x 40 cm

(10 x 16 inches) and cut out six 12 cm (5 inch) circles. Put on a greased baking tray and brush with egg yolk. Spread a tablespoon of pesto on each, leaving a 2 cm (3/4 inch) border. Divide the zucchini among the pastries and top with tomato halves. Bake for

15 minutes, or until golden. Top with olives, capers and black pepper.

NUTRITION PER SERVE
Protein 15 g; Fat 60 g; Carbohydrate 35 g;
Dietary Fibre 6 g; Cholesterol 80 mg;
3040 kJ (725 cal)

Roast the tomatoes for 30 minutes, then brush with the vinegar and oil.

Add the grated Parmesan to the pesto and process briefly until well mixed.

Arrange a few grilled zucchini slices over the pesto, leaving a clear border.

HIGH-TOP VEGETABLE PIE

Preparation time: 25 minutes +
    20 minutes refrigeration
Total cooking time: 1 hour 30 minutes
Serves 6

PASTRY
1 cup (125 g/4 oz) plain flour
60 g (2 oz) chilled butter, chopped
1 egg yolk
2 teaspoons poppy seeds
1–2 tablespoons iced water

30 g (1 oz) butter
2 tablespoons oil
1 onion, cut into thin wedges
1 leek, sliced
3 potatoes, cut into large chunks
300 g (10 oz) orange sweet potato,
    cut into large chunks
300 g (10 oz) pumpkin, cut into large
    chunks
200 g (6½ oz) swede, peeled and cut
    into large chunks
1 cup (250 ml/8 fl oz) vegetable stock
1 red capsicum, cut into large pieces
200 g (6½ oz) broccoli, cut into large
    florets
2 zucchini, cut into large pieces
1 cup (125 g/4 oz) grated vintage
    Cheddar

1 Preheat the oven to moderately hot 200°C (400°F/Gas 6). To make the pastry, sift the flour into a large bowl and add the butter. Rub the butter in with your fingertips until it resembles fine breadcrumbs. Make a well in the centre and add the egg yolk, poppy seeds and water and mix with a flat-bladed knife, using a cutting action, until the mixture comes together in beads. Gently gather the dough together and lift out onto a lightly floured work surface. Press the dough together into a ball and flatten it slightly into a disc, wrap in plastic wrap and refrigerate for 20 minutes.
2 Roll the dough out between two sheets of baking paper, then remove the top sheet and invert the pastry over a 23 cm (9 inch) pie plate. Use a small ball of pastry to help press the pastry into the plate then trim the edge. Prick the base with a fork and

bake for 15–20 minutes, or until dry to the touch and golden.
3 To make the filling, heat the butter and oil in a large saucepan, add the onion and leek and cook over medium heat for 5 minutes, or until soft and golden. Add the potato, sweet potato, pumpkin and swede and cook, stirring occasionally, until the vegetables start to soften. Add the stock and simmer for 30 minutes.
4 Add the remaining vegetables, reduce the heat and simmer for 20 minutes, or until the vegetables are

soft—some may break up slightly. The mixture should be just mushy. Season to taste with salt and pepper. Allow the mixture to cool a little.
5 Spoon the mixture into the shell, sprinkle with cheese and cook under a medium grill for 5–10 minutes, or until the cheese is golden brown.

NUTRITION PER SERVE
Protein 14 g; Fat 27 g; Carbohydrate 32 g;
Dietary Fibre 6.5 g; Cholesterol 90 mg;
1790 kJ (428 cal)

Prick the base of the pastry all over with a fork and bake until dry and golden.

Cook the vegetables until they are very soft when tested with a knife.

SPINACH PIE

Preparation time: 45 minutes +
  1 hour refrigeration
Total cooking time: 55 minutes
Serves 6

PASTRY
2 cups (250 g/8 oz) plain flour
30 g (1 oz) chilled butter, chopped
1/4 cup (60 ml) olive oil

FILLING
500 g (1 lb) English spinach leaves
2 teaspoons olive oil
1 onion, finely chopped
3 spring onions, finely chopped
200 g (6 1/2 oz) feta, crumbled
2 tablespoons chopped fresh flat-leaf
  parsley
1 tablespoon chopped fresh dill
2 tablespoons grated kefalotyri cheese
1/4 cup (45 g/1 1/2 oz) cooked white
  rice
1/4 cup (40 g/1 1/2 oz) pine nuts,
  toasted and roughly chopped
1/4 teaspoon ground nutmeg
1/2 teaspoon ground cumin
3 eggs, lightly beaten

1 Lightly grease a shallow 17 x 26 cm (7 x 10 inch) tin. To make the pastry, sift the flour and 1/2 teaspoon salt into a large bowl. Rub in the butter until it resembles fine breadcrumbs. Make a well in the centre and add the oil. Using your hands, mix together. Add 1/2 cup (125 ml/4 fl oz) warm water and mix with a flat-bladed knife, in a cutting action, until the mixture comes together in beads. Gently gather the dough together and lift out onto a lightly floured surface. Press into a ball and flatten into a disc. Wrap in plastic wrap and refrigerate for 1 hour.
2 Trim and wash the spinach, then coarsely chop the leaves and stems. Wrap in a tea towel and squeeze out as much moisture as possible. Heat the oil in a frying pan, add the onion and spring onion and cook over low heat, without browning, for 5 minutes, or until softened. Place in a bowl with the spinach and the remaining filling ingredients and mix well. Season.
3 Preheat the oven to moderately hot 200°C (400°F/Gas 6). Roll out just over

half the pastry between two sheets of baking paper, remove the top sheet and invert the pastry into the tin. Use a small ball of pastry to help press the pastry into the tin, allowing any excess to hang over the sides. Spoon the filling into the tin. Roll out the remaining pastry until large enough to cover the top. Place over the filling and press the two pastry edges firmly together to seal. Use a small sharp knife to trim away any extra pastry. Brush the top with a little oil, then score three strips lengthways, then on

the diagonal to make a diamond pattern on the surface. Make two slits in the top to allow steam to escape.
4 Bake for 45–50 minutes, covering with foil if the surface becomes too brown. The pie is cooked when it slides when the tin is gently shaken. Turn out onto a rack for 10 minutes, then cut into pieces and serve.

NUTRITION PER SERVE
Protein 19 g; Fat 33 g; Carbohydrate 39 g; Dietary Fibre 5 g; Cholesterol 133 mg; 2207 kJ (527 cal)

Line the tin with the pastry, then spoon the spinach filling into the tin.

Score a diamond pattern in the pastry, then make two slits so steam can escape.

FETA, TOMATO AND OLIVE PIZZA

Preparation time: 30 minutes +
  1 hour rising
Total cooking time: 50 minutes
Serves 4–6

PIZZA BASE
7 g (1/4 oz) sachet dry yeast
3/4 cup (90 g/3 oz) plain flour
3/4 cup (110 g/31/2 oz) wholemeal
    plain flour
1 tablespoon olive oil

1 tablespoon oil
2 onions, sliced
2 teaspoons soft brown sugar
1–2 tablespoons olive paste
250 g (8 oz) cherry tomatoes, halved
200 g (61/2 oz) feta cheese, crumbled
3 tablespoons shredded fresh basil

1 To make the dough, mix the yeast and flours in a large bowl. Make a well in the centre and add the olive oil and 1/2 cup (125 ml/4 fl oz) warm water. Mix well, adding a little more water if necessary, then gather together with your hands. Turn out and knead on a lightly floured surface for 5 minutes. Place in a lightly oiled bowl, cover with plastic wrap and leave in a draught-free place for 1 hour.
2 Meanwhile, heat the oil in a frying pan and cook the onion over medium–low heat for 20 minutes, stirring regularly. Add the sugar and cook, stirring, for 1–2 minutes, or until caramelized. Set aside to cool.
3 Preheat the oven to hot 220°C (425°F/Gas 7). Punch down the dough and knead for 1 minute. Roll out to a 30 cm (12 inches) round (it will shrink as you roll it), then tuck the edge of the dough under to create a rim. Sprinkle an oven tray lightly with polenta or brush with oil, and place the dough on the tray.
4 Spread the paste over the dough, leaving a narrow border, then top with the onion. Arrange the tomato halves over the onion, and sprinkle with feta and basil. Bake for 25 minutes.

NUTRITION PER SERVE (6)
Protein 11 g; Fat 15 g; Carbohydrate 25 g;
Dietary Fibre 4 g; Cholesterol 23 mg;
1170 kJ (279 cal)

Pour the olive oil and 1/2 cup (125 ml) warm water into the well.

Turn the dough out onto a lightly floured surface and knead.

Fold the edge of the dough under to give the pizza a rim.

Arrange the tomato halves over the onion and sprinkle the feta and basil on top.

ROAST VEGETABLE TART

Preparation time: 30 minutes
Total cooking time: 1 hour 45 minutes
Serves 4–6

2 slender eggplants, halved and cut
    into thick slices
350 g (11 oz) pumpkin, chopped
2 zucchini, halved and cut into thick
    slices
1–2 tablespoons olive oil
1 large red capsicum, chopped
1 teaspoon olive oil, extra
1 red onion, cut into thin wedges
1 tablespoon Korma curry paste
plain yoghurt, to serve

PASTRY
1¹/₂ cups (185 g/6 oz) plain flour
125 g (4 oz) butter, chopped
²/₃ cup (100 g/3¹/₂ oz) roasted
    cashews, finely chopped
1 teaspoon cumin seeds
2–3 tablespoons chilled water

1 Preheat the oven to moderately hot
200°C (400°F/Gas 6). Put the eggplant,
pumpkin and zucchini on a lined oven
tray, then brush with oil and bake for
30 minutes. Turn, add the capsicum
and bake for 30 minutes. Cool.
2 Meanwhile, heat the extra oil in a
frying pan and cook the onion for
2–3 minutes, or until soft. Add the
curry paste and cook, stirring, for
1 minute, or until fragrant and well
mixed. Cool. Reduce the oven to
moderate 180°C (350°F/Gas 4).
3 To make the pastry, sift the flour
into a large bowl and add the butter.
Rub the butter into the flour with your
fingertips until it resembles fine
breadcrumbs. Stir in the cashews and
cumin seeds. Make a well in the centre
and add the water. Mix with a flat-
bladed knife, using a cutting action,
until the mixture comes together in
beads. Gather the dough together and
lift out onto a sheet of baking paper.
Flatten to a disc, then roll out to a
35 cm (14 inch) circle.
4 Lift onto an oven tray and spread
the onion mixture over the pastry,
leaving a wide border. Arrange the
other vegetables over the onion, piling
them slightly higher in the centre.
Working your way around, fold the
edge of the pastry in pleats over the
vegetables. Bake for 45 minutes, or
until the pastry is golden. Serve
immediately with plain yoghurt.

NUTRITION PER SERVE (6)
Protein 9 g; Fat 34 g; Carbohydrate 33 g;
Dietary Fibre 5 g; Cholesterol 54 mg;
1959 kJ (470 cal)

Spread the onion mixture over the pastry, leaving
a good wide border for turning over.

Fold the edge of the pastry over the vegetables in
rough pleats.

VEGETABLE SAMOSAS

Preparation time: 35 minutes +
  20 minutes refrigeration
Total cooking time: 30 minutes
Makes 32

4 cups (500 g/1 lb) plain flour
2 tablespoons oil

VEGETABLE FILLING
600 g (1¹/₄ lb) waxy potatoes
185 g (6 oz) cauliflower florets,
  chopped
2 tablespoons vegetable oil
1 onion, chopped
2 cloves garlic, finely chopped
2 tablespoons grated fresh ginger
2 tablespoons mild curry powder
²/₃ cup (100 g/3¹/₂ oz) frozen peas
2 tablespoons lemon juice
oil, for deep-frying

1 In a food processor, process the flour and 1 teaspoon of salt for 5 seconds. Add the combined oil and 1 cup (250 ml/8 fl oz) of warm water. Process in short bursts until the mixture just comes together. Turn out onto a floured surface and gather into a ball. Cover with plastic wrap and refrigerate for 20 minutes.
2 To make the vegetable filling, chop the potatoes into quarters and cook until tender, then cool and finely dice. Boil or steam the cauliflower until tender, cool and finely dice. Heat the oil in a large frying pan and cook the onion over medium heat for 5 minutes, or until soft. Add the garlic, ginger and curry powder and cook for 2 minutes. Add the potato, cauliflower, peas and lemon juice and mix well. Remove from the heat and cool.
3 Divide the dough into 16 portions.

On a lightly floured surface, roll each portion into a 15 cm (6 inch) round, cut the rounds in half and put a tablespoon of the mixture in the middle of each semi-circle. Brush the edge with a little water and fold the pastry over the mixture, pressing the edges to seal.
4 Heat a deep-fat fryer, or fill a deep pan one third full of oil and heat until a cube of bread browns in 15 seconds.

Deep-fry the samosas in batches for 1 minute, or until golden. Drain on paper towels and serve hot with mango chutney, sweet chilli sauce or natural yoghurt.

NUTRITION PER SAMOSA
Protein 2.5 g; Fat 3.5 g; Carbohydrate 15 g; Dietary Fibre 1.5 g; Cholesterol 0 mg; 410 kJ (95 cal)

Process the flour, salt, oil and water until the mixture just comes together.

Add the potato, cauliflower, peas and lemon juice to the onion mixture.

Brush the edge of the dough with water, then fold the filling over the top and seal.

BLUE CHEESE AND ONION FLAN

Preparation time: 40 minutes +
    20 minutes refrigeration
Total cooking time: 1 hour 40 minutes
Serves 8

2 tablespoons olive oil
1 kg (2 lb) red onions, very thinly sliced
1 teaspoon soft brown sugar
2 cups (250 g/8 oz) plain flour
100 g (3¹/₂ oz) cold butter, cubed
³/₄ cup (180 ml/6 fl oz) cream
3 eggs
100 g (3¹/₂ oz) blue cheese, crumbled
1 teaspoon freshly chopped lemon
    thyme or thyme leaves

1 Heat the oil in a heavy-based pan over low heat. Add the onion and sugar and cook, stirring regularly, for 45 minutes, or until the onion is soft and lightly golden.
2 Process the flour and butter in a food processor for 15 seconds. Add 1–2 tablespoons of iced water and process in short bursts until the mixture just comes together. Turn out onto a floured surface and gather into a ball. Cover with plastic wrap and refrigerate for 10 minutes.
3 Preheat the oven to moderate 180°C (350°F/Gas 4). Roll out the pastry thinly on a lightly floured surface to fit a greased 22 cm (9 inch) round loose-based flan tin. Trim any excess pastry. Chill for 10 minutes. Line with

crumpled baking paper and fill with baking beads or rice. Put on a baking tray and bake for 10 minutes. Remove the paper and beads, then bake for 10 minutes, or until lightly golden and dry to the touch.
4 Cool, then gently spread the onion over the base of the pastry shell. Whisk together the cream, eggs, blue cheese, thyme and pepper to taste. Pour into the pastry shell and bake for 35 minutes, or until firm.

NUTRITION PER SERVE
Protein 9 g; Fat 30 g; Carbohydrate 25 g;
Dietary Fibre 1.5 g; Cholesterol 145 mg;
1718 kJ (410 cal)

Turn the dough out onto a lightly floured surface and gather into a ball.

Roll the pastry out thinly and line the greased flan tin, trimming away any excess.

Spread the onion over the cooled pastry base, then pour in the cream mixture.

PIZZA-TOPPED FOCACCIA

Preparation time: 30 minutes +
    1 hour 30 minutes standing
Total cooking time: 40 minutes
Serves 4

7 g (¹/₄ oz) sachet dry yeast
1 teaspoon sugar
2 tablespoons olive oil
2¹/₂ cups (310 g/10 oz) plain flour,
    sifted

PIZZA TOPPING
1 tablespoon tomato paste
1 large red capsicum, thinly sliced
125 g (4 oz) marinated artichoke
    hearts, quartered
¹/₄ cup (30 g/1 oz) black olives, pitted
200 g (6¹/₂ oz) bocconcini, thickly
    sliced

1 Combine the yeast, ³/₄ cup (185 ml/ 6 fl oz) of warm water and the sugar in a bowl and set aside in a warm place for 5–10 minutes, or until frothy. Put the oil, flour and 1 teaspoon salt in a large bowl, add the frothy yeast and mix to a soft dough.

2 Turn the dough out onto a lightly floured surface and knead for 10 minutes, or until smooth and elastic. Roll into a ball and place in a large oiled bowl. Cover with oiled plastic wrap and set aside in a warm place for 1 hour, or until the dough has doubled in size.

3 Preheat the oven to moderate 180°C (350°F/Gas 4). Punch down the dough with your fist to expel any air, and knead for 1 minute. Roll into a flat disc large enough to fit into a greased 23 cm (9 inch) springform tin. Press into the tin, cover with a tea towel and leave to rise for about 20 minutes.

4 Spread the tomato paste over the dough and arrange the other topping ingredients, except for the bocconcini, on top. Bake for 20 minutes, remove from the oven and spread the slices of bocconcini over the top, then bake for a further 20 minutes, or until the dough is well risen and firm to the touch in the centre. Cool on a wire rack before cutting and serving.

NUTRITION PER SERVE
Protein 25 g; Fat 20 g; Carbohydrate 60 g;
Dietary Fibre 5 g; Cholesterol 30 mg;
2235 kJ (535 cal)

Bocconcini are small balls of mozzarella. Cut them into thick slices with a sharp knife.

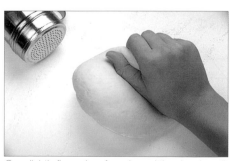

On a lightly floured surface, knead the dough until smooth and elastic.

Arrange the capsicum, artichokes and olives over the tomato paste.

ROASTED PUMPKIN AND SPINACH QUICHE

Preparation time: 20 minutes
Total cooking time: 1 hour 50 minutes
Serves 4–6

500 g (1 lb) butternut pumpkin
1 red onion, cut into small wedges
2 tablespoons olive oil
1 clove garlic, crushed
1 teaspoon salt
4 eggs
$1/2$ cup (125 ml/4 fl oz) cream
$1/2$ cup (125 ml/4 fl oz) milk
1 tablespoon parsley, chopped
1 tablespoon chopped coriander
1 teaspoon wholegrain mustard
6 sheets filo pastry
50 g ($1^3/4$ oz) English spinach,
   blanched
1 tablespoon grated Parmesan

1 Preheat the oven to moderately hot 190°C (375°F/Gas 5). Slice the pumpkin into 1 cm ($1/2$ inch) pieces leaving the skin on. Place the pumpkin, onion, 1 tablespoon of the olive oil, garlic and salt in a roasting tin. Roast for 1 hour, or until lightly golden and cooked.
2 Whisk together the eggs, cream, milk, herbs and mustard. Season with salt and pepper.
3 Grease a loose-based fluted flan tin or ovenproof dish measuring 22 cm (9 inches) across the base. Brush each sheet of filo pastry with oil and then line the flan tin with the six sheets. Fold the sides down, tucking them into the tin to form a crust.
4 Heat a baking tray in the oven for 10 minutes. Place the flan tin on the tray and arrange all the vegetables over the base. Pour the egg mixture over the vegetables and sprinkle with the Parmesan.
5 Bake for 35–40 minutes, or until the filling is golden brown and set.

NUTRITION PER SERVE (6)
Protein 10 g; Fat 20 g; Carbohydrate 15 g;
Dietary Fibre 2 g; Cholesterol 155 mg;
1200 kJ (285 cal)

Roast the vegetables until lightly golden and cooked through.

Line the flan tin with the six sheets of filo pastry.

Fold the sides of the filo pastry down and tuck them into the tin to form a crust.

Pour the mixture of egg and cream over the vegetables in the tin.

ARTICHOKE AND PROVOLONE QUICHES

Preparation time: 40 minutes +
   30 minutes refrigeration
Total cooking time: 35 minutes
Serves 6

2 cups (250 g/8 oz) plain flour
125 g (4 oz) cold butter, chopped
1 egg yolk

FILLING
1 small eggplant, sliced
6 eggs, lightly beaten
3 teaspoons wholegrain mustard

150 g (5 oz) provolone cheese, grated
200 g (6½ oz) marinated artichokes,
   sliced
125 g (4 oz) semi-dried tomatoes

1 Process the flour and butter in a processor for about 15 seconds until crumbly. Add the egg yolk and 3 tablespoons of water. Process in short bursts until the mixture comes together. Add a little extra water if you think the dough is a bit too dry. Turn out onto a floured surface and gather into a ball. Cover with plastic wrap and refrigerate for at least 30 minutes.
2 Preheat the oven to moderately hot 190°C (375°F/Gas 5) and grease six

11 cm (4½ inch) oval pie tins.
3 To make the filling, brush the sliced eggplant with olive oil and place under a grill until golden. Combine the eggs, mustard and cheese in a jug.
4 Roll out the pastry and line the tins. Trim away the excess pastry and decorate the edges. Place one eggplant slice and a few artichokes and tomatoes in each tin, pour the egg mixture over the top and bake for 25 minutes, or until golden.

NUTRITION PER QUICHE
Protein 20 g; Fat 30 g; Carbohydrate 35 g;
Dietary Fibre 4 g; Cholesterol 290 mg;
2025 kJ (480 cal)

Gather the pastry into a ball and cover with plastic wrap to refrigerate.

Brush each slice of eggplant with a little olive oil and then grill until golden.

Place one slice of eggplant in the bottom of each lined pie tin.

MUSHROOM QUICHE WITH PARSLEY PASTRY

Preparation time: 30 minutes +
  50 minutes refrigeration
Total cooking time: 1 hour
Serves 4–6

PASTRY
1¼ cups (155 g/5 oz) plain flour
¼ cup (15 g/½ oz) chopped fresh
  parsley
90 g (3 oz) cold butter, chopped
1 egg yolk

MUSHROOM FILLING
30 g (1 oz) butter
1 red onion, chopped
175 g (6 oz) button mushrooms, sliced
1 teaspoon lemon juice
⅓ cup (20 g/¾ oz) chopped fresh
  parsley
⅓ cup (20 g/¾ oz) chopped chives
1 egg, lightly beaten
⅓ cup (80 ml/2¾ oz) cream

1 To make the pastry, process the flour, parsley and butter for 15 seconds, or until crumbly. Add the egg yolk and 2 tablespoons of water. Process in short bursts until the mixture comes together. Add a little extra water if needed. Turn out onto a floured surface and gather into a ball. Cover with plastic wrap and refrigerate for at least 30 minutes.
2 Roll out the pastry between 2 sheets of baking paper until big enough to fit a loose-based flan tin measuring 35 x 10 cm (14 x 4 inches) across the base. Fit into the tin and trim off any excess pastry by rolling the rolling pin across the top of the tin. Refrigerate for 20 minutes. Preheat the oven to moderately hot 190°C (375°F/Gas 5).

Cover the pastry with baking paper and fill evenly with baking beads. Bake for 15 minutes. Remove the paper and beads and bake for a further 10 minutes, or until the pastry has dried out. Reduce the oven to moderate 180°C (350°F/Gas 4).
3 To make the mushroom filling, melt the butter in a pan and cook the onion for 2–3 minutes until soft. Add the mushrooms and cook, stirring, for 2–3 minutes, or until soft. Stir in the

lemon juice and herbs. Mix the egg and cream in a small jug and season well with salt and pepper.
4 Spread the mushroom mixture into the pastry shell and pour over the combined egg and cream. Bake for 25–30 minutes, or until set.

NUTRITION PER SERVE (6)
Protein 6 g; Fat 25 g; Carbohydrate 20 g; Dietary Fibre 2 g; Cholesterol 130 mg; 1350 kJ (320 cal)

Place the flour and parsley in a food processor and add the butter.

Use the rolling pin to lift the pastry into the flan tin, then roll over the top to trim off the excess.

Pour the combined egg and cream over the mushroom filling.

FRENCH SHALLOT TATIN

Preparation time: 45 minutes
 + 20 minutes refrigeration
Total cooking time: 1 hour
Serves 4–6

750 g (1½ lb) French shallots
50 g (1¾ oz) butter
2 tablespoons olive oil
⅓ cup (60 g/2 oz) soft brown sugar
3 tablespoons balsamic vinegar

PASTRY
1 cup (125 g/4 oz) plain flour
60 g (2 oz) cold butter, chopped
2 teaspoons wholegrain mustard
1 egg yolk

1 Peel the shallots, leaving the bases intact and tips exposed—to do this easily, put the unpeeled shallots in a bowl and cover with boiling water for 30 seconds. Drain and cool. This will make them easier to peel.
2 Heat the butter and olive oil in a large pan. Cook the shallots for 15 minutes over low heat, then remove. Add the sugar, vinegar and 3 tablespoons of water to the pan and stir to dissolve the sugar. Add the shallots and simmer over low heat for 15–20 minutes, turning occasionally.
3 Preheat the oven to moderately hot 200°C (400°F/Gas 6). To make the pastry, process the flour and butter until crumbly. Add the mustard, egg yolk and 1 tablespoon of water. Process in short bursts until the mixture comes together. Add a little extra water if necessary. Turn the mixture out onto a floured surface and quickly gather into a ball. Cover with plastic wrap and refrigerate for 20 minutes.

4 Grease a shallow 20 cm (8 inch) round sandwich tin. Pack the shallots tightly into the tin and pour over any syrup from the pan. Roll out the pastry on a sheet of baking paper to a circle, 1 cm (½ inch) larger than the tin. Lift the pastry into the tin and lightly push it down so it is slightly moulded over the shallots. Bake for 20–25 minutes, or until golden brown. Cool for 5 minutes on a wire rack. Place a serving dish over the tin and turn the tart out.

NUTRITION PER SERVE (6)
Protein 5 g; Fat 25 g; Carbohydrate 25 g;
Dietary Fibre 2 g; Cholesterol 75 mg;
1360 kJ (325 cal)

Return the shallots to the brown sugar and balsamic vinegar mixture in the pan.

Arrange the shallots over the base of the tin so that they are tightly packed together.

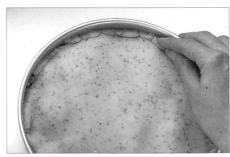

Lightly push the edge of the pastry down so that it moulds over the shallots.

MUSHROOM AND RICOTTA FILO TART

Preparation time: 35 minutes
Total cooking time: 40 minutes
Serves 6

60 g (2 oz) butter
270 g (9 oz) field mushrooms, sliced
2 cloves garlic, crushed
1 tablespoon Marsala
1 teaspoon thyme leaves
1/2 teaspoon chopped rosemary
  leaves
pinch of freshly grated nutmeg
5 sheets filo pastry
75 g (2 1/2 oz) butter, melted

200 g (6 1/2 oz) ricotta cheese
2 eggs, lightly beaten
1/2 cup (125 ml/4 fl oz) sour cream
1 tablespoon chopped parsley

1 Preheat the oven to moderate 180°C (350°F/Gas 4). Melt the butter in a frying pan and add the mushrooms. Cook over high heat for a few minutes, until they begin to soften. Add the garlic and cook for another minute. Stir in the Marsala, thyme, rosemary and nutmeg. Remove the mushrooms from the pan and drain off any liquid.
2 Work with one sheet of filo pastry at a time, keeping the rest covered with a damp tea towel to stop them drying out. Brush the sheets with melted

butter and fold in half. Place on top of each other to line a shallow 23 cm (9 inch) loose-based flan tin, allowing the edges to overhang.
3 Beat the ricotta, eggs and cream together and season to taste. Spoon half the mixture into the tin, then add the mushrooms. Top with the rest of the ricotta mixture. Bake for 35 minutes, or until firm. Sprinkle with the chopped parsley to serve.

NUTRITION PER SERVE
Protein 9 g; Fat 35 g; Carbohydrate 9 g;
Dietary Fibre 2 g; Cholesterol 160 mg;
1515 kJ (360 cal)

Remove the mushrooms from the pan, draining off as much liquid as possible.

Brush the filo with melted butter, fold in half and layer into the tin.

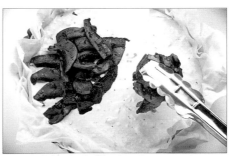
Layer half the ricotta filling into the pastry, then spread the mushrooms over the top.

POTATO, LEEK AND SPINACH QUICHE

Preparation time: 1 hour +
  50 minutes refrigeration
Total cooking time: 2 hours
Serves 6–8

2 cups (250 g/8 oz) plain flour
125 g (4 oz) cold butter, chopped

FILLING
3 potatoes
30 g (1 oz) butter
2 tablespoons oil
2 cloves garlic, crushed
2 leeks, sliced
500 g (1 lb) English spinach, trimmed
1 cup (125 g/4 oz) grated Cheddar
4 eggs
1/2 cup (125 ml/4 fl oz) cream
1/2 cup (125 ml/4 fl oz) milk

1 Place the flour in a food processor, add the butter and process for about 15 seconds until the mixture is crumbly. Add 2–3 tablespoons of water and process in short bursts until the mixture just comes together when you squeeze a little between your fingers. Add a little extra water if you think the dough is too dry. Turn out onto a floured surface and quickly bring the mixture together into a ball. Cover the pastry with plastic wrap and refrigerate for at least 30 minutes. Roll the pastry out between two sheets of baking paper until it is large enough to line a deep loose-based fluted flan tin measuring 21 cm (8 1/2 inches) across the base. Place on a baking tray and refrigerate for 20 minutes.
2 Peel and thinly slice the potatoes. Melt the butter and oil together in a frying pan and add the garlic and sliced potatoes. Gently turn the potatoes until they are coated, then cover and cook for 5 minutes over low heat. Remove the potatoes with a slotted spoon, drain on paper towels and set aside. Add the leeks to the pan and cook until they are softened, then remove from the heat.
3 Wash the spinach and put in a large saucepan with just the water clinging to the leaves. Cover the pan and cook for 2 minutes, or until it has just wilted. Cool the spinach and squeeze out any excess water, then spread the leaves out on a paper towel or a tea towel to allow to dry.
4 Preheat the oven to moderate 180°C (350°F/Gas 4). Cover the pastry shell with baking paper and fill evenly with baking beads. Bake for 15 minutes. Remove the paper and beads and bake for a further 15 minutes.
5 Spread half the cheese over the bottom of the pastry base and top with half the potatoes, half the spinach and half the leeks. Repeat these layers again. In a large jug, mix together the eggs, cream and milk and pour over the layered mixture. Bake for 1 hour 20 minutes, or until the filling is firm. Serve warm or cold.

NUTRITION PER SERVE (8)
Protein 15 g; Fat 35 g; Carbohydrate 35 g;
Dietary Fibre 5 g; Cholesterol 180 mg;
2150 kJ (510 cal)

NOTE: Spinach can be kept in a plastic bag and stored for up to 3 days in the refrigerator. It can often be very gritty, so wash thoroughly in a few changes of water. When cooking the spinach, you don't need to add any extra water, just heat it with the water still clinging to the leaves.

Squeeze a little of the pastry with your fingers: it should stick together.

Roll the pastry out between two sheets of baking paper.

Lift out the potatoes with a slotted spoon and drain on paper towels.

Cover the pan and cook the spinach for 2 minutes, or until it has just wilted.

Use your hands to squeeze out the excess water from the cooled spinach.

Build up layers of cheese, potato, spinach and leek in the pastry case.

81

CHARGRILLED VEGETABLE PIE WITH POLENTA PASTRY

Preparation time: 1 hour +
  50 minutes refrigeration
Total cooking time: 55 minutes
Serves 4–6

POLENTA PASTRY
1 cup (125 g/4 oz) plain flour
1/2 cup (75 g/21/2 oz) polenta
90 g (3 oz) cold butter, cubed
90 g (3 oz) cream cheese, cubed

1 kg (2 lb) eggplant, sliced lengthways
2 large tablespoons olive oil
1–2 cloves garlic, crushed
2 red capsicums, halved and seeded
8 cherry tomatoes, halved
handful of small basil leaves
2 teaspoons baby capers
1 teaspoon balsamic vinegar
1 teaspoon olive oil, extra

1 Place the flour, polenta, butter and cream cheese in a food processor. Process in short bursts until the mixture just comes together. Add 1–2 teaspoons of cold water if needed. Turn out onto a floured surface and quickly bring together into a ball. Cover with plastic wrap and refrigerate for at least 30 minutes.
2 Brush the eggplant with the combined olive oil and garlic and grill for 10–12 minutes, turning once and brushing 2–3 times during cooking. Grill the capsicum, skin-side-up, for 5–8 minutes, until the skin has blackened. Cool in a plastic bag, remove the skin and slice. Grill the tomatoes, cut-side-up, for 2–3 minutes.
3 Roll out the pastry on baking paper to fit a shallow 21 x 28 cm

(81/2 x 11 inch) loose-based flan tin. Press well into the sides and trim off any excess. Refrigerate for 20 minutes. Preheat the oven to moderately hot 190°C (375°F/Gas 5). Cover the pastry shell with baking paper and fill with baking beads. Bake for 15 minutes. Remove the paper and beads and bake the pastry shell for 15 minutes, or until it is cooked.

4 Layer the pastry with capsicum, eggplant, tomato halves, some basil leaves and capers. Brush with the combined balsamic vinegar and oil before serving.

NUTRITION PER SERVE (6)
Protein 7 g; Fat 25 g; Carbohydrate 30 g; Dietary Fibre 6 g; Cholesterol 55 mg; 1600 kJ (380 cal)

Crush the garlic; halve and seed the capsicums and halve the cherry tomatoes.

Process the mixture in short bursts until it just comes together.

Roll out the pastry on a sheet of baking paper until large enough to fit the tin.

TOMATO AND GOAT'S CHEESE PIE

Preparation time: 30 minutes +
 20 minutes refrigeration
Total cooking time: 30 minutes
Serves 6

1¹/₂ cups (185 g/6 oz) plain flour
100 g (3¹/₂ oz) cold butter, chopped
3 tablespoons grated mature Cheddar

FILLING
1 egg yolk, lightly beaten
3 tablespoons dried breadcrumbs
4–5 tomatoes, sliced
100 g (3¹/₂ oz) goat's cheese
1 tablespoon olive oil
2 tablespoons small basil leaves or
 shredded basil

1 Place the flour and butter in a food processor and process until crumbly. Add the Cheddar, ¹/₂ teaspoon of salt and 2–3 tablespoons of water. Process in short bursts until the mixture just comes together, adding a little extra water if necessary. Turn the mixture out onto a floured surface and quickly bring it together into a ball. Cover the pastry with plastic wrap and refrigerate for at least 20 minutes.

2 Preheat the oven to moderate 180°C (350°F/Gas 4). Roll out the pastry on a lightly floured surface into a circle about 35 cm (14 inches) in diameter. Wrap the pastry around a rolling pin and carefully lift it onto a greased baking tray. Carefully unroll the pastry into the tray.

3 Brush most of the egg yolk lightly over the pastry and sprinkle with the breadcrumbs. Arrange the slices of tomato on the pastry so that they overlap in a circle leaving a wide

border. Crumble the goat's cheese over the top of the tomatoes. Turn the edge of the pastry in over the tomato filling and brush with the remaining egg yolk (mix with a little milk if there's not much egg left).

4 Bake for 30 minutes, or until the pastry is golden and the cheese has melted. Then drizzle with the olive oil and season well with salt and freshly ground black pepper. Scatter the top of the pie with the basil leaves to serve.

NUTRITION PER SERVE
Protein 10 g; Fat 25 g; Carbohydrate 30 g;
Dietary Fibre 3 g; Cholesterol 95 mg;
1620 kJ (385 cal)

Process the flour and butter until crumbly, then add the cheese.

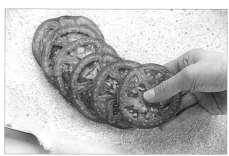

Lay the slices of tomato on the pastry and breadcrumbs so that they overlap.

Turn in the pastry edge over the tomato and goat's cheese filling.

THAI THREE MUSHROOM TART

Preparation time: 25 minutes
Total cooking time: 1 hour 10 minutes
Serves 8

375 g (12 oz) block puff pastry
1 teaspoon sesame oil
2 teaspoons oil
150 g (5 oz) shiitake mushrooms, trimmed
150 g (5 oz) button mushrooms, halved
150 g (5 oz) oyster mushrooms, halved
1/2 cup (125 ml/4 fl oz) coconut milk
1 stalk lemon grass, chopped
1 1/2 teaspoons grated fresh ginger
1 clove garlic, chopped
2 tablespoons chopped coriander leaves and stems
1 egg
1 tablespoon plain flour
1 spring onion, sliced diagonally

1 Preheat the oven to hot 210°C (415°F/Gas 6–7). Grease a shallow 19 cm x 28 cm (7 1/2 x 11 inch) rectangular loose-based flan tin, or a 25 cm (10 inch) round loose-based flan tin. Roll out the pastry to line the base and sides of the tin and trim off any excess. Prick all over with a fork. Bake for 20 minutes, or until crisp, then cool. While cooling, gently press down the pastry if it has puffed too high. Reduce the oven to moderately hot 200°C (400°F/Gas 6).

2 Heat the oils in a pan, add the shiitake and button mushrooms and stir until lightly browned. Add the oyster mushrooms, then cool. Pour away any liquid.
3 Process the coconut milk, lemon grass, ginger, garlic and coriander until fairly smooth. Add the egg and flour and blend in short bursts until combined. Season to taste.
4 Pour the mixture into the pastry, add the mushrooms and then the spring onion. Bake for 30 minutes, or until the filling has set.

NUTRITION PER SERVE
Protein 5 g; Fat 15 g; Carbohydrate 20 g; Dietary Fibre 2 g; Cholesterol 35 mg; 1045 kJ (250 cal)

Trim the shiitake mushrooms and halve the oyster and button mushrooms.

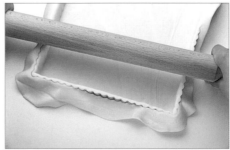
Trim the excess pastry quickly and easily by running a rolling pin over the tin.

Add the egg and flour to the coconut milk mixture and blend in short bursts.

CHEESE 'N' TATTIE PIE

Preparation time: 45 minutes
Total cooking time: 40 minutes
Serves 6–8

1 kg (2 lb) new potatoes, unpeeled, cooked and sliced
1 cup (125 g/4 oz) grated Cheddar
1 clove garlic, crushed
2 tablespoons chopped chives
2 tablespoons chopped marjoram
1/3 cup (80 ml/2³/4 fl oz) thick cream
2 eggs
2 sheets ready-rolled puff pastry
1 egg yolk, beaten, to glaze

1 Preheat the oven to hot 220°C (425°F/Gas 7). Place half the potatoes, overlapping the slices, in the base of a large dish, and season generously with salt and freshly ground black pepper. Sprinkle with half the cheese, garlic, chives and marjoram. Top with another layer of potato, cheese, garlic, chives and marjoram. Pour over the mixed cream and eggs.
2 Cut each pastry sheet into quarters, and each quarter into three equal lengths. Place the strips, overlapping, around the top of the pie, leaving the centre open. Press down the edges so that the pastry sticks to the pie dish, then trim the edge. Combine the egg

yolk with a little water and brush the top of the pie.
3 Bake for 15 minutes; reduce the heat to moderate 180°C (350°F/Gas 4), and bake for a further 15–20 minutes, or until the pastry is puffed and golden and the filling is set. Leave to stand for 10 minutes before serving.

NUTRITION PER SERVE (8)
Protein 15 g; Fat 20 g; Carbohydrate 30 g; Dietary Fibre 3 g; Cholesterol 115 mg; 1620 kJ (385 cal)

Top with another layer of potato slices, cheese, garlic, marjoram and chives.

Overlap the pastry strips around the top of the pie, leaving the centre open.

Brush the top of the pie with a little combined egg yolk and water.

Pasta

RICOTTA LASAGNE

Preparation time: 1 hour
Total cooking time: 1 hour 30 minutes
Serves 8

500 g (1 lb) fresh spinach lasagne
    sheets
1/2 cup (30 g/1 oz) fresh basil leaves,
    coarsely chopped
2 tablespoons fresh breadcrumbs
3 tablespoons pine nuts
2 teaspoons paprika
1 tablespoon grated Parmesan

RICOTTA FILLING
750 g (1 1/2 lb) ricotta cheese
1/2 cup (50 g/1 2/3 oz) grated
    Parmesan
pinch of nutmeg

TOMATO SAUCE
1 tablespoon olive oil
2 onions, chopped
2 cloves garlic, crushed
800 g (1 lb 10 oz) can crushed
    tomatoes
1 tablespoon tomato paste

BECHAMEL SAUCE
60 g (2 oz) butter
1/2 cup (60 g/2 oz) plain flour
2 cups (500 ml/16 fl oz) milk
2 eggs, lightly beaten
1/3 cup (35 g/1 1/4 oz) grated
    Parmesan

1 Lightly grease a 25 x 32 cm
(10 x 13 inch) baking dish. Cut the
pasta sheets into large pieces and
cook, two or three at a time, in boiling
water for 3 minutes. Drain and spread
on damp tea towels until needed.
2 To make the ricotta filling, put the
ricotta and Parmesan cheeses, nutmeg
and a good grinding of black pepper
in a bowl and mix together well.

3 To make tomato sauce, heat the oil
in a frying pan, add the onion and
cook for about 10 minutes, stirring
occasionally, until very soft. Add the
garlic and cook for 1 more minute.
Add the tomato and tomato paste and
stir until well combined. Stir until the
mixture comes to the boil. Reduce the
heat and simmer uncovered for
15 minutes, or until thickened,
stirring occasionally.
4 To make the béchamel sauce, heat
the butter in a small pan. When
starting to foam, add the flour and stir
for 3 minutes, or until just coloured.
Remove from the heat; add the milk
gradually, stirring after each addition,
then return to the heat and stir until
sauce boils and thickens. Remove
from the heat and stir in the eggs.
Return to moderate heat and stir until
almost boiling, but do not boil. Add
the cheese and season to taste. Put
plastic wrap directly onto the surface
of the sauce to prevent a skin
forming. Preheat the oven to 200°C
(400°F/Gas 6).
5 Put a layer of lasagne sheets in the
dish. Spread with a third of the ricotta
filling, sprinkle with basil, then top
with a third of the tomato sauce.
Repeat the layers, finishing with pasta.
6 Pour over the béchamel sauce and
spread until smooth, then sprinkle
with the combined breadcrumbs, pine
nuts, paprika and Parmesan. Bake for
45 minutes, or until browned. Leave
for 10 minutes before serving.

NUTRITION PER SERVE
Protein 28 g; Fat 30 g; Carbohydrate 60 g;
Dietary Fibre 4.5 g; Cholesterol 130 mg;
2622 kJ (625 cal)

NOTE: Leaving the lasagne to stand
before serving will help it to firm up
and makes it easier to cut.

SWEET POTATO RAVIOLI

Preparation time: 45 minutes
Total cooking time: 1 hour 10 minutes
Serves 6

500 g (1 lb) orange sweet potato, cut
    into large pieces
1/4 cup (60 ml/2 fl oz) olive oil
150 g (5 oz) ricotta cheese
1 tablespoon chopped fresh basil
1 clove garlic, crushed
2 tablespoons grated Parmesan
2 x 250 g (8 oz) packets egg won ton
    wrappers
60 g (2 oz) butter
4 spring onions, sliced on the diagonal
2 cloves garlic, crushed, extra
300 ml (10 fl oz) cream
baby basil leaves, to serve

1 Preheat the oven to hot 220°C
(425°F/Gas 7). Place the sweet potato
on a baking tray and drizzle with oil.
Bake for 40 minutes, or until tender.
2 Transfer the sweet potato to a bowl
with the ricotta, basil, garlic and
Parmesan and mash until smooth.
3 Cover the won ton wrappers with a
damp tea towel. Place 2 level
teaspoons of the sweet potato mixture
into the centre of one wrapper and
brush the edges with a little water. Top
with another wrapper. Place onto a
baking tray lined with baking paper
and cover with a tea towel. Repeat
with the remaining ingredients to
make 60 ravioli, placing a sheet of
baking paper between each layer.
4 Melt the butter in a frying pan. Add
the spring onion and garlic and cook
over medium heat for 1 minute. Add
the cream, bring to the boil, then
reduce the heat and simmer for
4–5 minutes, or until the cream has
reduced and thickened. Keep warm.
5 Bring a large saucepan of water to
the boil. Cook the ravioli in batches for
2–4 minutes, or until just tender. Drain
well. Ladle the hot sauce over the top
of the ravioli, garnish with the basil
leaves and serve immediately.

NUTRITION PER SERVE
Protein 11 g; Fat 40 g; Carbohydrate 35 g;
Dietary Fibre 2.5 g; Cholesterol 105 mg;
2351 kJ (560 cal)

Drizzle the chunks of sweet potato with oil and
bake until golden.

Cover the filling with a won ton wrapper, lining it
up with the bottom wrapper.

Simmer the cream mixture until it has reduced
and thickened.

Cook the ravioli in batches so that the pan is not
overcrowded. Cook until tender.

WARM PESTO PASTA SALAD

Preparation time: 20 minutes
Total cooking time: 20 minutes
Serves 4

PESTO
2 cloves garlic, crushed
1 teaspoon sea salt
3 tablespoons pine nuts, toasted
2 cups (60 g/2 oz) fresh basil
1/2 cup (50 g/1³/4 oz) grated
    Parmesan
1/3 cup (80 ml/2³/4 fl oz) extra virgin
    olive oil

500 g (1 lb) orecchiette or shell pasta
2 tablespoons olive oil
150 g (5 oz) jar capers, drained and
    patted dry
2 tablespoons extra virgin olive oil
2 cloves garlic, chopped
3 tomatoes, seeded and diced
300 g (10 oz) thin asparagus spears,
    cut in half and blanched
2 tablespoons balsamic vinegar
200 g (6¹/2 oz) rocket, trimmed and
    cut into short lengths
Parmesan shavings, to garnish

1 To make the pesto, place the garlic, sea salt and pine nuts in a food processor or blender and process until combined. Add the basil and Parmesan and process until finely minced. With the motor running, add the oil in a thin steady stream and blend until smooth.
2 Cook the pasta in a large saucepan of boiling water until *al dente*, then drain well.
3 Meanwhile, heat the oil in a frying pan, add the capers and fry over high heat, stirring occasionally, for 4–5 minutes, or until crisp. Remove from the pan and drain on crumpled paper towels.
4 In the same frying pan, heat the extra virgin olive oil over medium heat

and add the garlic, tomato and asparagus. Cook for 1–2 minutes, or until warmed through, tossing well. Stir in the balsamic vinegar.
5 Drain the pasta and transfer to a large serving bowl. Add the pesto and toss, coating the pasta well. Cool slightly. Add the tomato mixture and rocket and season to taste with salt and cracked black pepper. Toss well and sprinkle with the capers and Parmesan. Serve warm.

NUTRITION PER SERVE
Protein 22 g; Fat 45 g; Carbohydrate 90 g;
Dietary Fibre 9 g; Cholesterol 12 mg;
3629 kJ (868 cal)

Fry the capers over high heat, stirring occasionally, until crisp.

Add the pesto and toss thoroughly through the pasta. Allow to cool a little.

PUMPKIN AND BASIL LASAGNE

Preparation time: 20 minutes
Total cooking time: 1 hour 25 minutes
Serves 4

650 g (1 lb 5 oz) pumpkin
2 tablespoons olive oil
500 g (1 lb) ricotta cheese
1/3 cup (50 g/1 3/4 oz) pine nuts, toasted
3/4 cup (35 g/1 oz) fresh basil
2 cloves garlic, crushed
35 g (1 oz) Parmesan, grated
125 g (4 oz) fresh lasagne sheets
185 g (6 oz) mozzarella, grated

1 Preheat the oven to moderate 180°C (350°F/Gas 4). Lightly grease a baking tray. Cut the pumpkin into thin slices and arrange in a single layer on the tray. Brush with oil and cook for 1 hour, or until softened, turning halfway through cooking.
2 Place the ricotta, pine nuts, basil, garlic and Parmesan in a bowl and mix well with a wooden spoon.
3 Brush a square 20 cm (8 inch) ovenproof dish with oil. Cook the pasta according to the packet instructions. Arrange one third of the pasta sheets over the base of the dish and spread with the ricotta mixture. Top with half of the remaining lasagne sheets.

4 Arrange the pumpkin evenly over the pasta with as few gaps as possible. Season with salt and cracked black pepper and top with the final layer of pasta sheets. Sprinkle with mozzarella. Bake for 20–25 minutes, or until the cheese is golden. Leave for 10 minutes, then cut into squares.

NUTRITION PER SERVE
Protein 24 g; Fat 32 g; Carbohydrate 33 g; Dietary Fibre 4.5 g; Cholesterol 37 mg; 2166 kJ (517 cal)

NOTE: If the pasta has no cooking instructions, blanch them one at a time until softened. Then drain and spread on tea towels to dry.

Mix together the ricotta, pine nuts, basil, garlic and Parmesan.

Cook the pasta according to the packet instructions until *al dente*.

Place the pumpkin on top of the lasagne sheet, leaving as few gaps as possible.

HERB RAVIOLI

Preparation time: 1 hour + 30 minutes
  standing
Total cooking time: 10 minutes
Serves 4

300 g (10 oz) plain flour
3 eggs, beaten
3 tablespoons oil
1 cup (250 g/8 oz) ricotta cheese
2 tablespoons grated Parmesan
2 teaspoons chopped fresh chives
1 tablespoon chopped flat-leaf parsley
2 teaspoons chopped fresh basil
1 teaspoon chopped fresh lemon
  thyme or thyme
1 egg, beaten, extra

1 Sift the flour into a bowl and make a well in the centre. Gradually mix in the eggs and oil. Turn out onto a lightly floured surface and knead for 6 minutes, or until smooth. Cover with plastic wrap and leave for 30 minutes.
2 To make the filling, mix the ricotta, Parmesan and herbs. Season well.
3 Divide the dough into four portions and shape each into a log. Keeping the unworked portions covered, take one portion and flatten it with one or two rolls of a rolling pin. With machine rollers set to the widest setting, crank the dough through two or three times. Fold it into thirds, turn the dough by 90 degrees and feed it through again. If the dough feels sticky, flour it lightly each time it is rolled. Repeat the rolling and folding 8–10 times until the dough feels smooth and elastic. Reduce the width of the rollers by one setting and pass the dough through without folding it. Repeat, setting the rollers one notch closer each time until you have reached a thickness of 2 mm

(¹/₆ inch). Roll another sheet slightly larger than the first and cover with a tea towel.
4 Spread the smaller sheet out onto a work surface. Spoon 1 teaspoon of the filling at 5 cm (2 inch) intervals. Brush the beaten egg between the filling along the cutting lines. Place the larger sheet on top. Press the two sheets together along the cutting line. Cut the ravioli with a pastry wheel or knife. Transfer to a lightly floured baking

tray. Repeat with the remaining dough and filling. Can be stored in the refrigerator for 1–2 days.
5 Cook the ravioli in a large pan of salted boiling water for 5–8 minutes and top with a sauce of your choice.

NUTRITION PER SERVE
Protein 25 g; Fat 30 g; Carbohydrate 55 g;
Dietary Fibre 3 g; Cholesterol 215 mg;
2395 kJ (570 cal)

Mix together the ricotta, Parmesan and herbs and season with salt and pepper.

Brush the beaten egg between the filling along the cutting lines.

Press the two sheets of dough together and cut the ravioli with a pastry wheel.

PASTA WITH RICOTTA, CHILLI AND HERBS

Preparation time: 15 minutes
Total cooking time: 20 minutes
Serves 4

500 g (1 lb) spiral pasta or penne
3 tablespoons olive oil
3 cloves garlic, crushed
2 teaspoons very finely chopped fresh
    chilli

1 cup (30 g/1 oz) fresh flat-leaf parsley
    leaves, roughly chopped
1/2 cup (15 g/1/2 oz) fresh basil leaves,
    shredded
1/2 cup (15 g/1/2 oz) fresh oregano
    leaves, roughly chopped
200 g (61/2 oz) ricotta cheese, cut into
    small cubes

1 Add the pasta to a large pan of rapidly boiling water and cook until *al dente*. Drain and return to the pan. Meanwhile, heat the oil in a non-stick heavy-based frying pan. Add the garlic and chilli to the frying pan and stir for 1 minute over low heat.
2 Pour the contents of the frying pan over the pasta and add the herbs. Season to taste and toss well.
3 Add the cubes of ricotta to the pasta and serve immediately.

NUTRITION PER SERVE
Protein 20 g; Fat 20 g; Carbohydrate 90 g;
Dietary Fibre 7 g; Cholesterol 24 mg;
2635 kJ (630 cal)

Heat the oil in a frying pan and cook the garlic and chilli for 1 minute over low heat.

Pour the contents of the frying pan over the pasta and add the herbs and salt and pepper.

Cut the fresh ricotta into small cubes and add to the pasta salad.

GREEN OLIVE AND EGGPLANT TOSS

Preparation time: 20 minutes
Total cooking time: 20 minutes
Serves 4

500 g (1 lb) fettuccine or tagliatelle
1 cup (185 g/6 oz) green olives
1 large eggplant
2 tablespoons olive oil
2 cloves garlic, crushed
½ cup (125 ml/4 fl oz) lemon juice
2 tablespoons chopped fresh parsley
½ cup (50 g/1¾ oz) freshly grated
Parmesan

1 Cook the pasta in a large pan of rapidly boiling water until it is *al dente*. Drain and return to the pan. While the pasta is cooking, chop the olives (removing the pits) and cut the eggplant into small cubes.
2 Heat the oil in a heavy-based frying pan. Add the garlic and stir for 30 seconds. Add the eggplant and cook over medium heat, stirring frequently, for 6 minutes or until the eggplant is tender.
3 Add the olives, lemon juice and salt and pepper to the pan. Tip the sauce into the pasta and toss well. Serve sprinkled with parsley and Parmesan.

NUTRITION PER SERVE
Protein 20 g; Fat 17 g; Carbohydrate 92 g;
Dietary Fibre 10 g; Cholesterol 12 mg;
2572 kJ (615 cal)

While the pasta is cooking, dice the eggplant and chop the olives.

Cook the garlic for 30 seconds, then add the eggplant and cook until tender.

Add the olives, lemon juice and salt and pepper to the frying pan, then tip over the pasta.

PASTA ALFREDO

Preparation time: 10 minutes
Total cooking time: 15 minutes
Serves 4–6

500 g (1 lb) pasta (see NOTE)
90 g (3 oz) butter
1¹/₂ cups (150 g/5 oz) freshly
    grated Parmesan
1¹/₄ cups (315 ml/10 fl oz) cream
3 tablespoons chopped
    fresh parsley

1 Cook the pasta in a large pan of rapidly boiling salted water until *al dente*. Drain and return to the pan.
2 While the pasta is cooking, melt the butter in a pan over low heat. Add the Parmesan and cream and bring to the boil, stirring constantly. Reduce the heat and simmer, stirring, until the sauce has thickened slightly. Add the parsley and salt and pepper, to taste, and stir until well combined.
3 Add the sauce to the pasta and toss well so the sauce coats the pasta. Garnish with chopped herbs or sprigs of fresh herbs such as thyme.

NUTRITION PER SERVE (6):
Protein 20 g; Fat 40 g; Carbohydrate 60 g;
Dietary Fibre 4 g; Cholesterol 125 mg;
2875 kJ (685 cal)

NOTE: Traditionally fettucine is used with this sauce, but you can try any pasta. Try to time the sauce so it is ready just as the pasta is cooked.

It is best to use a block of Parmesan and grate your own each time you need it.

To chop parsley, use a large sharp knife. A swivel action is easiest, holding the point of the knife.

PASTA NAPOLITANA

Preparation time: 20 minutes
Total cooking time: 1 hour
Serves 4–6

2 tablespoons olive oil
1 onion, finely chopped
1 carrot, finely chopped
1 celery stick, finely chopped
500 g (1 lb) very ripe tomatoes,
    chopped
2 tablespoons chopped fresh parsley
2 teaspoons sugar
500 g (1 lb) pasta (see NOTE)

1 Heat the oil in a heavy-based pan.
Add the onion, carrot and celery,
cover and cook for 10 minutes over
low heat, stirring occasionally.
2 Add the tomato, parsley, sugar and
1/2 cup (125 ml/4 fl oz) of water. Bring
to the boil, reduce the heat to low,
cover and simmer for 45 minutes,
stirring occasionally. Season. If
necessary, add up to 3/4 cup (185 ml/
6 fl oz) more water.
3 About 15 minutes before serving,
cook the pasta in a large pan of rapidly
boiling salted water until *al dente*.
Drain and return to the pan. Pour the
sauce over the pasta and gently toss.

NUTRITION PER SERVE (6):
Protein 10 g; Fat 7 g; Carbohydrate 65 g;
Dietary Fibre 6 g; Cholesterol 0 mg;
1540 kJ (365 cal)

NOTE: Traditionally, spaghetti is
served with this sauce, but you can
use any pasta. We have shown
penne rigate.

HINT: The sauce can be reduced to a
more concentrated version by
cooking it uncovered so the moisture
evaporates, for a longer period. Store it
in the refrigerator and add water or
stock to thin it, if necessary, when you
are reheating.

Dice the vegetables quite finely before cooking in
the hot oil.

The tomatoes should be very ripe to give this
sauce the best flavour.

Pestos & Tapenades

They are best known as pasta sauces, but pestos and tapenades are also great for spicing up vegetables and soups or serving as dips. Sterilise your jars first with boiling water, then dry in a warm oven.

TRADITIONAL PESTO

Whiz 2 cups (60 g/2 oz) basil leaves, $1/4$ cup (40 g/$1^1/4$ oz) lightly toasted pine nuts, 2 coarsely chopped large cloves of garlic and a pinch of salt in a food processor or blender. With the motor running, slowly pour in $1/3$ cup (80 ml/$2^3/4$ fl oz) extra virgin olive oil. Add $1/2$ cup (50 g/$1^3/4$ oz) freshly grated Parmesan and some black pepper and process until just combined. Transfer to a sterilised jar and cover the surface with a thin layer of extra virgin olive oil. Seal

and refrigerate for up to a week. Serve as a pasta sauce, a dip, or a dressing for vegetables.
Makes about 1 cup (250 g/8 oz).

RED PESTO

Put a 200 g ($6^1/2$ oz) jar sun-dried tomatoes in oil, $1/3$ cup (10 g/$1/4$ oz) fresh basil leaves, $1/3$ cup (7 g/$1/4$ oz) fresh flat-leaf parsley leaves, 2 chopped cloves garlic, 2 teaspoons rinsed and drained capers and 4 tablespoons lightly toasted pine nuts in a food

processor or blender. Process until finely minced. Keep the motor running while you pour in 2 tablespoons red wine vinegar and $1/2$ cup (125 ml/ 4 fl oz) extra virgin olive oil. When these are thoroughly blended, add 2 tablespoons freshly grated Parmesan and some pepper. Transfer to a sterilised jar and cover the surface with a thin coating of extra virgin olive oil. Seal and refrigerate for up to 2 weeks. Serve as a pasta sauce if thinned with a little more olive oil, or a dip for crudités.
Makes about $1^1/4$ cups (310 g/10 oz).

ROCKET AND PECAN PESTO

Whiz 60 g (2 oz) young rocket leaves, 1/3 cup (7 g/1/4 oz) flat-leaf parsley, 12 large pecan halves and 2 coarsely chopped large cloves garlic in a food processor or blender. With the motor running, slowly pour in 1/2 cup (125 ml/4 fl oz) extra virgin olive oil. Add 1/3 cup (35 g/1 1/4 oz) grated Parmesan and mix well. Lightly season with salt. Put the pesto in a sterilised jar and cover the surface with a thin coating of extra virgin olive oil. Seal and refrigerate for up to a week. Serve as a dip with crudités and crusty bread or as a pasta sauce.
Makes about 3/4 cup (185 g/6 oz).

OLIVE TAPENADE

Place 1 tablespoon rinsed and drained capers, 1 small clove garlic, 1 cup (125 g/4 oz) sliced pitted black or green olives and 2 tablespoons lemon juice in a food processor or blender. Process until finely chopped. While the motor is still running, pour in 2 tablespoons extra virgin olive oil and 1 1/2 tablespoons Cognac. Season to taste with black pepper. Transfer to a sterilised jar. Seal and refrigerate for up to 2 weeks. Serve as a spread for bread or with crudités.
Makes about 1 1/4 cups (310 g/10 oz).

NORTH AFRICAN TAPENADE

Put a pinch of saffron in a small bowl with 1 teaspoon hot water and set aside. Whiz 2/3 cup (140 g/4 1/2 oz) pitted green olives, 1/4 teaspoon dried oregano, 2 tablespoons toasted pine nuts, 1 chopped clove garlic and 1/8 teaspoon ground cumin in a food processor or blender. With the motor running, add 3 teaspoons lime juice, 3 tablespoons extra virgin olive oil and the saffron and water mixture. Stop processing as soon as the ingredients are blended and transfer to a sterilised jar. Seal and store in the refrigerator for up to 2 weeks. Delicious as a pasta sauce when thinned with a little more olive oil, or on bruschetta.
Makes about 1 cup (250 g/8 oz).

From left to right: Traditional pesto; Red pesto; Rocket and pecan pesto; Olive tapenade; North African tapenade.

SPINACH AND RICOTTA CANNELLONI

Preparation time: 45 minutes
Total cooking time: 1 hour
Serves 4

FILLING
30 g (1 oz) butter
1 small onion, finely chopped
2 cloves garlic, crushed
3 bunches English spinach, trimmed
    and finely shredded
300 g (10 oz) ricotta cheese
1 tablespoon fresh oregano

SAUCE
1 tablespoon olive oil
1 small onion, finely chopped
2 cloves garlic, crushed
440 g (14 oz) can peeled whole
    tomatoes
1/2 cup (125 ml/4 fl oz) tomato pasta
    sauce
1 teaspoon dried oregano
2 teaspoons Dijon mustard
1 tablespoon balsamic vinegar
1 teaspoon sugar

375 g (12 oz) packet fresh lasagne
1/2 cup (75 g/21/2 oz) grated
    mozzarella
1/2 cup (50 g/13/4 oz) finely grated
    Parmesan

1 Preheat the oven to moderate 180°C (350°F/Gas 4). Cut the pasta sheets into twelve 12 cm squares. Bring a pan of salted water to the boil, blanch the lasagne in batches for 1–2 minutes, then drain flat on a damp tea towel.
2 Melt the butter in a pan and cook the onion and garlic for 3–5 minutes, or until the onion softens. Add the spinach and cook for 5 minutes, or

until wilted and the moisture has evaporated. Cool then mix with the ricotta and oregano in a food processor until smooth. Season.
3 To make the sauce, heat the oil in a pan, add the onion and garlic and cook over low heat for 8–10 minutes. Add the rest of the sauce ingredients. Bring to the boil, then reduce the heat and simmer for 10–15 minutes, or until the sauce thickens.
4 Lightly grease a 2 litre (64 fl oz) casserole. Spread a third of the sauce over the base. Spoon 11/2 tablespoons

of spinach mixture onto one side of each lasagne square, leaving a small border. Roll up the pasta to cover the filling and place in the dish seam-side-down. Repeat with all the sheets. Spoon in the remaining sauce and sprinkle with the cheeses. Bake for 30–35 minutes, or until bubbling. Leave for 5 minutes before serving.

NUTRITION PER SERVE
Protein 25 g; Fat 27 g; Carbohydrate 35 g;
Dietary Fibre 5 g; Cholesterol 70 mg;
1970 kJ (470 cal)

Blanch the lasagne sheets in batches in salted boiling water.

Lay the lasagne squares out flat on a clean damp tea towel to drain.

Spoon the spinach mixture onto one side of the pasta square and then roll up into a tube.

MACARONI CHEESE

Preparation time: 15 minutes
Total cooking time: 35 minutes
Serves 4

225 g (7 oz) macaroni
80 g (2¾ oz) butter
1 onion, finely chopped
3 tablespoons plain flour
2 cups (500 ml/16 fl oz) milk
2 teaspoons wholegrain mustard
250 g (8 oz) Cheddar, grated
30 g (1 oz) fresh breadcrumbs

1 Cook the pasta in rapidly boiling salted water until *al dente*. Drain.

Preheat the oven to moderate 180°C (350°F/Gas 4) and grease a casserole.
2 Melt the butter in a large pan over low heat and cook the onion for 5 minutes, or until softened. Stir in the flour and cook for 1 minute, or until pale and foaming. Remove from the heat and gradually stir in the milk. Return to the heat and stir until the sauce boils and thickens. Reduce the heat and simmer for 2 minutes. Stir in the mustard and about three-quarters of the cheese. Season to taste.
3 Mix the pasta with the cheese sauce. Spoon into the dish and sprinkle the breadcrumbs and remaining cheese over the top. Bake for 15 minutes, or until golden brown and bubbling.

NUTRITION PER SERVE
Protein 30 g; Fat 45 g; Carbohydrate 60 g; Dietary Fibre 4 g; Cholesterol 130 mg; 3087 kJ (737 cal)

Cook the onion in the butter over medium heat until softened.

FETTUCCINE WITH ZUCCHINI

Preparation time: 15 minutes
Total cooking time: 15 minutes
Serves 4–6

500 g (1 lb) tagliatelle or fettuccine
60 g (2 oz) butter
2 cloves garlic, crushed
500 g (1 lb) zucchini, grated
3/4 cup (75 g/2¹/2 oz) grated
   Parmesan cheese

1 cup (250 ml/8 fl oz) olive oil
16 basil leaves (see HINT)

1 Cook the pasta in a large pan of rapidly boiling water until *al dente*. Drain and return to the pan.
2 Meanwhile, heat the butter in a deep heavy-based pan over low heat until it is foaming. Add the garlic and cook for 1 minute. Add the zucchini and cook, stirring occasionally, for 1–2 minutes or until the zucchini has softened.
3 Add the sauce to the pasta. Add the Parmesan cheese and toss well.

4 To make basil leaves crisp, heat the oil in a small pan, add two leaves at a time and cook for 1 minute or until crisp. Drain on paper towels. Serve with the pasta.

NUTRITION PER SERVE (6)
Protein 15 g; Fat 53 g; Carbohydrate 60 g;
Dietary Fibre 5.5 g; Cholesterol 37 mg;
3245 kJ (775 cal)

HINT: Basil leaves can be fried up to 2 hours in advance. Store in an airtight container after cooling.

Coarsely grate the zucchini and then fry with the garlic until softened.

Toss the zucchini into the pasta and then add the grated Parmesan.

Fry the basil leaves in a little oil until they are crisp, then drain on paper towels.

PUMPKIN RIGATONI

Preparation time: 15 minutes
Total cooking time: 25 minutes
Serves 4–6

3 tablespoons pine nuts
30 g (1 oz) butter
2 leeks, white part only, finely sliced
1 kg (2 lb) pumpkin, diced
1/2 teaspoon ground nutmeg
500 g (1 lb) rigatoni or large penne
1 1/4 cups (300 ml/10 fl oz) cream

1 Toast the pine nuts by stirring over low heat in a non-stick frying pan until lightly golden. Alternatively, spread on a baking tray and grill—be sure to check often as they brown quickly.
2 Heat the butter in a large pan over low heat. Add the leek, cover the pan and cook, stirring occasionally, for 5 minutes. Add the pumpkin and nutmeg, cover and cook for 8 minutes.
3 Meanwhile, cook the pasta in a large pan of boiling water until *al dente* Drain and keep warm.
4 Add the cream and 3 tablespoons

water to the pumpkin and bring the sauce to the boil. Cook, stirring occasionally, for 8 minutes or until tender. Pour over the pasta. Sprinkle with the pine nuts to serve.

NUTRITION PER SERVE
Protein 15 g; Fat 30 g; Carbohydrate 72 g;
Dietary Fibre 7 g; Cholesterol 80 mg;
2612 kJ (625 cal)

Cut off the dark green leaves of the leek and slice the white part finely.

Heat the butter in a large pan and cook the sliced leek for 5 minutes.

Add the cream and a little water to the pumpkin sauce and bring to the boil.

TORTELLINI WITH MUSHROOM SAUCE

Preparation time: 25 minutes
Total cooking time: 1 hour 30 minutes
Serves 4

PASTA
2 cups (250 g/8 oz) plain flour
pinch of salt
3 eggs
1 tablespoon olive oil

FILLING
125 g (4 oz) packet frozen spinach,
    thawed, excess liquid removed
125 g (4 oz) ricotta cheese
2 tablespoons grated Parmesan
    cheese
1 egg, beaten

SAUCE
1 tablespoon olive oil
1 clove garlic, crushed
125 g (4 oz) mushrooms, sliced
1 cup (250 ml/8 fl oz) cream
3 tablespoons grated Parmesan
    cheese

3 tablespoons grated Parmesan
    cheese, to serve
3 tablespoons finely chopped fresh
    parsley, to serve

1 To make the pasta, sift the flour and salt onto a board. Make a well in the centre of the flour. Whisk together the eggs, oil and 1 tablespoon water. Add this gradually to the flour, working in with your hands until the mixture forms a ball. Add a little more water if necessary. Knead on a lightly floured surface for 5 minutes or until the dough is smooth and elastic. Put in a lightly oiled bowl, cover with plastic wrap and leave for 30 minutes.

2 To make the filling, mix together the drained spinach, ricotta, Parmesan, egg, and salt and pepper. Set aside.

3 To make the sauce, heat the oil in a frying pan. Add the garlic and stir over low heat for 30 seconds. Add the mushrooms and cook for 3 minutes. Pour in the cream.

4 Roll out the dough on a lightly floured surface until about 1 mm thick. Using a floured cutter, cut into 5 cm (2 inch) rounds. Spoon about 1/2 teaspoon of filling in the centre of each round. Brush a little water around the edge. Fold each round in half to form a semi-circle. Press the edges together firmly. Wrap each semi-circle around your forefinger to make a ring. Press the ends of the dough together firmly.

5 Cook the tortellini in batches in a large pan of rapidly boiling water for about 8 minutes each batch—until the pasta is *al dente*. Drain well and return to the pan. Keep warm.

6 Return the sauce to the heat. Bring to the boil then reduce the heat and simmer for 3 minutes. Add the Parmesan cheese and salt and pepper and stir well. Toss the sauce and tortellini together and serve immediately in warmed bowls.

7 Mix together the Parmesan and chopped parsley and serve as an accompaniment to the pasta.

NUTRITION PER SERVE
Protein 27 g; Fat 52 g; Carbohydrate 49 g;
Dietary Fibre 5 g; Cholesterol 299 mg;
3220 kJ (770 cal)

Knead the pasta dough on a lightly floured surface until smooth and elastic.

Mix together the spinach, ricotta, Parmesan and egg to make the filling.

Fry the garlic and mushrooms and then pour in the cream to make the sauce.

Spoon a little filling into the centre of each round, then fold over and twist round your finger.

Cook the tortellini in batches so that you don't overcrowd the pan.

Reheat the sauce and then toss well with the tortellini and serve immediately.

SPAGHETTI WITH GORGONZOLA SAUCE

Preparation time: 10 minutes
Total cooking time: 20 minutes
Serves 4–6

375 g (12 oz) spaghetti or bucatini
30 g (1 oz) butter
1 stick celery, finely chopped

1¼ cups (300 ml/10 fl oz) cream
250 g (8 oz) ricotta cheese, beaten until smooth
200 g (6½ oz) gorgonzola cheese, diced

1 Cook the pasta in a large pan of rapidly boiling water until *al dente*. Drain and return to the pan.
2 Heat the butter and cook the celery for 2 minutes. Add the cream, ricotta and gorgonzola and season well.
3 Bring to the boil, stirring constantly, then simmer over low heat for 1 minute. Add the sauce to the pasta and toss well.

NUTRITION PER SERVE
Protein 20 g; Fat 42 g; Carbohydrate 46 g; Dietary Fibre 3 g; Cholesterol 134 mg; 2698 kJ (645 cal)

Gorgonzola is a rich, strong Italian blue-veined cheese which pairs beautifully with celery.

Heat the butter in a pan and cook the celery for a couple of minutes to just soften.

Bring the sauce to the boil, then reduce the heat to low and let it simmer for 1 minute.

TORTELLINI WITH NUTTY HERB SAUCE

Preparation time: 15 minutes
Total cooking time: 10 minutes
Serves 4–6

500 g (1 lb) cheese tortellini or ravioli
60 g (2 oz) butter
100 g (3½ oz) walnuts, chopped

100 g (3½ oz) pine nuts
2 tablespoons chopped fresh parsley
2 teaspoons chopped fresh thyme
¼ cup (60 g/2 oz) ricotta cheese
3 tablespoons cream

1 Cook the pasta in rapidly boiling water until *al dente*. Drain and return to the pan.
2 Heat the butter in a heavy-based pan until foaming. Add the walnuts and pine nuts and stir for 5 minutes, or until golden brown. Add the parsley, thyme and salt and pepper.
3 Beat the ricotta with the cream. Toss the sauce and pasta together and top with ricotta cream. Serve immediately.

NUTRITION PER SERVE
Protein 12 g; Fat 40 g; Carbohydrate 13 g;
Dietary Fibre 3 g; Cholesterol 58 mg;
1943 kJ (465 cal)

Chop the walnuts finely with a large knife. This recipe also works well with hazelnuts.

Cook the walnuts and pine nuts in the foaming butter until they are golden brown.

Beat the ricotta and cream together and use as a topping for the pasta.

PASTA PRIMAVERA

Preparation time: 25 minutes
Total cooking time: 10–15 minutes
Serves 4

500 g (1 lb) pasta (see NOTE)
1 cup (155 g/5 oz) frozen broad beans
200 g (6¹/₂ oz) sugar snap peas
155 g (5 oz) asparagus spears
30 g (1 oz) butter
1 cup (250 ml/8 fl oz) cream
60 g (2 oz) freshly grated Parmesan

1 Cook the pasta in a large pan of rapidly boiling salted water until *al dente*. Drain and return to the pan to keep warm.
2 Cook the beans in a pan of boiling water for 2 minutes. Plunge them into iced water and then drain. Remove and discard the skins from the broad beans—you can usually just squeeze them out, otherwise carefully slit the skins first.
3 Trim the stalks from the peas and break the woody ends from the asparagus spears. Cut the asparagus into short lengths.
4 Melt the butter in a heavy-based frying pan. Add the vegetables, cream and Parmesan. Simmer gently over medium heat for 3–4 minutes, or until the peas and asparagus are bright green and just tender. Season with some salt and pepper. Pour the sauce over the warm pasta and toss to combine. Serve immediately.

NUTRITION PER SERVE
Protein 30 g; Fat 35 g; Carbohydrate 95 g;
Dietary Fibre 12 g; Cholesterol 105 mg;
3420 kJ (815 cal)

NOTE: Traditionally, primavera is served with spaghetti. Here it is shown with spaghettini, a thin spaghetti.

After cooking, the broad beans should slip easily out of their skins.

Trim the stalks from the sugar snap peas and snap the woody ends from the asparagus.

PASTA POMODORO

Preparation time: 15 minutes
Total cooking time: 10–15 minutes
Serves 4

500 g (1 lb) pasta
1¹/₂ tablespoons olive oil
1 onion, very finely chopped
2 x 400 g (13 oz) cans Italian
　　tomatoes, chopped
¹/₄ cup (7 g/¹/₄ oz) fresh basil leaves

1 Cook the pasta in a large pan of rapidly boiling salted water until *al dente*. Drain and return to the pan to keep warm.
2 Heat the oil in a large frying pan.

Add the onion and cook over medium heat until softened. Stir in the chopped tomato and simmer for 5–6 minutes, or until the sauce has reduced slightly and thickened. Season with salt and freshly ground pepper. Stir in the basil leaves and cook for another minute.

3 Pour the sauce over the warm pasta and gently toss. Serve immediately.

NUTRITION PER SERVE:
Protein 20 g; Fat 10 g; Carbohydrate 95 g;
Dietary Fibre 10 g; Cholesterol 5 mg;
2295 kJ (545 cal)

To finely chop an onion, cut it in half and slice horizontally, without cutting all the way through.

Then make cuts close together across one way, then in the opposite direction, to make dice.

Salads

MEXICANA SALAD

Preparation time: 40 minutes +
  overnight standing
Total cooking time: 1 hour
Serves 10–12

250 g (8 oz) black-eyed beans
250 g (8 oz) red kidney beans
500 g (1 lb) sweet potato
1 large red onion, chopped
1 large green capsicum,
  chopped
3 ripe tomatoes, chopped
1/4 cup (15 g/1/2 oz) chopped basil
3 flour tortillas
1 tablespoon oil
2 tablespoons grated Parmesan
1/4 cup (60 g/2 oz) sour cream

DRESSING
1 clove garlic, crushed
1 tablespoon lime juice
2 tablespoons olive oil

GUACAMOLE
3 avocados
2 tablespoons lemon juice
1 clove garlic, crushed
1 small red onion, chopped
1 small red chilli, chopped
1/4 cup (60 g/2 oz) sour cream
2 tablespoons hot ready-made taco
  sauce

1 Soak the beans in a large bowl of cold water overnight. Drain and cook in a large pan of rapidly boiling water for 30 minutes, or until just tender. Skim off any scum that appears on the surface during cooking. Do not overcook or they will become mushy. Drain and set aside to cool.

2 Chop the sweet potato into large pieces and cook in boiling water until tender. Drain and combine with the onion, capsicum, tomato and beans. Stir in the basil.

3 To make the dressing, shake the ingredients in a jar until combined. Pour over the salad and toss to coat.

4 Preheat the oven to moderate 180°C (350°F/Gas 4). Using a small knife, cut cactus shapes or large triangles out of the tortillas, brush lightly with the oil and sprinkle with Parmesan. Bake for 5–10 minutes, or until they are crisp and golden.

5 To make the guacamole, mash the avocados with the lemon juice. Add the garlic, onion, chilli, sour cream and taco sauce and mix well.

6 Pile the guacamole in the centre of the salad, top with the sour cream and arrange the cactus shapes on top.

NUTRITION PER SERVE (12)
Protein 15 g; Fat 25 g; Carbohydrate 40 g;
Dietary Fibre 10 g; Cholesterol 15 mg;
1735 kJ (415 cal)

Combine the sweet potato with the onion, capsicum, tomato and beans.

Using a small sharp knife, cut cactus shapes out of the tortillas.

FRESH BEETROOT AND GOAT'S CHEESE SALAD

Preparation time: 20 minutes
Total cooking time: 30 minutes
Serves 4

1 kg fresh beetroot (about 4 bulbs
 with leaves)
200 g (6$^{1}/_{2}$ oz) green beans
1 tablespoon red wine vinegar
2 tablespoons extra virgin olive oil
1 clove garlic, crushed
1 tablespoon drained capers,
 coarsely chopped
100 g (3$^{1}/_{2}$ oz) goat's cheese

1 Trim the leaves from the beetroot. Scrub the bulbs and wash the leaves well. Simmer the whole bulbs in a large saucepan of boiling-water, covered, for 30 minutes, or until tender when pierced with the point of a knife. (The cooking time may vary depending on the size of the bulbs.)

2 Meanwhile, bring a saucepan of water to the boil, add the beans and cook for 3 minutes, or until just tender. Remove with a slotted spoon and plunge into a bowl of cold water. Drain well. Add the beetroot leaves to the same saucepan of boiling water and cook for 3–5 minutes, or until the leaves and stems are tender. Drain, plunge into a bowl of cold water, then drain again well.

3 Drain and cool the beetroots, then peel the skins off and cut the bulbs into thin wedges.

4 To make the dressing, put the red wine vinegar, oil, garlic, capers, $^{1}/_{2}$ teaspoon salt and $^{1}/_{2}$ teaspoon pepper in a screw-top jar and shake.
5 To serve, divide the beans and beetroot (leaves and bulbs) among four serving plates. Crumble the goat's cheese over the top and drizzle with the dressing.

NUTRITION PER SERVE
Protein 12 g; Fat 18 g; Carbohydrate 22 g;
Dietary Fibre 9 g; Cholesterol 25 mg;
1256 kJ (300 cal)

Remove the skin from the beetroot, then cut into thin wedges.

Cook the beetroot leaves for 3–5 minutes, or until they are tender.

ASPARAGUS AND MUSHROOM SALAD

Preparation time: 20 minutes
Total cooking time: 10 minutes
Serves 4

155 g (5 oz) asparagus spears
1 tablespoon wholegrain mustard
1/4 cup (60 ml/2 fl oz) orange juice
2 tablespoons lemon juice
1 tablespoon lime juice
1 tablespoon orange zest
2 teaspoons lemon zest
2 teaspoons lime zest

2 cloves garlic, crushed
1/4 cup (90 g/3 oz) honey
400 g (13 oz) button mushrooms,
   halved
150 g (5 oz) rocket
1 red capsicum, cut into strips

1 Snap the woody ends from the asparagus spears and cut in half on the diagonal. Cook in boiling water for 1 minute, or until just tender. Drain, plunge into cold water and set aside.
2 Place the mustard, citrus juice and zest, garlic and honey in a large saucepan and season with pepper. Bring to the boil, then reduce the heat

and add the mushrooms, tossing for 2 minutes. Cool.
3 Remove the mushrooms from the sauce with a slotted spoon. Return the sauce to the heat, bring to the boil, then reduce the heat and simmer for 3–5 minutes, or until reduced and syrupy. Cool slightly.
4 Toss the mushrooms, rocket leaves, capsicum and asparagus. Put on a plate and drizzle with the sauce.

NUTRITION PER SERVE
Protein 6 g; Fat 0 g; Carbohydrate 25 g;
Dietary Fibre 5 g; Cholesterol 0 mg;
550 kJ (132 cal)

Use a zester to remove the zest of the orange, lemon and lime.

Toss the mushrooms in the mustard, juices, zest, garlic and honey.

Remove the mushrooms and simmer the sauce until it is reduced and syrupy.

TOMATO, HALOUMI AND SPINACH SALAD

Preparation time: 15 minutes +
   2 hours marinating
Total cooking time: 1 hour
Serves 4

200 g (6¹/2 oz) haloumi cheese
¹/4 cup (60 ml/2 fl oz) olive oil
2 cloves garlic, crushed
1 tablespoon chopped fresh oregano
1 tablespoon chopped fresh marjoram
8 egg (Roma) tomatoes, halved
1 small red onion, cut into 8 wedges
   with base intact

¹/4 cup (60 ml/2 fl oz) olive oil, extra
2 tablespoons balsamic vinegar
150 g (5 oz) baby English spinach
   leaves

1 Cut the haloumi into 1 cm (¹/2 inch) slices lengthways and put in a shallow dish. Mix together the oil, garlic and herbs and pour over the haloumi. Marinate, covered, for 1–2 hours.
2 Preheat the oven to moderately hot 200°C (400°F/Gas 6). Place the tomato and onion in a single layer in a roasting tin, drizzle with 2 tablespoons of the extra olive oil and 1 tablespoon of the vinegar and sprinkle with salt and cracked black pepper. Bake for

50–60 minutes, or until golden.
3 Meanwhile, heat a non-stick frying pan over medium heat. Drain the haloumi and cook for 1 minute each side, or until golden brown.
4 Divide the spinach leaves among four serving plates and top with the tomato and onion. Whisk together the remaining olive oil and balsamic vinegar in a small bowl and drizzle over the salad. Top with the haloumi.

NUTRITION PER SERVE
Protein 14 g; Fat 27 g; Carbohydrate 6.5 g;
Dietary Fibre 4 g; Cholesterol 26 mg;
1333 kJ (320 cal)

Cut the onion into eight wedges, keeping the base intact.

Arrange the tomatoes and onion in a single layer in a roasting tin and bake until golden.

Drain the marinated haloumi and cook for a minute on each side, until golden brown.

VIETNAMESE SALAD

Preparation time: 30 minutes +
   10 minutes standing + 30 minutes
   refrigeration
Total cooking time: Nil
Serves 4–6

200 g (6¹/2 oz) dried rice vermicelli
1 cup (140 g/4¹/2 oz) crushed peanuts
¹/2 cup (10 g/¹/4 oz) fresh Vietnamese
   mint leaves, torn
¹/2 cup (15 g/¹/2 oz) firmly packed
   fresh coriander leaves
¹/2 red onion, cut into thin wedges
1 green mango, cut into julienne strips
1 Lebanese cucumber, halved
   lengthways and thinly sliced on the
   diagonal

LEMON GRASS DRESSING
¹/2 cup (125 ml/4 fl oz) lime juice
1 tablespoon shaved palm sugar
¹/4 cup (60 ml/2 fl oz) seasoned rice
   vinegar
2 stems lemon grass, finely chopped
2 red chillies, seeded and finely
   chopped
3 kaffir lime leaves, shredded

1 Place the rice vermicelli in a bowl and cover with boiling water. Leave for 10 minutes, or until soft, then drain, rinse under cold water and cut into short lengths.
2 Place the vermicelli, three-quarters of the peanuts, the mint, coriander, onion, mango and cucumber in a large bowl and toss together.
3 To make the dressing, place all the ingredients in a jar with a lid and shake together.
4 Toss the salad and dressing and refrigerate for 30 minutes. Sprinkle with the remaining nuts to serve.

NUTRITION PER SERVE (6)
Protein 6.5 g; Fat 13 g; Carbohydrate 19 g;
Dietary Fibre 3 g; Cholesterol 0 mg;
926 kJ (221 cal)

Cut the green mango into julienne strips (the size and shape of matchsticks).

Using scissors, cut the rice vermicelli into shorter, more manageable lengths.

Put the salad ingredients in a bowl and toss well, reserving some of the peanuts to garnish.

TABBOULEH

Preparation time: 25 minutes +
  30 minutes refrigeration
Total cooking time: Nil
Serves 8

1 cup (175 g/6 oz) burghul
2 teaspoons olive oil
1 cup (30 g/1 oz) chopped fresh flat-
  leaf parsley
1 cup (50 g/1¾ oz) chopped fresh
  mint

¾ cup (90 g/3 oz) finely chopped
  spring onions
4 Roma (egg) tomatoes, chopped
½ cup (125 ml/4 fl oz) olive oil
½ cup (125 ml/4 fl oz) lemon juice
2 cloves garlic, crushed

1 Put the burghul in a bowl and pour
in 1 cup (250 ml/8 fl oz) boiling water.
Mix in the olive oil, then set aside for
10 minutes. Stir again and cool.
2 Add the herbs, spring onion and
tomato to the burghul and mix well.
Whisk the oil, lemon juice and garlic

together and add to the burghul. Mix
gently and season well. Cover and
chill for 30 minutes before serving.

NUTRITION PER SERVE
Protein 6 g; Fat 20 g; Carbohydrate 7.5 g;
Dietary Fibre 5 g; Cholesterol 0 mg;
1028 kJ (245 cal)

VARIATION: Burghul is also sold as
bulgur or cracked wheat. If you prefer,
use couscous instead of the burghul in
this recipe.

Roma tomatoes are also known as 'egg' or 'plum'
tomatoes because of their shape.

Soak the burghul in boiling water and then mix
with the olive oil.

Add the herbs, spring onion and tomato to the
burghul and mix well.

CHICKPEA AND ROAST VEGETABLE SALAD

Preparation time: 25 minutes +
  30 minutes standing
Total cooking time: 40 minutes
Serves 8

500 g (1 lb) butternut pumpkin, cubed
2 red capsicums, halved
4 slender eggplants, cut in half
  lengthways
4 zucchini, cut in half lengthways
4 onions, quartered
olive oil, for brushing

2 x 300 g (10 oz) cans chickpeas,
  rinsed and drained
2 tablespoons chopped fresh flat-leaf
  parsley

DRESSING
1/3 cup (80 ml/2³/4 fl oz) olive oil
2 tablespoons lemon juice
1 clove garlic, crushed
1 tablespoon chopped fresh thyme

1 Preheat the oven to hot 220°C
(425°F/Gas 7). Brush two baking trays
with oil and lay out the vegetables in a
single layer. Brush lightly with oil.
2 Bake for 40 minutes, or until the

vegetables are tender and begin to
brown slightly on the edges. Cool.
Remove the skins from the capsicum if
you want. Chop the capsicum,
eggplant and zucchini into pieces,
then put the vegetables in a bowl with
the chickpeas and half the parsley.
3 Whisk together all the dressing
ingredients. Season, then toss with the
vegetables. Leave for 30 minutes, then
sprinkle with the rest of the parsley.

NUTRITION PER SERVE
Protein 8.5 g; Fat 12 g; Carbohydrate 20 g;
Dietary Fibre 7.5 g; Cholesterol 0 mg;
935 kJ (225 cal)

Rinse the chickpeas under cold running water
then drain thoroughly.

Chop the roasted capsicum, eggplant and
zucchini into small pieces.

Put the olive oil, lemon juice, garlic and thyme in a
bowl and whisk together.

LEEK AND CAPER SALAD

Preparation time: 20 minutes
Total cooking time: 20 minutes
Serves 6

5 leeks, white part only
1/3 cup (80 ml/2³/4 fl oz) olive oil
2 tablespoons sherry vinegar
2 tablespoons baby capers, rinsed

1 Cut the leeks in half lengthways and wash under cold running water. Cut them into 5 cm (2 inch) lengths, then cut in half again lengthways. Heat the oil in a large heavy-based pan, add the leeks and stir until coated with the oil. Cover and cook over low heat for 15–20 minutes, or until the leeks are soft and tender (but don't let them brown or burn). Cool for 10 minutes.
2 Stir through the vinegar and season to taste with salt and pepper. Transfer to a serving dish and scatter with the baby capers (if baby capers are unavailable, use chopped ordinary-sized capers).

NUTRITION PER SERVE
Protein 1.5 g; Fat 13 g; Carbohydrate 2.5 g;
Dietary Fibre 2 g; Cholesterol 0 mg;
550 kJ (130 cal)

Trim the leeks and wash them thoroughly under cold running water.

Add the leeks to the pan and stir until they are covered with the oil.

Add the vinegar to the cooled leeks and stir until they are well coated.

CAPONATA

Preparation time: 20 minutes +
  24 hours refrigeration
Total cooking time: 40 minutes
Serves 8

1 kg (2 lb) eggplant, cubed
3/4 cup (185 ml/6 fl oz) olive oil
200 g (6 1/2 oz) zucchini, cubed
1 red capsicum, thinly sliced
2 onions, finely sliced
4 celery sticks, sliced
400 g (13 oz) can crushed tomatoes
3 tablespoons red wine vinegar
2 tablespoons sugar
2 tablespoons drained capers
24 green olives, pitted (see NOTE)
2 tablespoons pine nuts, toasted

1 Put the eggplant in a colander, sprinkle with salt and leave to drain.
2 Heat 3 tablespoons of the oil in a large frying pan and fry the zucchini and capsicum for 5–6 minutes, or until the zucchini is lightly browned. Transfer to a bowl. Add a little more oil to the pan and gently fry the onion and celery for 6–8 minutes, or until softened but not brown. Transfer to the bowl.
3 Rinse the eggplant and pat dry. Add 1/4 cup (60 ml/2 fl oz) of the oil to the pan, increase the heat and brown the eggplant in batches. Keep adding more oil to each batch. Drain on paper towels and set aside.
4 Remove any excess oil from the pan and return the vegetables to the pan, except the eggplant.
5 Add 1/4 cup (60 ml/2 fl oz) water and the tomatoes. Reduce the heat and simmer for 10 minutes. Add the remaining ingredients and eggplant and mix well. Remove from the

heat and cool. Cover and leave for 24 hours in the refrigerator. Add some pepper, and more vinegar if needed.

NUTRITION PER SERVE
Protein 3.5 g; Fat 25 g; Carbohydrate 8.5 g;
Dietary Fibre 5.5 g; Cholesterol 0 mg;
1160 kJ (280 cal)

NOTE: Green olives stuffed with red pimentos can be used instead of pitted green olives.

STORAGE TIME: Caponata will keep, covered, in the refrigerator for up to 5 days.

You can remove the stones from the olives with an olive pitter.

Increase the heat under the oil and brown the eggplant in batches.

Add the water and crushed tomatoes to the pan and allow to simmer.

FENNEL WITH PECORINO CHEESE

Preparation time: 15 minutes
Total cooking time: 25 minutes
Serves 4

4 fennel bulbs
1 clove garlic, crushed
1/2 lemon, sliced
2 tablespoons olive oil
1 teaspoon salt

3 tablespoons butter, melted
2 tablespoons grated Pecorino
cheese

1 Cut the top shoots and base off the fennel and remove the tough outer layers. Cut into segments and place in a pan with the garlic, lemon, oil and salt. Cover with water and bring to the boil. Reduce the heat and simmer for 20 minutes, or until just tender.
2 Drain well and place in a heatproof dish. Drizzle with the butter. Sprinkle

with the cheese and season to taste.
3 Place under a preheated grill until the cheese has browned. Best served piping hot.

NUTRITION PER SERVE
Protein 4 g; Fat 23 g; Carbohydrate 3 g;
Dietary Fibre 2.5 g; Cholesterol 43 mg;
990 kJ (235 cal)

NOTE: If Pecorino (a hard sheep's milk cheese) is not available, then use Parmesan instead.

Trim the tops and bases from the fennel and remove the tough outer layers.

Sprinkle grated Pecorino cheese over the fennel and brown under a grill.

Cut the fennel into segments and put in a pan with the garlic, lemon, oil and salt.

POTATO SALAD

Preparation time: 30 minutes
Total cooking time: 5 minutes
Serves 4

600 g (1¼ lb) potatoes, unpeeled, cut
 into bite-sized pieces
1 small onion, finely chopped
1 small green capsicum, chopped
2–3 celery sticks, finely chopped
¼ cup (15 g/½ oz) finely chopped
 parsley

DRESSING
¾ cup (185 g/6 oz) mayonnaise
1–2 tablespoons vinegar or lemon
 juice
2 tablespoons sour cream

1 Cook the potato in a large pan of
boiling water for 5 minutes, or until
just tender (pierce with a small sharp
knife—if the potato comes away easily
it is ready). Drain and cool completely.
2 Combine the onion, capsicum,
celery and parsley (reserving a little for
garnishing) with the cooled potato in a
large salad bowl.

3 To make the dressing, mix together
the mayonnaise, vinegar and sour
cream. Season with salt and pepper.
Pour over the salad and toss gently to
combine, without breaking the potato.
Garnish with the remaining parsley.

NUTRITION PER SERVE
Protein 6 g; Fat 20 g; Carbohydrate 30 g;
Dietary Fibre 4 g; Cholesterol 30 mg;
1355 kJ (320 cal)

NOTE: Any potato is suitable for this
recipe. Most potatoes are delicious
with their skins left on.

Cut the potatoes into bite-sized pieces, leaving
the skins on.

Combine the onion, capsicum, celery and parsley
with the cooled potato.

Mix together the mayonnaise, vinegar and sour
cream and season, to taste.

GREEK SALAD

Preparation time: 20 minutes
Total cooking time: Nil
Serves 6–8

6 tomatoes, cut into thin wedges
1 red onion, cut into thin rings
2 Lebanese cucumbers, sliced

1 cup (185 g/6 oz) Kalamata olives
200 g (6½ oz) feta cheese
½ cup (125 ml/4 fl oz) extra virgin
  olive oil
dried oregano, to sprinkle

1 Combine the tomato wedges with
the onion rings, sliced cucumber and
Kalamata olives in a large bowl.
Season to taste with salt and freshly

ground black pepper.
2 Break up the feta into large pieces
with your fingers and scatter over the
top of the salad. Drizzle with the olive
oil and sprinkle with some oregano.

NUTRITION PER SERVE (8)
Protein 6 g; Fat 25 g; Carbohydrate 3 g;
Dietary Fibre 2 g; Cholesterol 15 mg;
1060 kJ (250 cal)

Cut the tomatoes into thin wedges, and cut the
red onion into thin rings.

Combine the tomato, onion, cucumber and
olives in a large bowl.

Good feta should break up and crumble nicely.
Just use your fingers.

HOKKIEN NOODLE SALAD

Preparation time: 20 minutes
Total cooking time: Nil
Serves 8

900 g (1³/₄ lb) Hokkien noodles
6 spring onions, sliced diagonally
1 large red capsicum, thinly sliced
200 g (6¹/₂ oz) snow peas, sliced
1 carrot, sliced diagonally
60 g (2 oz) fresh mint, chopped
60 g (2 oz) fresh coriander, chopped
100 g (3¹/₂ oz) roasted cashew nuts

SESAME DRESSING
2 teaspoons sesame oil
1 tablespoon peanut oil
2 tablespoons lime juice
2 tablespoons kecap manis (see
    NOTE)
3 tablespoons sweet chilli sauce

1 Gently separate the noodles and place in a large bowl, cover with boiling water and leave for 2 minutes. Rinse and drain.
2 Put the noodles in a large bowl, and add spring onions, capsicum, snow peas, carrot, mint and coriander. Toss together well.

3 To make the dressing, whisk together the oils, lime juice, kecap manis and sweet chilli sauce. Pour the dressing over the salad and toss again. Sprinkle the cashew nuts over the top and serve immediately.

NUTRITION PER SERVE
Protein 10 g; Fat 9 g; Carbohydrate 35 g; Dietary Fibre 4.5 g; Cholesterol 0 mg; 1115 kJ (265 cal)

NOTE: If you can't find kecap manis, you can use soy sauce sweetened with a little soft brown sugar.

Top and tail the snow peas, then finely slice lengthways with a sharp knife.

Separate the noodles, then put them in a large bowl and cover with boiling water.

Whisk together the oils, lime juice, kecap manis and sweet chilli sauce.

121

GADO GADO

Preparation time: 30 minutes
Total cooking time: 35 minutes
Serves 4

6 new potatoes, unpeeled
2 carrots, cut into thick strips
250 g (8 oz) snake beans, cut into
    10 cm (4 inch) lengths
2 tablespoons peanut oil
250 g (8 oz) firm tofu, cubed
100 g (3¹/₂ oz) baby English spinach
2 Lebanese cucumbers, cut into thick
    strips
1 large red capsicum, thickly sliced
100 g (3¹/₂ oz) bean sprouts
5 hard-boiled eggs

PEANUT SAUCE
1 tablespoon peanut oil
1 onion, finely chopped
²/₃ cup (160 g/5¹/₂ oz) peanut butter
¹/₄ cup (60 ml/2 fl oz) kecap manis
2 tablespoons ground coriander
2 teaspoons chilli sauce
³/₄ cup (185 ml/6 fl oz) coconut cream
1 teaspoon grated palm sugar
1 tablespoon lemon juice

1 Cook the potatoes in boiling water until tender. Drain and cool slightly. Cut into quarters. Cook the carrots and beans separately in pans of boiling water until just tender. Plunge into iced water, then drain.
2 Heat the oil in a non-stick frying pan and cook the tofu in batches until crisp. Drain on paper towels.
3 To make the peanut sauce, heat the oil in a pan over low heat and cook the onion for 5 minutes, or until golden. Add the peanut butter, kecap manis, coriander, chilli sauce and coconut cream. Bring to the boil, reduce the heat and simmer for 5 minutes. Add the sugar and juice and stir until dissolved.
4 Arrange the vegetables and tofu on a plate. Halve the eggs and place in the centre. Serve with the sauce.

NUTRITION PER SERVE
Protein 35 g; Fat 55 g; Carbohydrate 35 g; Dietary Fibre 15 g; Cholesterol 265 mg; 3175 kJ (755 cal)

Cut the cucumbers and capsicum into thick strips for dipping in the sauce.

Cook the snake beans quickly in a large saucepan of boiling water.

Heat the oil and cook the tofu in batches until crisp and golden brown.

Add the peanut butter, kecap manis, coriander, chilli sauce and coconut cream.

WALDORF SALAD

Preparation time: 20 minutes
Total cooking time: Nil
Serves 4–6

2 red and 2 green apples
2 tablespoons lemon juice
1/4 cup (30 g/1 oz) walnut pieces
4 celery sticks, sliced
1 cup (250 g/8 oz) mayonnaise

1 Quarter the apples, remove and discard the seeds and cores, and cut the apples into small pieces.
2 Place the diced apple in a large bowl, drizzle with the lemon juice and toss to coat (this will prevent the apple discolouring). Add the walnut pieces and celery and mix well.
3 Add the mayonnaise to the apple mixture and toss until well coated. Spoon the salad into a lettuce-lined bowl and serve immediately.

NUTRITION PER SERVE (6)
Protein 2 g; Fat 15 g; Carbohydrate 20 g; Dietary Fibre 3 g; Cholesterol 15 mg; 1020 kJ (240 cal)

NOTE: Waldorf salad can be made up to 2 hours in advance and stored, covered, in the refrigerator. It is named after the Waldorf-Astoria hotel in New York where it was first served.

Using both red and green apples gives the finished salad a colourful appearance.

Pour the lemon juice over the apples and toss to coat—this will prevent them browning.

Add the mayonnaise to the apple mixture and toss until well coated.

Oils & Vinegars

Spice up your marinades, vinaigrettes and dressings with these delicious recipes, or simply enjoy the oil with fresh crusty bread. If you sterilise the storage jar first by rinsing it with boiling water and placing it in a warm oven until it is completely dry, most oils and vinegars will keep for up to 6 months.

TARRAGON VINEGAR

Warm 2 cups (500 ml/16 fl oz) white wine vinegar over low heat. Gently bruise 25 g (³/₄ oz) fresh tarragon leaves in your hands and put in a 2-cup (500 ml/16 fl oz) sterilised wide-necked jar. Pour in the vinegar, seal with a non-metallic lid and shake well. Allow to stand in a warm place for 2 weeks to infuse. Strain and return to the clean sterilised bottle. Add a fresh sprig of tarragon, seal and label. Store in a cool, dark place for up to 6 months. Makes 2 cups (500 ml/16 fl oz).

CHILLI OIL

Place 6 dried chillies and 1 teaspoon chilli powder in a heavy-based pan. Add 3 cups (750 ml/24 fl oz) olive oil, bring to the boil, then lower the heat and simmer for 5 minutes (if it gets too hot the oil will change flavour). Cover with plastic wrap and leave in a cool, dark place for 3 days. Strain the oil into a 3-cup (750 ml/24 fl oz) sterilised bottle. Discard the chillies and add new chillies for decoration. Makes 3 cups (750 ml/24 fl oz). Store in a cool, dark place for up to 6 months.

PARMESAN OIL

Combine 2 cups (500 ml/16 fl oz) olive oil and 100 g (3¹/₂ oz) finely grated Reggiano Parmesan in a small pan. Stir over low heat for 10–15 minutes, or until the Parmesan starts to melt and clump together. Remove from the heat and allow to cool. Strain into a 2-cup (500 ml/16 fl oz) sterilised bottle and add 20 g (³/₄ oz) shaved Parmesan. Seal and label. Store in a cool, dark place for up to 6 months. Makes 2 cups (500 ml/16 fl oz).

INDIAN OIL

Place 1 teaspoon each of garam masala, coriander seeds, cardamom pods and fennel seeds, 3 allspice berries, 3 curry leaves and 1 small dried chilli in a bowl and lightly crush with the back of a spoon. Place in a sterilised bottle with 3 cups (750 ml/ 24 fl oz) peanut or canola oil. Seal and leave for 3 days in a cool, dark place. Strain into a 3-cup (750 ml/24 fl oz) sterilised bottle. Store in a cool, dark place for up to 3 months. Makes about 3 cups (750 ml/24 fl oz).

SPICY APPLE AND CINNAMON VINEGAR

Combine 2 cups (500 ml/16 fl oz) white wine vinegar, 1/3 cup (30 g/1 oz) finely chopped dried apple slices, 1/4 teaspoon black peppercorns, 2 bay leaves, 1/4 teaspoon yellow mustard seeds, 2 cinnamon sticks, 2 sprigs fresh thyme and 1 garlic clove in a 2-cup (500 ml/16 fl oz) sterilised jar or bottle. Seal and leave in a cool, dark place for 2 weeks. Strain the vinegar and pour into warm sterilised jars. Store in a cool, dark place for up to 6 months. Makes about 2 cups (500 ml/16 fl oz).

RASPBERRY VINEGAR

Place 2 1/3 cups (290 g/10 oz) fresh or thawed frozen raspberries in a non-metallic bowl and crush gently with the back of a spoon. Over low heat, warm 2 cups (500 ml/16 fl oz) white wine vinegar. Add the vinegar to the raspberries and mix well. Pour into a 2-cup (500 ml/16 fl oz) sterilised jar and keep in a warm place for 2 weeks, shaking regularly. Strain through a muslin-lined sieve into a small pan. Add 2 teapoons caster sugar and stir over medium heat until the sugar has dissolved. Pour into a warm sterilised jar or bottle. Add 2–3 raspberries, if desired, seal and label. Store in a cool, dark place for up to 6 months. Makes about 2 cups (500 ml/16 fl oz).

SPICED MALT VINEGAR

Place 2 cups (500 ml/16 fl oz) malt vinegar in a pan. Add a 1 cm piece (10 g) fresh ginger cut into four pieces. Add 1 cinnamon stick, 2 teaspoons allspice berries, 1/2 teaspoon black peppercorns, 1 teaspoon brown mustard seeds, 10 cloves and warm over low heat. Pour into a warm, sterilised, 2-cup (500 ml/16 fl oz) wide-necked jar and seal with a non-metallic lid. Stand in a warm place for 2 weeks. Put some peppercorns into a sterilised 2-cup (500 ml/16 fl oz) bottle. Strain and pour the vinegar into the bottle. Seal and store in a cool, dark place for up to 6 months. Makes 2 cups (500 ml/16 fl oz).

From left to right: Tarragon vinegar; Chilli oil; Parmesan oil; Raspberry vinegar; Spicy apple and cinnamon vinegar; Spiced malt vinegar; Indian oil.

125

LEMON, FENNEL AND ROCKET SALAD

Preparation time: 25 minutes
Total cooking time: 5 minutes
Serves 4

2 lemons
2 oranges
1 large fennel bulb or 2 baby fennel
200 g (6¹/₂ oz) rocket
100 g (3¹/₂ oz) pecans, chopped
¹/₂ cup (90 g/3 oz) stuffed green
    olives, halved lengthways

TOASTED SESAME DRESSING
1 tablespoon sesame oil
1 tablespoon sesame seeds
¹/₄ cup (60 ml/2 fl oz) olive oil
2 tablespoons white wine vinegar
1 teaspoon French mustard

1 Peel the lemons and oranges, removing all the white pith. Cut the fruit into thin slices and remove any seeds. Thinly slice the fennel. Wash and dry the rocket leaves and tear into pieces. Chill the salad while making the dressing.
2 To make the dressing, heat the oil in a small pan over moderate heat. Add the sesame seeds and fry, stirring constantly, until lightly golden. Remove from the heat and cool. Pour the mixture into a small jug, whisk in the remaining ingredients and season with salt and ground black pepper.
3 Combine the fruit, fennel, rocket, pecans and olives in a shallow serving bowl. Drizzle with the dressing.

NUTRITION PER SERVE
Protein 6 g; Fat 40 g; Carbohydrate 10 g;
Dietary Fibre 9 g; Cholesterol 0 mg;
1820 kJ (435 cal)

Cut the peeled lemons and oranges into thin slices and remove any seeds.

Using a large, sharp knife, thinly slice the fennel bulb crossways.

Stir the sesame seeds in the sesame oil until they are lightly golden.

STUFFED MUSHROOM SALAD

Preparation time: 25 minutes
Total cooking time: Nil
Serves 4

20 button mushrooms
1/4 cup (60 g/2 oz) pesto, chilled
100 g (3 1/2 oz) rocket leaves
1 green oakleaf lettuce
12 small black olives
1/3 cup (50 g/1 3/4 oz) sliced semi-dried
    or sun-dried tomatoes
1 tablespoon roughly chopped
    basil
Parmesan shavings, to serve

DRESSING
1/3 cup (80 ml/2 3/4 fl oz) olive oil
1 tablespoon white wine vinegar
1 teaspoon Dijon mustard

1 Trim the mushroom stalks level with the caps and scoop out the remaining stalk with a melon baller. Spoon the pesto into the mushrooms.
2 To make the dressing, whisk together all the ingredients. Season with salt and pepper, to taste.
3 Arrange the rocket and lettuce leaves on a serving plate and top with the mushrooms, olives, tomato and basil. Drizzle the dressing over the salad and top with the Parmesan shavings. Serve immediately.

NUTRITION PER SERVE
Protein 9 g; Fat 35 g; Carbohydrate 2 g;
Dietary Fibre 3 g; Cholesterol 15 mg;
1525 kJ (365 cal)

HINT: Home-made pesto is preferable for this recipe. To make your own, process 1 cup (30 g/1 oz) loosely packed basil leaves, 2 tablespoons pine nuts and 1/4 cup (25 g/3/4 oz) grated Parmesan in a food processor to form a smooth paste. Gradually pour in 1/4 cup (60 ml/2 fl oz) olive oil in a steady stream with the motor running. Process until combined.

Draw a vegetable peeler across a block of Parmesan to make the shavings.

Trim the mushroom stalks so they are level with the caps.

Spoon the chilled pesto into the mushroom caps. Home-made pesto will give the best flavour.

WARM RADICCHIO SALAD WITH CRUSHED TOMATO VINAIGRETTE

Preparation time: 40 minutes
Total cooking time: 25 minutes
Serves 4

4–5 tablespoons olive oil
6 cloves garlic, thinly sliced
7 Roma (egg or plum) tomatoes, cored and halved
3 tablespoons extra virgin olive oil
2 tablespoons red wine vinegar
1 teaspoon honey
920 g (1 lb 14 oz) chicory
1 onion, halved and sliced
1 radicchio lettuce

1 Heat half the olive oil in a small frying pan, add the garlic and fry over moderately high heat for a few minutes, or until lightly browned. Drain on paper towels.
2 Heat a little more olive oil in the frying pan and cook the tomatoes, cut-side-down, over moderate heat until browned and very soft. Turn to brown the other side. Transfer to a bowl to cool, then peel and discard the skins. Coarsely mash the flesh with a fork.
3 To make the vinaigrette, whisk together about half of the crushed tomatoes, the extra virgin olive oil, the vinegar and the honey. Season with salt and freshly ground black pepper.
4 Trim the coarse stems from the chicory, wash the leaves very well and

drain. Cut into short lengths. Heat the rest of the olive oil in the frying pan, add the onion and cook until transparent. Add the chicory and stir until just wilted. Add the remaining tomatoes and stir until well combined. Season with salt and black pepper.
5 Tear any large radicchio leaves into smaller pieces. Toss through the chicory mixture. Transfer to a large serving bowl, drizzle with the tomato vinaigrette and sprinkle with the garlic. Serve immediately.

NUTRITION PER SERVE
Protein 7 g; Fat 35 g; Carbohydrate 9 g; Dietary Fibre 8 g; Cholesterol 0 mg; 1620 kJ (385 cal)

Fry the garlic in the oil over moderate heat until lightly browned.

Cook the tomatoes until they are browned and very soft.

Tear any large radicchio leaves into smaller pieces and toss with the chickory.

SUMMER BREAD SALAD

Preparation time: 20 minutes
Total cooking time: 15 minutes
Serves 6–8

2 red capsicums
2 yellow capsicums
6 Roma (egg or plum) tomatoes, cut
    into large chunks
100 g (3½ oz) capers, drained
100 g (3½ oz) black olives
150 g (5 oz) bocconcini, halved
1 Italian wood-fired loaf
2 cups (60 g/2 oz) basil leaves

DRESSING
4 cloves garlic, finely chopped
¼ cup (60 ml/2 fl oz) red wine vinegar
½ cup (125 ml/4 fl oz) extra virgin
    olive oil

1 Cut the capsicums into large pieces, removing the seeds and white membrane. Place, skin-side-up, under a hot grill, until the skin blackens and blisters. Cool in a plastic bag or under a tea towel, then peel away the skin and cut into thick strips.
2 Put the capsicum, tomato, capers, olives and bocconcini in a bowl and toss to combine.

3 Put the dressing ingredients in a screw-top jar and shake well.
4 Cut the bread into large pieces and put in a bowl. Drizzle with the dressing and mix until well coated. Toss gently with the capsicum mixture and basil leaves.

NUTRITION PER SERVE (8)
Protein 15 g; Fat 25 g; Carbohydrate 35 g;
Dietary Fibre 4 g; Cholesterol 25 mg;
1870 kJ (445 cal)

NOTE: This dish is based on the Tuscan favourite that uses leftover crusty bread to make a salad.

Put the grilled capsicum pieces in a plastic bag until cool enough to handle.

Put the grilled capsicum, tomato, capers, olives and bocconcini in a bowl and toss together.

Using a bread knife, cut the wood-fired loaf into large pieces.

129

ORANGE POPPY SEED ROASTED VEGETABLES

Preparation time: 20 minutes
Total cooking time: 50 minutes
Serves 6–8

500 g (1 lb) new potatoes, unpeeled, halved
6 parsnips, peeled and quartered lengthways
500 g (1 lb) orange sweet potato, cut into large pieces
335 g (11 oz) baby carrots, with stalks
6 pickling onions, halved

⅓ cup (80 ml/2¾ fl oz) oil
2 tablespoons poppy seeds
200 g (6½ oz) Brie cheese, thinly sliced

ORANGE DRESSING
½ cup (125 ml/4 fl oz) orange juice
2 cloves garlic, crushed
1 tablespoon Dijon mustard
1 teaspoon white wine vinegar
1 teaspoon sesame oil

1 Preheat the oven to moderately hot 200°C (400°F/Gas 6). Place all the vegetables and the oil in a large deep baking dish. Toss the vegetables to coat with the oil. Bake for 50 minutes, or until the vegetables are crisp and tender, tossing every 15 minutes. Sprinkle with the poppy seeds.
2 Whisk together all the dressing ingredients.
3 Pour the dressing over the warm vegetables and toss to coat. Transfer to a large bowl, top with the Brie and serve immediately, while still warm.

NUTRITION PER SERVE (8)
Protein 10 g; Fat 20 g; Carbohydrate 35 g;
Dietary Fibre 6 g; Cholesterol 25 mg;
1510 kJ (360 cal)

Quarter the parsnips lengthways and cut the sweet potato into large pieces.

Roast the vegetables until they are tender, then sprinkle with the poppy seeds.

Pour the dressing over the warm vegetables and toss to coat.

ASPARAGUS AND RED CAPSICUM SALAD

Preparation time: 20 minutes
Total cooking time: 15 minutes
Serves 4

2 red capsicums
1/3 cup (80 ml/2¾ fl oz) virgin olive oil
1 clove garlic, crushed
2 tablespoons lemon juice
2 tablespoons chopped basil
2 tablespoons pine nuts
310 g (10 oz) fresh asparagus
small black olives

1 Cut the capsicums into large pieces, removing the seeds and white membrane. Place, skin-side-up, under a hot grill until the skin blackens and blisters. Cool under a tea towel or in a plastic bag, then carefully peel away and discard the skin. Finely dice the capsicum flesh.

2 Put the olive oil, garlic, lemon juice and basil in a small bowl and whisk to combine. Add the capsicum and pine nuts, and season with salt and pepper.

3 Remove the woody ends from the asparagus (hold each spear at both ends and bend gently—the woody end will snap off at its natural breaking point). Plunge the asparagus into a large frying pan of boiling water and cook for 3 minutes, or until just tender. Drain and plunge into a bowl of iced water, then drain again and gently pat dry with paper towels.

4 Arrange the asparagus on a large serving platter and spoon the dressing over the top. Garnish with the black olives and perhaps a few lemon wedges to squeeze over the top.

NUTRITION PER SERVE
Protein 4 g; Fat 25 g; Carbohydrate 5 g;
Dietary Fibre 3 g; Cholesterol 0 mg;
1100 kJ (260 cal)

Grill the capsicum pieces until the skin blackens and blisters.

Add the diced capsicum and pine nuts to the other dressing ingredients.

Cook the asparagus in boiling water, then plunge into cold water and pat dry with paper towels.

ROAST BEETROOT AND ONION WEDGE SALAD

Preparation time: 30 minutes
Total cooking time: 1 hour 30 minutes
Serves 4–6

4 medium beetroot
3 red onions
1/3 cup (80 ml/2³/4 fl oz) oil
20 g (³/4 oz) butter
1 teaspoon ground cumin
1 teaspoon soft brown sugar
2 tablespoons orange juice
2 tablespoons orange zest
chopped chives, to garnish

SOUR CREAM DRESSING
150 g (5 oz) sour cream
2 tablespoons chopped chives
1 tablespoon chopped thyme
1 teaspoon lemon juice

1 Preheat the oven to moderate 180°C (350°F/Gas 4). Trim the leafy tops from the beetroot, leaving a short stalk, and wash thoroughly. Keep the beetroot whole to avoid bleeding during baking. Cut each onion into 6 large wedges, leaving the bases intact so the wedges hold together. Put the oil, beetroot and onion in a large baking dish and bake for 1 hour 15 minutes. Put the beetroot and onion on separate plates and cool slightly. Peel the skins from the beetroot. Trim the tops and tails, and cut into wedges.
2 Heat the butter in a frying pan, add the cumin and brown sugar, and cook for 1 minute. Add the orange juice and simmer for 5 minutes, or until the juice has reduced slightly. Add the baked beetroot wedges and orange zest, and stir gently over low heat for 2 minutes.
3 To make the dressing, mix together the sour cream, chives, thyme and lemon juice. Arrange the cooked beetroot and onion wedges on a large plate and drizzle the dressing over the top. Garnish with the chopped chives.

NUTRITION PER SERVE (6)
Protein 3 g; Fat 25 g; Carbohydrate 10 g;
Dietary Fibre 4 g; Cholesterol 40 mg;
1185 kJ (280 cal)

Trim the leafy tops from the beetroot, leaving a short stalk on each one.

Cut the onions into wedges, leaving as much of the base intact as possible.

Add the beetroot wedges and orange zest to the pan and cook over low heat.

MARINATED TOFU AND CARROT SESAME SALAD

Preparation time: 30 minutes
+ 1 hour marinating
Total cooking time: 15 minutes
Serves 4

500 g (1 lb) firm tofu
2 tablespoons grated fresh ginger
2 spring onions, finely sliced
1 tablespoon mirin
1/4 cup (60 ml/2 fl oz) soy sauce
1 teaspoon sesame oil
oil, for cooking
2 Lebanese cucumbers
2 carrots, peeled
1/4 Chinese cabbage, shredded
100 g (3 1/2 oz) crispy fried egg
    noodles
50 g (1 3/4 oz) roasted peanuts, roughly
    chopped
mint leaves, to garnish

DRESSING
1 tablespoon grated lime rind
1 tablespoon sugar
2 tablespoons lime juice
1/4 cup (60 ml/2 fl oz) olive oil
2 tablespoons shredded mint leaves

1 Cut the tofu into 1 cm (1/2 inch) thick triangles. Put in a shallow dish with the ginger, spring onion, mirin, soy sauce and sesame oil. Cover and refrigerate for 1 hour.
2 Heat 2 tablespoons of the oil in a large non-stick frying pan. Add the tofu and cook, in batches, over high heat until crisp and golden. Drain on paper towels.
3 Cut the cucumbers and carrots into paper-thin ribbons with a vegetable peeler. Arrange the cabbage on a large platter and top with the cucumber,

carrot and the fried tofu.
4 Gently whisk together the dressing ingredients and drizzle over the salad. Sprinkle with the noodles and nuts and garnish with mint leaves.

NUTRITION PER SERVE
Protein 20 g; Fat 30 g; Carbohydrate 20 g;
Dietary Fibre 5 g; Cholesterol 10 mg;
1690 kJ (400 cal)

Marinate the tofu in the ginger, spring onion, mirin, soy sauce and sesame oil.

Fry the marinated tofu in batches so that you don't overcrowd the pan.

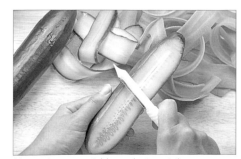

Use a sharp vegetable peeler to cut the cucumbers and carrots into ribbons.

WILD MUSHROOM SALAD

Preparation time: 15 minutes
Total cooking time: 15 minutes
Serves 4

100 g (3¹/₂ oz) hazelnuts
1 mizuna lettuce
90 g (3 oz) baby curly endive
60 g (2 oz) baby English spinach
2 tablespoons hazelnut oil
2 tablespoons light olive oil
500 g (1 lb) wild mushrooms
    (enoki, shimeji, Shiitake, oyster)
150 g (5 oz) strong blue cheese,
    crumbled

TOMATO MUSTARD VINAIGRETTE
¹/₂ cup (125 ml/4 fl oz) light olive oil
2 tablespoons tarragon vinegar
1 teaspoon tomato mustard

1 Preheat the oven to moderate 180°C (350°F/Gas 4). Put the hazelnuts on a baking tray and cook for 10 minutes, shaking the tray occasionally. Remove from the oven, cool, and remove the skins by rubbing the nuts together in a tea towel. Coarsely chop the nuts.
2 Remove the tough lower stems from the mizuna and endive, and tear the larger leaves into bite-sized pieces. Wash the mizuna, endive and spinach under cold water, dry completely and refrigerate until well chilled.
3 To make the vinaigrette, whisk the ingredients together and season well.
4 Heat the oils in a frying pan and sauté the mushrooms for 3–4 minutes, or until beginning to soften. Remove from the heat and cool slightly, then stir in the vinaigrette. Arrange the salad greens on serving plates. Spoon the mushrooms over the top and sprinkle with cheese and hazelnuts.

NUTRITION PER SERVE
Protein 10 g; Fat 75 g; Carbohydrate 20 g;
Dietary Fibre 4 g; Cholesterol 40 mg;
3375 kJ (805 cal)

NOTE: Chestnut mushrooms or chanterelles can also be used. Pink oyster mushrooms, if available, make this salad look particularly attractive.

Rub the hazelnuts together in a tea towel to remove the skins.

Remove the tough lower stems from the baby curly endive.

Sauté the mushrooms until they are just beginning to soften.

SPICY LENTIL SALAD

Preparation time: 30 minutes
Total cooking time: 1 hour 10 minutes
Serves 6

1 cup (220 g/7 oz) brown rice
1 cup (185 g/6 oz) brown lentils
1 teaspoon turmeric
1 teaspoon ground cinnamon
6 cardamom pods
3 star anise
2 bay leaves
1/4 cup (60 ml/2 fl oz) sunflower oil
1 tablespoon lemon juice
250 g (8 oz) broccoli florets
2 carrots, cut into julienne strips
1 onion, finely chopped
2 cloves garlic, crushed
1 red capsicum, finely chopped
1 teaspoon garam masala
1 teaspoon ground coriander
1 1/2 cups (250 g/8 oz) fresh or frozen
     peas, thawed

MINT AND YOGHURT DRESSING
1 cup (250 g/8 oz) plain yoghurt
1 tablespoon lemon juice
1 tablespoon chopped fresh mint
1 teaspoon cumin seeds

1 Put 3 cups (750 ml/24 fl oz) water with the rice, lentils, turmeric, cinnamon, cardamom, star anise and bay leaves in a pan. Stir well and bring to the boil. Reduce the heat, cover and simmer gently for 50–60 minutes, or until the liquid is absorbed. Remove the whole spices. Transfer the mixture to a large bowl. Whisk 2 tablespoons of the oil with the lemon juice and fork through the rice mixture.
2 Boil, steam or microwave the broccoli and carrots until tender. Drain and refresh in cold water.

3 Heat the remaining oil in a large pan and add the onion, garlic and capsicum. Stir-fry for 2–3 minutes, then add the garam masala and coriander, and stir-fry for a further 1–2 minutes. Add the vegetables and toss to coat in the spice mixture. Add to the rice and fork through to combine. Cover and refrigerate until cold.
4 To make the dressing, mix the

yoghurt, lemon juice, mint and cumin seeds together, and season with salt and pepper. Spoon the salad into individual serving bowls or onto a platter and serve with the dressing.

NUTRITION PER SERVE
Protein 20 g; Fat 15 g; Carbohydrate 50 g;
Dietary Fibre 10 g; Cholesterol 7 mg;
1605 kJ (380 cal)

Add the cardamom pods, star anise and bay leaves to the pan.

Add the vegetables and toss to coat with the spice mixture.

Mix the yoghurt, lemon juice, mint and cumin seeds together to make a dressing.

Stir-fries

POTATO NOODLES WITH VEGETABLES

Preparation time: 30 minutes + soaking
Total cooking time: 25 minutes
Serves 4

300 g (10 oz) dried potato starch
   noodles
30 g (1 oz) dried cloud-ear fungus
1/4 cup (60 ml/2 fl oz) sesame oil
2 tablespoons vegetable oil
3 cloves garlic, finely chopped
4 cm (11/2 inch) piece of fresh ginger,
   grated
2 spring onions, finely chopped
2 carrots, cut into short matchsticks
2 spring onions, extra, cut into short
   lengths
500 g (1 lb) baby bok choy or
   250 g (8 oz) English spinach,
   roughly chopped
1/4 cup (60 ml/2 fl oz) shoshoyu
   (Japanese soy sauce)
2 tablespoons mirin
1 teaspoon sugar
2 tablespoons sesame seed and
   seaweed sprinkle

1 Cook the dried potato noodles in boiling water for about 5 minutes or until translucent. Drain and then rinse under cold running water until cold. (Thoroughly rinsing the noodles will remove any excess starch.) Roughly chop the noodles into lengths of about 15 cm (6 inches), to make them easier to eat with chopsticks.

2 Pour boiling water over the fungus and soak for 10 minutes. Drain thoroughly and chop roughly. Heat 1 tablespoon of the sesame oil with the vegetable oil in a large, heavy-based pan or wok. Add the garlic, ginger and spring onion to the pan and cook for 3 minutes over medium heat, stirring regularly. Add the carrot sticks and stir-fry for 1 minute.

3 Add the noodles, extra spring onion, bok choy, remaining sesame oil, shoshoyu, mirin and sugar. Toss well, cover and cook over low heat for 2 minutes.

4 Add the drained fungus, cover the pan and cook for another 2 minutes. Sprinkle with the sesame seed and seaweed sprinkle. Serve immediately.

NUTRITION PER SERVE
Protein 5 g; Fat 11 g; Carbohydrate 20 g;
Dietary Fibre 3 g; Cholesterol 0 mg;
830 kJ (198 cal)

NOTE: Japanese soy sauce is lighter and sweeter than Chinese soy sauce. It is available from Asian speciality stores, along with potato starch noodles (Korean vermicelli) and cloud-ear fungus.

Make the noodles easier to eat by roughly chopping them with kitchen scissors.

Add the noodles, spring onion, bok choy, sesame oil, shoshoyu, mirin and sugar.

ASIAN GREENS WITH TERIYAKI TOFU DRESSING

Preparation time: 15 minutes
Total cooking time: 20 minutes
Serves 6

650 g (1 lb 5 oz) baby bok choy
500 g (1 lb) choy sum
440 g (14 oz) snake beans, topped and tailed
1/4 cup (60 ml/2 fl oz) oil
1 onion, thinly sliced
1/3 cup (60 g/2 oz) soft brown sugar
1/2 teaspoon ground chilli

2 tablespoons grated fresh ginger
1 cup (250 ml/8 fl oz) teriyaki sauce
1 tablespoon sesame oil
600 g (1 1/4 lb) silken firm tofu, drained

1 Cut the baby bok choy and choy sum widthways into thirds. Cut the snake beans into long lengths.
2 Heat a wok over high heat, add 1 tablespoon of the oil and swirl to coat the side. Cook the onion in batches for 3–5 minutes, or until crisp. Remove with a slotted spoon and drain on paper towels.
3 Heat 1 tablespoon of the oil in the wok, add half the greens and stir-fry for 2–3 minutes, or until wilted.

Remove and keep warm. Repeat with the remaining oil and greens. Remove. Drain any liquid from the wok.
4 Add the combined sugar, chilli, ginger and teriyaki sauce to the wok and bring to the boil. Simmer for 1 minute. Add the sesame oil and tofu and simmer for 2 minutes, turning once—the tofu will break up. Divide the greens among serving plates, then top with the dressing. Sprinkle with the fried onion to serve.

NUTRITION PER SERVE
Protein 19 g; Fat 11 g; Carbohydrate 20 g;
Dietary Fibre 11 g; Cholesterol 1 mg;
1093 kJ (260 cal)

Cut the baby bok choy and choy sum widthways into thirds.

Cook the combined greens in two batches until the leaves are wilted.

Cook the tofu for a couple of minutes and then turn with a spatula—the tofu will break up.

TAMARI ROASTED ALMONDS WITH SPICY GREEN BEANS

Preparation time: 10 minutes
Total cooking time: 25 minutes
Serves 4–6

1 tablespoon sesame oil
2¹/2 cups (500 g/1 lb) jasmine rice
2 tablespoons sesame oil, extra
1 long red chilli, seeded and finely chopped
2 cm (³/4 inch) piece of fresh ginger, peeled and grated
2 cloves garlic, crushed

375 g (12 oz) green beans, cut into short lengths
¹/2 cup (125 ml/4 fl oz) hoisin sauce
1 tablespoon soft brown sugar
2 tablespoons mirin
250 g (8 oz) tamari roasted almonds, roughly chopped (see NOTE)

1 Preheat the oven to moderately hot 200°C (400°F/Gas 6). Heat the oil in a 1.5 litre (48 fl oz) ovenproof dish. Add the rice and stir to coat with oil. Stir in 1 litre (32 fl oz) boiling water. Cover and bake for 20 minutes, or until all the water is absorbed. Keep warm.
2 Meanwhile, heat the extra oil in a wok or large frying pan and cook the chilli, ginger and garlic for 1 minute, or until lightly browned. Add the beans, hoisin sauce and sugar and stir-fry for 2 minutes. Stir in the mirin and cook for 1 minute, or until the beans are tender but still crunchy.
3 Remove from the heat and stir in the almonds. Serve on a bed of the rice.

NUTRITION PER SERVE (6)
Protein 15 g; Fat 34 g; Carbohydrate 80 g; Dietary Fibre 9.5 g; Cholesterol 0 mg; 2874 kJ (687 cal)

NOTE: Tamari roasted almonds are available from health-food stores.

When chopping chillies, it's a good idea to wear rubber gloves to prevent chilli burns.

Cook the rice in the oven until all the water has been absorbed.

Stir-fry the beans for 2 minutes, tossing to coat them in the sauce.

UDON NOODLE STIR-FRY

Preparation time: 15 minutes
Total cooking time: 10 minutes
Serves 4

500 g (1 lb) fresh udon noodles
1 tablespoon oil
6 spring onions, cut into short lengths
3 cloves garlic, crushed
1 tablespoon grated fresh ginger
2 carrots, cut into short lengths
150 g (5 oz) snow peas, cut in half on the diagonal
100 g (3¹/2 oz) bean sprouts

500 g (1 lb) choy sum, cut into short lengths
2 tablespoons Japanese soy sauce
2 tablespoons mirin
2 tablespoons kecap manis
2 sheets roasted nori, cut into thin strips

1 Bring a saucepan of water to the boil, add the noodles and cook for 5 minutes, or until tender and not clumped together. Drain and rinse under hot water.
2 Heat the oil in a wok until hot, then add the spring onion, garlic and ginger. Stir-fry over high heat for

1–2 minutes, or until soft. Add the carrot, snow peas and 1 tablespoon water, toss well, cover and cook for 1–2 minutes, or until the vegetables are just tender.
3 Add the noodles, bean sprouts, choy sum, soy sauce, mirin and kecap manis, then toss until the choy sum is wilted and coated with the sauce. Stir in the nori just before serving.

NUTRITION PER SERVE
Protein 25 g; Fat 7.5 g; Carbohydrate 95 g; Dietary Fibre 13 g; Cholesterol 22 mg; 2330 kJ (557 cal)

Cut the roasted nori sheets into very thin strips. It is available from Asian speciality shops.

Cook the udon noodles until they are tender and not clumped together.

Stir-fry the greens, noodles and sauces until the choy sum is wilted and coated with sauce.

TEMPEH STIR-FRY

Preparation time: 15 minutes
Total cooking time: 15 minutes
Serves 4

1 teaspoon sesame oil
1 tablespoon peanut oil
2 cloves garlic, crushed
1 tablespoon grated fresh ginger
1 red chilli, finely sliced
4 spring onions, sliced on the diagonal
300 g (10 oz) tempeh, diced
500 g (1 lb) baby bok choy leaves

800 g (1 lb 10 oz) Chinese broccoli, chopped
1/2 cup (125 ml/4 fl oz) mushroom oyster sauce
2 tablespoons rice vinegar
2 tablespoons fresh coriander leaves
3 tablespoons toasted cashew nuts

1 Heat the oils in a wok over high heat, add the garlic, ginger, chilli and spring onion and cook for 1–2 minutes, or until the onion is soft. Add the tempeh and cook for 5 minutes, or until golden. Remove and keep warm.

2 Add half the greens and 1 tablespoon water to the wok and cook, covered, for 3–4 minutes, or until wilted. Remove and repeat with the remaining greens and more water.
3 Return the greens and tempeh to the wok, add the sauce and vinegar and warm through. Top with the coriander and nuts. Serve with rice.

NUTRITION PER SERVE
Protein 23 g; Fat 15 g; Carbohydrate 12 g; Dietary Fibre 15 g; Cholesterol 0 mg; 2220 kJ (529 cal)

Stir-fry the garlic, ginger, chilli and spring onion for 1–2 minutes.

Add the tempeh to the wok and stir-fry for 5 minutes, or until golden.

Add the greens to the wok in two batches and cook until wilted.

ITALIAN FENNEL STIR-FRY

Preparation time: 20 minutes
Total cooking time: 5 minutes
Serves 4

1 tablespoon extra virgin olive oil
20 g (3/4 oz) butter
2 baby fennel bulbs (500 g/1 lb),
    thinly sliced
2 cloves garlic, thinly sliced
1 tablespoon lemon juice
250 g (8 oz) cherry tomatoes, halved
1/4 cup (7 g/1/4 oz) chopped fresh
    oregano

100 g (31/2 oz) small Kalamata olives
100 g (31/2 oz) feta cheese

1 Heat the wok until very hot, add the oil and butter, and swirl it around to coat the side. Stir-fry the fennel slices and garlic for 2 minutes, or until they begin to soften.
2 Add the lemon juice and tomatoes, and season with salt. Stir-fry for 2 minutes, then add the oregano and olives, and toss gently to combine.
3 Place in a serving dish and crumble the feta cheese over the top. Sprinkle with freshly cracked black pepper.

NUTRITION PER SERVE
Protein 6 g; Fat 15 g; Carbohydrate 5 g;
Dietary Fibre 4 g; Cholesterol 30 mg;
765 kJ (185 cal)

Trim the tops and bases from the fennel bulbs, then cut the bulbs into thin slices.

STIR-FRIED CAULIFLOWER WITH TOASTED NUTS

Preparation time: 30 minutes
Total cooking time: 20 minutes
Serves 4

2 tablespoons oil
2 tablespoons mild curry paste
1 tablespoon currants
1 tablespoon grated fresh ginger
4 spring onions, diagonally sliced

500 g (1 lb) cauliflower, cut into bite-sized florets
2 teaspoons sesame oil
150 g (5 oz) walnuts, toasted
150 g (5 oz) cashews, toasted
1 tablespoon sesame seeds

1 Heat the wok until very hot, add the oil and swirl it around. Stir-fry the curry paste for 3 minutes, or until fragrant. Add the currants, ginger, spring onion and cauliflower. Stir-fry for 4–5 minutes, adding about 1/3 cup

(80 ml/2¾ fl oz) water to moisten. Cover and steam for 1–2 minutes, or until the cauliflower is tender.
2 Season with salt and pepper, and drizzle with the sesame oil. Toss the toasted walnuts and cashews through the cauliflower mixture. Serve sprinkled with the sesame seeds.

NUTRITION PER SERVE
Protein 15 g; Fat 60 g; Carbohydrate 10 g; Dietary Fibre 8 g; Cholesterol 0 mg; 2750 kJ (655 cal)

Toast the walnuts and cashews by dry-frying them in the wok.

Heat the oil in the very hot wok and stir-fry the curry paste until it is fragrant.

Add the currants, ginger, spring onion and cauliflower, and toss well.

143

SPRING VEGETABLES WITH HERBED BUTTER

Preparation time: 20 minutes
Total cooking time: 10 minutes
Serves 6 as an accompaniment

2 tablespoons light olive oil
200 g (6¹/2 oz) asparagus, cut into short lengths
115 g (4 oz) baby corn, halved lengthways
250 g (8 oz) snow peas
250 g (8 oz) green beans, halved

300 g (10 oz) baby carrots, halved lengthways
2 cloves garlic, crushed
50 g (1³/4 oz) butter
¹/4 cup (15 g/¹/2 oz) finely chopped fresh parsley
¹/4 cup (15 g/¹/2 oz) finely chopped fresh chives
¹/4 cup (15 g/¹/2 oz) shredded fresh basil

1 Heat the wok until very hot, add the oil and swirl it around to coat the side. Stir-fry all the vegetables over high heat for 5 minutes. Cover and cook over low heat for 2 minutes, or until tender.
2 Add the crushed garlic, butter and all the fresh herbs, and toss until the butter has melted and the herbs have wilted slightly. Season well with salt and pepper and serve immediately as an accompaniment.

NUTRITION PER SERVE
Protein 3 g; Fat 12 g; Carbohydrate 8 g; Dietary Fibre 4 g; Cholesterol 20 mg; 695 kJ (165 cal)

Use a large sharp knife to finely chop the fresh parsley, chives and basil.

Stir-fry the asparagus, snow peas, beans, corn and carrot over high heat.

Add the garlic, butter and herbs to the tender vegetables and toss until the butter melts.

WILD MUSHROOMS WITH SPICES

Preparation time: 30 minutes
Total cooking time: 5 minutes
Serve 4

20 g (³/4 oz) butter
1 tablespoon oil
2 cloves garlic, crushed
1 teaspoon ground cumin
1 teaspoon ground coriander
¹/4 teaspoon sweet paprika
750 g (1¹/2 lb) mixed mushrooms (see NOTE), cleaned and trimmed

2 tablespoons dry sherry
4 spring onions, sliced
¹/4 cup (15 g/¹/2 oz) shredded fresh basil
2 tablespoons chopped fresh flat-leaf parsley

1 Heat the wok until very hot, add the butter and oil and swirl it around the wok. Stir-fry the garlic, cumin, coriander and paprika for 1–2 minutes, or until fragrant. Add the mushrooms and stir-fry for 2 minutes, tossing well.
2 Add the sherry and bring to the boil. Cover and cook for 30 seconds. Toss the spring onion and herbs through the mushroom mixture.

NUTRITION PER SERVE
Protein 7 g; Fat 9.5 g; Carbohydrate 4 g; Dietary Fibre 5.5 g; Cholesterol 15 mg; 580 kJ (140 cal)

NOTE: Mushrooms such as shimeji, oyster, swiss brown, enoki and button can be used in this recipe. If using enoki mushrooms, add them when the sherry is added as they cook faster than the other mushrooms.

Clean and trim the mushrooms, cutting any larger ones in half.

Stir-fry the garlic, cumin, coriander and paprika until fragrant.

Add the sherry and enoki mushrooms, and cover and cook for 2 minutes.

STIR-FRIED ASIAN GREENS AND MUSHROOMS

Preparation time: 20 minutes
Total cooking time: 5 minutes
Serves 4

20 stems Chinese broccoli
4 baby bok choy
100 g (3¹/₂ oz) shimeji or enoki
  mushrooms
100 g (3¹/₂ oz) shiitake mushrooms
1 tablespoon soy sauce
2 teaspoons crushed palm sugar
1 tablespoon oil
4 spring onions, cut into short pieces
5 cm (2 inch) fresh ginger, cut into thin
  strips
1–2 small red chillies, seeded and
  finely chopped
2–3 cloves garlic, crushed
125 g (4 oz) snow peas, halved
1–2 teaspoons seasoning sauce

1 Remove any tough outer leaves from the Chinese broccoli and bok choy. Cut into 4 cm (1¹/₂ inch) pieces across the leaves, including the stems. Wash thoroughly, then drain and dry thoroughly. Wipe the mushrooms with a paper towel and trim the ends. Slice the shiitake mushrooms thickly.
2 Combine the soy sauce and palm sugar with ¹/₄ cup (60 ml/2 fl oz) water. Set aside.
3 Heat the wok until very hot, add the oil and swirl it around to coat the side. Stir-fry the spring onion, ginger, chilli and garlic over low heat for 30 seconds, without browning. Increase the heat to high and add the Chinese broccoli, bok choy and snow peas. Stir-fry for 1–2 minutes, or until the vegetables are wilted.

4 Add the prepared mushrooms and soy sauce mixture. Stir-fry over high heat for 1–2 minutes, or until the mushrooms and sauce are heated through. Sprinkle with the seasoning sauce, to taste, and serve immediately.

NUTRITION PER SERVE
Protein 6.5 g; Fat 10 g; Carbohydrate 15 g;
Dietary Fibre 3 g; Cholesterol 0 mg;
780 kJ (185 cal)

You will need to gently separate the shimeji mushrooms from each other.

Trim the shiitake mushrooms and cut them into thick slices.

Peel the piece of ginger with a vegetable peeler or sharp knife and cut it into thin strips.

STIR-FRIED TOFU WITH ORANGE AND FRESH PINEAPPLE

Preparation time: 35 minutes
Total cooking time: 10 minutes
Serves 4

250 g (8 oz) firm tofu, cut into cubes
5 cm (2 inch) fresh ginger, grated
2 teaspoons finely grated orange rind
oil, for cooking
2 large onions, cut into thin wedges
3 cloves garlic, finely chopped
2 teaspoons soft brown sugar
2 teaspoons white vinegar

250 g (8 oz) fresh pineapple, cut into bite-sized pieces
1 tablespoon orange juice

1 Put the tofu, ginger, orange rind and some pepper in a glass or ceramic bowl. Stir, cover and refrigerate.
2 Heat the wok until very hot, add 1¹/₂ tablespoons of the oil and swirl it around to coat. Stir-fry the onion, garlic and brown sugar over medium heat for 2–3 minutes, or until the onion is soft and golden. Stir in the vinegar and cook for 2 minutes. Remove from the wok.
3 Reheat the wok and add the pineapple and orange juice. Stir-fry for

3 minutes over high heat, or until the pineapple is just soft and golden. Stir in the onion mixture, remove from the wok, cover and set aside.
4 Reheat the wok until very hot and add 1¹/₂ tablespoons of the oil. Stir-fry the tofu in two batches, tossing regularly until it is lightly crisp and golden. Drain on paper towels.
5 Return the tofu and the pineapple mixture to the wok, and toss to heat through. Season well and serve.

NUTRITION PER SERVE
Protein 6.5 g; Fat 3 g; Carbohydrate 15 g;
Dietary Fibre 3 g; Cholesterol 0 mg;
430 kJ (100 cal)

Drain the firm tofu, and cut it into bite-sized cubes with a sharp knife.

Stir-fry the onion, garlic and brown sugar until the onion is soft and golden.

Stir-fry the marinated tofu in two batches until it is lightly crisp and golden.

SPICY BROCCOLI AND CAULIFLOWER STIR-FRY

Preparation time: 15 minutes
Total cooking time: 10 minutes
Serves 4

1 teaspoon ground cumin
1 teaspoon ground coriander
2 tablespoons oil
2 cloves garlic, crushed
1 teaspoon grated fresh ginger
1/2 teaspoon chilli powder

1 onion, cut into wedges
200 g (6½ oz) cauliflower, cut into
    bite-sized florets
200 g (6½ oz) broccoli, cut into bite-
    sized florets
200 g (6½ oz) haloumi cheese, diced
1 tablespoon lemon juice

1 Heat the wok until very hot, add the cumin and coriander, and dry-fry the spices for 1 minute. Add the oil with the garlic, ginger and chilli powder, and stir-fry briefly. Add the onion and cook for 2–3 minutes, being careful not to burn the spices.

2 Add the cauliflower and broccoli, and stir-fry until they are cooked through but still crisp. Add the haloumi and toss well until the haloumi is coated with the spices and is just beginning to melt. Season well and serve sprinkled with lemon juice.

NUTRITION PER SERVE
Protein 12 g; Fat 15 g; Carbohydrate 3 g;
Dietary Fibre 4 g; Cholesterol 20 mg;
820 kJ (195 cal)

Haloumi cheese comes in a block—cut it into small cubes.

Dry-fry the ground cumin and coriander in a very hot wok.

Add the onion wedges to the spice mixture and toss to coat.

COLOURFUL CABBAGE STIR-FRY

Preparation time: 15 minutes
Total cooking time: 10 minutes
Serves 2

200 g (6¹/₂ oz) red cabbage
200 g (6¹/₂ oz) white cabbage
200 g (6¹/₂ oz) green cabbage
1 apple
oil, for cooking
1 teaspoon soft brown sugar
1 red onion, thinly sliced
1 red chilli, finely chopped
1 tablespoon chopped fresh thyme
1 tablespoon cider vinegar
²/₃ cup (100 g/3¹/₂ oz) chopped
   blanched almonds

1 Finely shred the three different varieties of cabbage. Wash thoroughly, drain and dry well in a tea towel. Core and slice the apple.
2 Heat the wok until very hot, add 1 tablespoon of the oil and swirl it around to coat the side. Add the apple and brown sugar, and stir-fry for 1–2 minutes, or until the apple caramelizes. Remove the apple from the wok and set aside.
3 Reheat the wok, add a little oil if necessary and stir-fry the sliced red onion for 1 minute. Add the chopped chilli, shredded red cabbage and white cabbage, and stir-fry for 2–3 minutes. Add the shredded green cabbage and stir-fry for 1 minute. Stir in the thyme and the caramelized apple, and season well. Pour in the cider vinegar, cover

and steam for 1 minute. Add the almonds and toss well until evenly distributed. Serve immediately.

NUTRITION PER SERVE
Protein 15 g; Fat 40 g; Carbohydrate 20 g;
Dietary Fibre 15 g; Cholesterol 0 mg;
2420 kJ (580 cal)

Finely shred the red, white and green cabbage before washing thoroughly.

PHAD THAI

Preparation time: 20 minutes
Total cooking time: 15 minutes
Serves 4

400 g (13 oz) flat rice-stick noodles
2 tablespoons peanut oil
2 eggs, lightly beaten
1 onion, cut into thin wedges
2 cloves garlic, crushed
1 small red capsicum, thinly sliced
100 g (3¹/₂ oz) deep-fried tofu puffs,
    cut into thin strips
6 spring onions, thinly sliced
¹/₂ cup (30 g/1 oz) chopped fresh
    coriander leaves

¹/₄ cup (60 ml/2 fl oz) soy sauce
2 tablespoons lime juice
1 tablespoon soft brown sugar
2 teaspoons sambal oelek
1 cup (90 g/3 oz) bean shoots
3 tablespoons chopped roasted
    unsalted peanuts

1 Cook the noodles in a saucepan of boiling water for 5–10 minutes, or until tender. Drain and set aside.
2 Heat a wok over high heat and add enough peanut oil to coat the bottom and side. When smoking, add the egg and swirl to form a thin omelette. Cook for 30 seconds, or until just set. Roll up, remove and thinly slice.
3 Heat the remaining oil in the wok.

Add the onion, garlic and capsicum and cook over high heat for 2–3 minutes, or until the onion softens. Add the noodles, tossing well. Stir in the omelette, tofu, spring onion and half the coriander.
4 Pour in the combined soy sauce, lime juice, sugar and sambal oelek, then toss to coat the noodles. Sprinkle with the bean shoots and top with roasted peanuts and the remaining coriander. Serve immediately.

NUTRITION PER SERVE
Protein 13 g; Fat 21 g; Carbohydrate 34 g;
Dietary Fibre 5 g; Cholesterol 90 mg;
1565 kJ (375 cal)

Buy deep-fried tofu puffs (rather than silken or firm tofu) and cut into thin strips.

Cook the egg, swirling the wok, to make a thin omelette, then roll up and thinly slice.

Stir in the omelette, tofu, spring onion and fresh coriander.

SWEET AND SOUR TOFU WITH NOODLES

Preparation time: 10 minutes
Total cooking time: 5 minutes
Serves 4

100 g (3¹/₂ oz) deep-fried tofu puffs
    (see NOTE)
2 tablespoons oil
1 onion, sliced
1 red capsicum, cut into squares
3 cloves garlic, crushed
2 teaspoons grated fresh ginger
500 g (1 lb) thin Hokkien noodles

³/₄ cup (120 g/4 oz) small chunks
    fresh pineapple
¹/₄ cup (60 ml/2 fl oz) pineapple juice
¹/₄ cup (60 ml/2 fl oz) hoisin sauce
¹/₄ cup (15 g/¹/₂ oz) roughly chopped
    fresh coriander

1 Slice the tofu puffs into three, then cut each slice into two or three pieces.
2 Heat the wok until very hot, add the oil and stir-fry the onion and capsicum for 1–2 minutes, or until beginning to soften. Add the garlic and ginger, stir-fry for 1 minute, then add the tofu and stir-fry for 2 minutes.
3 Add the noodles and pineapple chunks and toss until the mixture is combined and heated through. Add the pineapple juice, hoisin sauce and chopped coriander, and toss well. Serve immediately.

NUTRITION PER SERVE
Protein 10 g; Fat 15 g; Carbohydrate 65 g;
Dietary Fibre 3.5 g; Cholesterol 0 mg;
1830 kJ (435 cal)

NOTE: Deep-fried tofu puffs are available from the refrigerated section in Asian grocery stores and some supermarkets. They have a very different texture to ordinary tofu.

Use your fingers to gently pull apart the strands of Hokkien noodles before use.

Buy deep-fried tofu puffs, not silken tofu. Slice each tofu puff into three, then cut into pieces.

Stir-fry the onion and capsicum until they are beginning to soften.

GREEN BEANS WITH SHIITAKE MUSHROOMS

Preparation time: 15 minutes
Total cooking time: 12 minutes
Serves 4 as a main course, or 6–8 as
  an accompaniment

2 tablespoons sesame seeds
1 tablespoon oil
1 teaspoon sesame oil
5 spring onions, sliced

800 g (1 lb 10 oz) green beans
200 g (6¹/₂ oz) shiitake mushrooms
2 teaspoons finely chopped fresh
  ginger
2 tablespoons mirin
2 tablespoons soy sauce
1 tablespoon sugar

1 Heat the wok until very hot, add the
sesame seeds and stir-fry over high
heat until they are golden. Remove
from the wok and set aside.
2 Reheat the wok, add the oils and
swirl to coat the side. Add the spring
onion and beans, and stir-fry for
4 minutes. Add the mushrooms and
ginger, and cook for 4 minutes.
3 Pour in the mirin, soy sauce and
sugar, cover and cook for 2 minutes,
or until the beans are tender. Sprinkle
with the toasted sesame seeds.

NUTRITION PER SERVE (4)
Protein 7.5 g; Fat 12 g; Carbohydrate 10 g;
Dietary Fibre 7 g; Cholesterol 0 mg;
885 kJ (210 cal)

Peel the fresh ginger and chop it finely to make
up 2 teaspoons.

Dry-fry the sesame seeds over high heat until they
are golden.

Stir-fry the spring onion and beans in the oil and
sesame oil.

STIR-FRIED EGGPLANT WITH LEMON

Preparation time: 20 minutes +
  30 minutes standing
Total cooking time: 12 minutes
Serves 4

1 kg (2 lb) small eggplants
1 tablespoon salt
olive oil, for cooking
8 spring onions, sliced
3 cloves garlic, crushed
2 teaspoons cumin seeds
1 tablespoon ground coriander
1 teaspoon grated lemon rind

$^1/_3$ cup (80 ml/$2^3/_4$ fl oz) lemon juice
2 teaspoons soft brown sugar
2 tablespoons fresh coriander leaves

1 Peel the eggplants and cut into small cubes. Put in a colander and sprinkle with the salt. Leave for 30 minutes, then rinse under cold water and pat dry with paper towels.
2 Heat the wok until very hot, add $1^1/_2$ tablespoons of the oil and swirl it around to coat the side. Stir-fry the eggplant in two batches over high heat for 3–4 minutes, or until browned and cooked (use $1^1/_2$ tablespoons oil for each batch). Remove from the wok.
3 Return all the eggplant to the wok

and add the spring onion. Stir-fry for 1 minute, or until the eggplant is soft. Add the garlic and cumin seeds, and cook for 1 minute. Stir in the ground coriander and cook for 30 seconds. Add the lemon rind, juice and sugar, and toss well. Season with salt and black pepper and sprinkle with coriander leaves. Delicious served with buckwheat noodles.

NUTRITION PER SERVE
Protein 3.5 g; Fat 10 g; Carbohydrate 10 g;
Dietary Fibre 7 g; Cholesterol 0 mg;
640 kJ (155 cal)

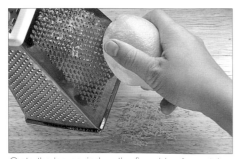
Grate the lemon rind on the fine side of a metal grater, avoiding the bitter pith underneath.

Put the eggplant cubes in a colander and sprinkle with the salt to draw out any bitter juices.

Stir-fry the eggplant in batches until it is browned and cooked through.

153

ASPARAGUS AND MUSTARD STIR-FRY

Preparation time: 10 minutes
Total cooking time: 10 minutes
Serves 2

480 g (15 oz) asparagus
1 tablespoon oil
1 red onion, sliced
1 clove garlic, crushed
1 tablespoon wholegrain mustard
1 teaspoon honey
1/2 cup (125 ml/4 fl oz) cream

1 Break the woody ends off the asparagus by holding both ends of the spear and bending gently until it snaps at its natural breaking point. Cut the asparagus into 5 cm (2 inch) lengths.
2 Heat the wok until very hot, add the oil and swirl to coat the side. Stir-fry the onion for 2–3 minutes, or until tender. Stir in the crushed garlic and cook for 1 minute. Add the asparagus to the wok and stir-fry for 3–4 minutes, or until tender, being careful not to overcook the asparagus.
3 Remove the asparagus from the wok, set it aside and keep it warm. Combine the wholegrain mustard, honey and cream. Add to the wok and bring to the boil, then reduce the heat and simmer for 2–3 minutes, or until the mixture reduces and thickens slightly. Return the asparagus to the wok and toss it through the cream mixture. Serve immediately.

NUTRITION PER SERVE
Protein 8.5 g; Fat 35 g; Carbohydrate 10 g;
Dietary Fibre 5 g; Cholesterol 85 mg;
1685 kJ (405 cal)

VARIATION: When asparagus is in season, white and purple asparagus are also available. Vary the recipe by using a mixture of the three colours. Do not overcook the purple asparagus or it will turn green as it cooks.

HINT: This dish can also be served on croutons, toasted ciabatta or toasted wholegrain bread as a smart starter or first course.

Gently bend the asparagus spear and the tough woody end will naturally snap off.

Stir-fry the sliced red onion over moderate heat for 2–3 minutes, or until tender.

PUMPKIN AND CASHEW STIR-FRY

Preparation time: 20 minutes
Total cooking time: 15 minutes
Serves 4–6

oil, for cooking
1 cup (155 g/5 oz) raw cashews
1 leek, white part only, sliced
2 teaspoons ground coriander
2 teaspoons ground cumin
2 teaspoons brown mustard seeds
2 cloves garlic, crushed

1 kg (2 lb) butternut pumpkin, cubed
3/4 cup (185 ml/6 fl oz) orange juice
1 teaspoon soft brown sugar

1 Heat the wok until very hot, add 1 tablespoon of the oil and swirl to coat. Stir-fry the cashews until golden, then drain on paper towels. Stir-fry the leek for 2–3 minutes, or until softened. Remove from the wok.
2 Reheat the wok, add 1 tablespoon of the oil and stir-fry the coriander, cumin, mustard seeds and garlic for 2 minutes, or until the spices are fragrant and the mustard seeds begin

to pop. Add the pumpkin and stir to coat well. Stir-fry for 5 minutes, or until the pumpkin is brown and tender.
3 Add the orange juice and sugar. Bring to the boil and cook for 5 minutes. Add the leek and three-quarters of the cashews and toss well. Top with the remaining cashews.

NUTRITION PER SERVE (6)
Protein 8 g; Fat 20 g; Carbohydrate 20 g; Dietary Fibre 4 g; Cholesterol 0 mg; 1240 kJ (295 cal)

Stir-fry the cashews in 1 tablespoon of the oil until they are golden.

Reheat the wok and stir-fry the coriander, cumin, mustard seeds and garlic.

Add the pumpkin and stir to coat well in the spices. Stir-fry until brown and tender.

THREE-BEAN STIR-FRY

Preparation time: 10 minutes
Total cooking time: 5 minutes
Serves 4

1 tablespoon oil
1 red onion, chopped
2 cloves garlic, crushed
1 tablespoon finely chopped fresh
   thyme
200 g (6¹/2 oz) green beans, cut into
   short lengths
300 g (10 oz) can cannellini beans,
   rinsed
1 cup (170 g/5¹/2 oz) chickpeas,
   rinsed and drained

150 g (5 oz) rocket
2 tablespoons finely chopped fresh
   parsley
3 tablespoons lemon juice

1 Heat the wok until very hot, add the
oil and swirl it around to coat the side.
Stir-fry the onion for 2 minutes. Add
the garlic and stir-fry until soft. Stir in
the thyme.
2 Add the green beans and stir-fry for
2–3 minutes, or until tender. Add the
cannellini beans and chickpeas, and
stir-fry until heated through. Season,
and spoon the mixture onto the rocket
on a platter. Sprinkle the parsley on
top and drizzle with the lemon juice
to serve.

NUTRITION PER SERVE
Protein 7 g; Fat 6 g; Carbohydrate 10 g;
Dietary Fibre 6.5 g; Cholesterol 0 mg;
530 kJ (125 cal)

Add the green beans to the onion, garlic and
thyme, and stir-fry until tender.

STIR-FRIED CRISP TOFU IN A HOT BEAN SAUCE

Preparation time: 35 minutes +
  30 minutes marinating
Total cooking time: 15 minutes
Serves 4

500 g (1 lb) firm tofu, cut into
    small cubes
2 tablespoons peanut oil
1/4 cup (60 ml/2 fl oz) soy sauce
2 teaspoons finely grated fresh ginger
oil, for cooking
3/4 cup (125 g/4 oz) rice flour
2 onions, cut into thin wedges
2 cloves garlic, finely chopped
2 teaspoons soft brown sugar
1/2 red capsicum, cut into short,
    thin strips
5 spring onions, cut into short pieces
2 tablespoons dry sherry
2 teaspoons finely grated orange rind
2 tablespoons hot bean paste

1 Place the tofu in a glass or ceramic bowl with the peanut oil. Add the soy sauce and ginger, cover and refrigerate for 30 minutes.
2 Drain the tofu, reserving the marinade, and toss several pieces at a time in the rice flour to coat heavily. Heat the wok until very hot, add about 1/4 cup (60 ml/2 fl oz) of the oil and swirl it around to coat the side. Add the tofu to the hot oil and stir-fry over medium heat for 1 1/2 minutes, or until golden all over. Remove from the wok and drain on paper towels. Repeat with the remaining tofu. Keep warm. Drain any oil from the wok.
3 Reheat the wok and stir-fry the onion, garlic and sugar for 3 minutes, or until golden. Add the capsicum,

spring onion, sherry, orange rind, bean paste and the reserved tofu marinade. Stir and bring to the boil. Return the tofu to the wok, toss to heat through, and serve.

NUTRITION PER SERVE
Protein 15 g; Fat 8 g; Carbohydrate 40 g;
Dietary Fibre 3 g; Cholesterol 0 mg;
1215 kJ (290 cal)

Marinate the tofu in the peanut oil and soy sauce for 30 minutes before cooking.

Drain the tofu in a sieve, then toss it in the rice flour to coat heavily.

Stir-fry the tofu until it is golden on all sides, then drain on paper towels.

MIXED BEANS WITH BALSAMIC AND LIME

Preparation time: 15 minutes
Total cooking time: 10 minutes
Serves 6

1 tablespoon oil
2 cloves garlic, crushed
1 red onion, cut into thin wedges
1 red capsicum, cut into short, thin
    strips
1 yellow capsicum, cut into short, thin
    strips
400 g (13 oz) can chickpeas, drained
400 g (13 oz) can red kidney beans,
    drained

2 teaspoons soft brown sugar
2 tablespoons balsamic vinegar
1/4 cup (60 ml/2 fl oz) lime juice
250 g (8 oz) cherry tomatoes, halved
1 Lebanese cucumber, chopped
1/4 cup (15 g/1/2 oz) chopped fresh
    coriander
butter lettuce leaves, to serve

1 Heat the wok until very hot, add the oil and swirl it around to coat the side. Stir-fry the garlic, onion and capsicum strips over moderate heat for 2–3 minutes, then remove from the wok and set aside.
2 Add the chickpeas and kidney beans to the wok, stir in the brown sugar and balsamic vinegar, and toss

for 2–3 minutes, or until reduced by half. Add the lime juice and toss until well combined.
3 Using two wooden spoons, stir in the cherry tomatoes, chopped cucumber, coriander and the onion and capsicum mixture. Quickly stir-fry until heated through and thoroughly mixed. Put a couple of lettuce leaves on each plate and spoon the stir-fry into the leaves to serve.

NUTRITION PER SERVE
Protein 10 g; Fat 5 g; Carbohydrate 25 g;
Dietary Fibre 9 g; Cholesterol 0 mg;
750 kJ (180 cal)

Peel the red onion and then cut it into thin wedges for quick stir-frying.

Remove the seeds from the capsicum and cut the flesh into short, thin strips.

Cut the cucumber lengthways into strips, then cut the strips into small pieces.

WARM STIR-FRIED SALAD

Preparation time: 15 minutes
Total cooking time: 5 minutes
Serves 2

2 tablespoons olive oil
1 red onion, sliced
1 red capsicum, cut into small
    squares
2 cloves garlic, thinly sliced
250 g (8 oz) cherry tomatoes, halved

150 g (5 oz) baby English spinach
    leaves
1/2 cup (25 g/3/4 oz) fresh basil leaves
125 g (4 oz) feta cheese, crumbled

1 Heat the wok until very hot, add the oil and swirl it around to coat the side. Add the onion, capsicum and garlic and stir-fry for 2 minutes, or until just beginning to soften. Add the tomatoes, spinach and basil, and stir-fry until the leaves have just wilted.
2 Transfer the mixture to a serving

plate and top with the crumbled feta cheese. Serve immediately.

NUTRITION PER SERVE
Protein 15 g; Fat 35 g; Carbohydrate 7 g;
Dietary Fibre 6 g; Cholesterol 45 mg;
1635 kJ (390 cal)

NOTE: Serve as a main course with crusty bread or pasta or heap onto crostini as a starter.

Remove the seeds from the capsicum and cut the flesh into squares.

Peel the cloves of garlic, then cut each clove into thin slices.

Good-quality feta cheese should crumble easily between your fingers.

FRAGRANT GREENS

Preparation time: 15 minutes
Total cooking time: 8 minutes
Serves 4

2 tablespoons oil
300 g (10 oz) broccoli, cut into
    small florets
150 g (5 oz) snake beans, cut into
    short lengths
3 spring onions, sliced
250 g (8 oz) cabbage,
    finely shredded
1 green capsicum, cut into strips
2 tablespoons lime juice
1 tablespoon soft brown sugar
1/4 cup (15 g/1/2 oz) fresh Thai basil,
    shredded (see NOTE)

1 Heat the wok until very hot, add the oil and swirl it around to coat the side. Stir-fry the broccoli and snake beans for 3–4 minutes, or until the vegetables are bright green and just tender. Add the spring onion, cabbage and capsicum, and continue stir-frying until just softened.
2 Combine the lime juice and brown sugar, stirring until the sugar has dissolved. Add to the wok with the basil. Toss to combine with the vegetables and serve immediately.

NUTRITION PER SERVE
Protein 6 g; Fat 10 g; Carbohydrate 9 g;
Dietary Fibre 7 g; Cholesterol 0 mg;
630 kJ (150 cal)

NOTE: You can include any suitable kind of green vegetable in this dish, including Asian greens. If you can't find Thai basil, use ordinary basil or coriander—either will give fragrance and flavour like Thai basil.

Top and tail the snake beans, and cut them into short lengths.

Using a large sharp knife, finely shred the cabbage so that it will stir-fry quickly.

Shred the Thai basil just before you need it, or it will turn black.

PROVENCALE STIR-FRY

Preparation time: 25 minutes
Total cooking time: 30 minutes
Serves 4

1 large eggplant, cut into thick
    batons
3/4 cup (90 g/3 oz) plain flour
oil, for cooking
2 onions, cut into wedges
2 cloves garlic, finely chopped
1/2 cup (125 ml/4 fl oz) white wine
150 g (5 oz) green beans
4 large zucchini, sliced
200 g (6 1/2 oz) button mushrooms
1/4 cup (15 g/1/2 oz) chopped fresh
    basil
2 tomatoes, chopped
2 tablespoons tomato paste

1 Toss the eggplant in the flour until it is lightly coated. Heat the wok until very hot, add about 2 tablespoons of the oil and swirl it around to coat the side. Stir-fry the eggplant in three or four batches over medium-high heat, tossing regularly for about 3 minutes, or until it is golden and just cooked. Add more oil to the wok with each batch. Remove from the wok and drain on paper towels. Season with salt and freshly ground black pepper.

2 Add the onion and garlic to the wok and stir-fry for 3 minutes, or until softened. Add the wine, beans and zucchini. Cook for 2 minutes, tossing regularly. Add the mushrooms and cook, covered, for 2 minutes. Stir in the basil, tomato and tomato paste. Cook for 1 minute, then season well with salt and pepper.

3 Arrange the tomato mixture on a plate, top with the eggplant and serve.

NUTRITION PER SERVE
Protein 9 g; Fat 6 g; Carbohydrate 25 g;
Dietary Fibre 8.5 g; Cholesterol 0 mg;
910 kJ (215 cal)

Trim the top of the eggplant and cut the eggplant into short, thick batons.

Use two spoons to toss the eggplant in the flour until it is lightly coated.

Stir-fry the floured eggplant in batches until it is golden and just cooked.

SESAME TOFU STIR-FRY

Preparation time: 20 minutes +
  30 minutes marinating
Total cooking time: 10 minutes
Serves 4

300 g (10 oz) firm tofu
2 teaspoons sesame oil
2 tablespoons soy sauce
1 tablespoon sesame seeds
2 tablespoons oil
3 zucchini, sliced
150 g (5 oz) button mushrooms,
  halved or quartered
1 large red capsicum, cut into squares
2 cloves garlic, crushed
3 cups (550 g/1 lb 2 oz) cold, cooked
  brown rice
1–2 tablespoons soy sauce, extra

1 Drain the tofu and pat dry with paper towels. Cut into cubes, place in a glass or ceramic bowl and add the sesame oil and soy sauce. Stir well and leave in the fridge to marinate for 30 minutes, stirring occasionally.
2 Heat the wok until very hot, add the sesame seeds and dry-fry until lightly golden. Tip onto a plate to cool.
3 Reheat the wok, add the oil and swirl it around to coat the side. Remove the tofu from the dish with a slotted spoon and reserve the marinade. Stir-fry the tofu over high heat, turning occasionally, for about 3 minutes, or until browned. Remove from the wok and set aside.
4 Add the vegetables and garlic, and cook, stirring often, until they are just tender. Add the rice and tofu, and stir-fry until heated through.

5 Add the toasted sesame seeds, the reserved marinade and extra soy sauce to taste. Toss to coat the tofu and vegetables, then serve immediately.

NUTRITION PER SERVE
Protein 15 g; Fat 20 g; Carbohydrate 50 g;
Dietary Fibre 5.5 g; Cholesterol 0 mg;
1815 kJ (435 cal)

Dry-fry the sesame seeds until they are lightly golden brown.

CHILLI NOODLE AND NUT STIR-FRY

Preparation time: 20 minutes
Total cooking time: 12 minutes
Serves 4

1½ tablespoons oil
1 tablespoon sesame oil
2–3 small red chillies, finely chopped
1 large onion, cut into thin wedges
4 cloves garlic, very thinly sliced
1 red capsicum, cut into strips
1 green capsicum, cut into strips
2 large carrots, cut into batons
100 g (3½ oz) green beans
2 celery sticks, cut into batons

2 teaspoons honey
500 g (1 lb) Hokkien noodles, gently
    separated
100 g (3½ oz) dry-roasted peanuts
100 g (3½ oz) honey-roast cashews
¼ cup (30 g/1 oz) chopped fresh
    garlic chives, or 4 spring onions,
    chopped
sweet chilli sauce and sesame oil, to
    serve

1 Heat the wok over low heat, add the oils and swirl them to coat the side. When the oil is warm, add the chilli and heat until the oil is very hot.
2 Add the onion and garlic, and stir-fry for 1 minute, or until the onion just softens. Add the capsicum, carrot and

beans, and stir-fry for 1 minute. Add the celery, honey and 1 tablespoon water, and season with salt and pepper. Toss well, then cover and cook for 1–2 minutes, or until the vegetables are just tender.
3 Add the noodles and nuts and toss well. Cook, covered, for 1–2 minutes, or until the noodles are heated through. Stir in the garlic chives and serve, drizzled with the sweet chilli sauce and sesame oil.

NUTRITION PER SERVE
Protein 20 g; Fat 45 g; Carbohydrate 75 g;
Dietary Fibre 7 g; Cholesterol 0 mg;
3330 kJ (795 cal)

Peel the cloves of garlic, then cut them into paper-thin slices.

Remove the seeds from the capsicum, and cut the flesh into strips.

Heat the oil until warm, then add the chilli and heat until the oil is very hot.

163

Grains, Pulses & Tofu

BROWN RICE AND CASHEW PATTIES WITH CORIANDER SAMBAL

Preparation time: 30 minutes + overnight soaking + 30 minutes refrigeration
Total cooking time: 2 hours
Serves 8

250 g dried chickpeas
3 cups (650 g/1 lb 5 oz) instant brown rice (see NOTE)
1 tablespoon oil
1 onion, finely chopped
125 g (4 oz) roasted cashew paste
1 egg
60 g (2 oz) tahini
1 teaspoon ground cumin
1 teaspoon ground turmeric
1 tablespoon lemon juice
1 vegetable stock cube
5 tablespoons tamari
1 small carrot, grated
1/2 cup (40 g/11/2 oz) fresh wholemeal breadcrumbs
oil, for shallow-frying
2 tablespoons oil, extra
310 g (10 oz) bok choy, trimmed and washed

CORIANDER AND COCONUT SAMBAL
90 g (3 oz) fresh coriander leaves
1 clove garlic, chopped
1 small fresh green chilli, seeded and finely chopped
1 teaspoon garam masala
2 tablespoons lime juice
1/4 cup (15 g/1/2 oz) shredded coconut

1 Soak the chickpeas in cold water overnight. Drain. Place in a large saucepan and cover with water. Bring to the boil and cook for 1–11/2 hours, or until cooked. Drain, reserving 2 tablespoons of the liquid.

2 Meanwhile, bring a saucepan of water to the boil and cook the rice over medium heat for 10–12 minutes, or until tender. Rinse well and drain. Keep warm.

3 Heat the oil in a frying pan and cook the onion for 2–3 minutes, or until golden. Set aside.

4 Mix the chickpeas, cashew paste, egg, tahini, cumin, turmeric, lemon juice, stock cube, reserved chickpea liquid and 2 tablespoons of the tamari in a food processor until smooth. Transfer to a large bowl and add the rice, onion, carrot and breadcrumbs and mix well. Divide the mixture into 16 even portions and form into patties about 1.5 cm thick. Refrigerate for 30 minutes.

5 To make the sambal, finely chop all the ingredients in a food processor. Refrigerate until ready to use.

6 To cook the patties, heat the oil in a large deep frying pan over medium heat and cook in batches for 3–4 minutes each side, or until golden and cooked through. Remove and keep warm. Wipe with a paper towel. In the same pan, heat the extra oil and add the bok choy and cook, tossing, for 1–2 minutes, or until wilted. Pour on the remaining 3 tablespoons tamari and toss through. Place the bok choy on eight serving plates and top with two patties. Spoon a dollop of chilled sambal on top and serve immediately.

NUTRITION PER SERVE
Protein 17 g; Fat 17 g; Carbohydrate 80 g; Dietary Fibre 11 g; Cholesterol 23 mg; 2294 kJ (548 cal)

NOTE: Instant (or quick-cook) rice has been cooked, then dehydrated so it takes less time to cook than the ordinary type.

CHICKPEA PATTIES WITH CARAMELIZED ONION

Preparation time: 20 minutes
Total cooking time: 30 minutes
Serves 4

1 tablespoon olive oil
1 red onion, finely chopped
2 cloves garlic, crushed
1 tablespoon ground cumin
2 x 310 g (10 oz) cans chickpeas
1/4 cup (30 g/1 oz) sunflower seeds
1/2 cup (30 g/1 oz) finely chopped
    fresh coriander leaves
2 eggs, lightly beaten
2/3 cup (75 g/21/2 oz) besan flour
oil, for shallow-frying

CARAMELIZED ONION
40 g (11/4 oz) butter
2 red onions, thinly sliced
3 teaspoons soft brown sugar
plain yoghurt, to serve

1 Heat the oil in a frying pan, add the onion and cook over medium heat for 3 minutes, or until soft. Add the garlic and cumin and cook for 1 minute. Allow to cool slightly.
2 Blend the drained chickpeas, sunflower seeds, coriander, egg and onion mixture in a food processor until smooth. Fold in the besan flour and season. Divide the mixture into eight portions and, using floured hands, form into patties. Heat 1 cm (1/2 inch) oil in a frying pan and cook

the patties in two batches over medium heat for 2–3 minutes each side, or until firm. Drain on paper towels. Keep warm.
3 To make the caramelized onion, melt the butter in a small frying pan and cook the onion over medium heat for 10 minutes, stirring occasionally. Add the sugar and cook for 1 minute, or until caramelized. Spoon over the patties with a dollop of yoghurt.

NUTRITION PER SERVE
Protein 35 g; Fat 38 g; Carbohydrate 70 g;
Dietary Fibre 23 g; Cholesterol 116 mg;
3170 kJ (757 cal)

NOTE: Besan flour is also known as chickpea flour.

Fold the besan flour (also known as chickpea flour) into the chickpea purée.

Shallow-fry the chickpea patties in batches, until firm and golden on both sides.

Cook the onion for 10 minutes, then stir in the sugar and cook until caramelized.

TOFU BURGERS

Preparation time: 25 minutes +
  30 minutes refrigeration
Total cooking time: 30 minutes
Serves 6

1 tablespoon olive oil
1 red onion, finely chopped
200 g (6½ oz) Swiss brown
    mushrooms, finely chopped
350 g (11 oz) hard tofu (see NOTE)
2 large cloves garlic
3 tablespoons chopped fresh basil
2 cups (200 g/6½ oz) dry wholemeal
    breadcrumbs
1 egg, lightly beaten
2 tablespoons balsamic vinegar
2 tablespoons sweet chilli sauce
1½ cups (150 g/5 oz) dry wholemeal
    breadcrumbs, extra
olive oil, for shallow-frying
6 wholemeal or wholegrain bread rolls
½ cup (125 g/4 oz) mayonnaise
100 g (3½ oz) semi-dried tomatoes
60 g (2 oz) rocket leaves
sweet chilli sauce, to serve

1 Heat the oil in a frying pan and cook the onion over medium heat for 2–3 minutes, or until soft. Add the mushrooms and cook for a further 2 minutes. Cool slightly.
2 Blend 250 g (8 oz) of the tofu with the garlic and basil in a food processor until smooth. Transfer to a large bowl and stir in the onion mixture, breadcrumbs, egg, vinegar and sweet chilli sauce. Grate the remaining tofu and fold through the mixture, then refrigerate for 30 minutes. Divide the mixture into six and form into patties, pressing together well. Coat them in the extra breadcrumbs.
3 Heat 1 cm (½ inch) oil in a deep

frying pan and cook the patties in two batches for 4–5 minutes each side, or until golden. Turn carefully to prevent them breaking up. Drain on crumpled paper towels and season with salt.
4 Halve the bread rolls and toast under a hot grill. Spread mayonnaise over both sides of each roll. Layer semi-dried tomatoes, a tofu patty and rocket leaves in each roll and drizzle with sweet chilli sauce.

NUTRITION PER SERVE
Protein 23 g; Fat 24 g; Carbohydrate 86 g; Dietary Fibre 10 g; Cholesterol 37 mg; 2740 kJ (653 cal)

NOTE: Hard tofu (not to be confused with 'firm' tofu) is quite rubbery and firm and won't break up during cooking. It's perfect for patties, stir-frying and pan-frying.

Mix the tofu, garlic and basil in a food processor until smooth.

Grate the remaining hard tofu and fold it into the mixture. Refrigerate for 30 minutes.

Be careful when you turn the patties during frying. You don't want them to break up.

TOFU WITH CARROT AND GINGER SAUCE

Preparation time: 25 minutes +
    overnight marinating
Total cooking time: 30 minutes
Serves 6

2 x 300 g (10 oz) packets firm tofu
1/2 cup (125 ml/4 fl oz) freshly
    squeezed orange juice
1 tablespoon soft brown sugar
1 tablespoon soy sauce
2 tablespoons chopped fresh
    coriander leaves
2 cloves garlic, crushed
1 teaspoon grated fresh ginger
2–3 tablespoons oil
1 kg (2 lb) baby bok choy, cut into
    quarters lengthways

CARROT AND GINGER SAUCE
300 g (10 oz) carrots, chopped
2 teaspoons grated fresh ginger
2/3 cup (170 ml/51/2 fl oz) orange juice
1/2 cup (125 ml/4 fl oz) vegetable
    stock

1 Drain the tofu, then slice each block into six lengthways. Place in a single layer in a flat non-metallic dish. Mix the juice, sugar, soy sauce, coriander, garlic and ginger in a jug, then pour over the tofu. Cover and refrigerate overnight, turning once.
2 Drain the tofu, reserving the marinade. Heat the oil in a large frying pan and cook the tofu in batches over high heat for 2–3 minutes each side, or until golden. Remove and keep warm. Bring the marinade to the boil in a saucepan, then reduce the heat and

simmer for 1 minute. Remove from the heat and keep warm.
3 Heat a wok, add the bok choy and 1 tablespoon water and cook, covered, over medium heat for 2–3 minutes, or until tender. Remove and keep warm.
4 Put all the sauce ingredients in a saucepan, bring to the boil, then reduce the heat and simmer, covered, for 5–6 minutes, or until the carrot is tender. Transfer to a food processor and blend until smooth.
5 To serve, divide the bok choy among six plates. Top with some sauce, then the tofu and drizzle on a little of the marinade before serving.

NUTRITION PER SERVE
Protein 14 g; Fat 14 g; Carbohydrate 14 g;
Dietary Fibre 8.5 g; Cholesterol 0 mg;
1034 kJ (246 cal)

Use a non-metallic dish for marinating in acidic liquids such as orange juice.

Cook the tofu slices in batches until golden brown on both sides.

Blend the carrot and ginger sauce in a food processor until smooth.

GREEN PILAU WITH CASHEWS

Preparation time: 15 minutes
Total cooking time: 1 hour 10 minutes
Serves 6

200 g (6¹/2 oz) baby English spinach
²/3 cup (100 g/3¹/2 oz) cashew nuts,
    chopped
2 tablespoons olive oil
6 spring onions, chopped
1¹/2 cups (300 g/10 oz) long-grain
    brown rice
2 cloves garlic, finely chopped
1 teaspoon fennel seeds

2 tablespoons lemon juice
2¹/2 cups (600 ml/20 fl oz) vegetable
    stock
3 tablespoons chopped fresh mint
3 tablespoons chopped fresh flat-leaf
    parsley

1 Preheat the oven to moderate 180°C
(350°F/Gas 4). Shred the English
spinach leaves.
2 Place the cashew nuts on a baking
tray and roast for 5–10 minutes, or
until golden brown—watch carefully.
3 Heat the oil in a large frying pan
and cook the spring onion over
medium heat for 2 minutes, or until
soft. Add the rice, garlic and fennel

seeds and cook, stirring frequently, for
1–2 minutes, or until the rice is evenly
coated. Increase the heat to high,
add the lemon juice, stock and
1 teaspoon salt and bring to the boil.
Reduce to low, cover and cook for
45 minutes without lifting the lid.
4 Remove from the heat and sprinkle
with the spinach and herbs. Leave,
covered, for 8 minutes, then fork the
spinach and herbs through the rice.
Season. Serve sprinkled with cashews.

NUTRITION PER SERVE
Protein 6 g; Fat 12 g; Carbohydrate 32 g;
Dietary Fibre 3.5 g; Cholesterol 0 mg;
1091 kJ (260 cal)

Wash the spinach thoroughly, trim away any
stalks and shred the leaves.

Stir the rice until it is evenly coated and starts to
stick to the pan.

Fork the spinach and herbs through the rice and
sprinkle with cashews to serve.

COUSCOUS VEGETABLE LOAF

Preparation time: 20 minutes
+ cooling + overnight refrigeration
Total cooking time: 10 minutes
Serves 6

1 litre (32 fl oz) vegetable stock
500 g (1 lb) instant couscous
30 g (1 oz) butter
3 tablespoons olive oil
2 cloves garlic, crushed
1 onion, finely chopped
1 tablespoon ground coriander
1 teaspoon ground cinnamon
1 teaspoon garam masala
250 g (8 oz) cherry tomatoes,
    quartered
1 zucchini, diced
130 g (4¹/₂ oz) can corn kernels,
    drained
8 large fresh basil leaves
150 g (5 oz) sun-dried capsicums in oil
1 cup (60 g/2 oz) chopped fresh basil
¹/₃ cup (80 ml/2³/₄ fl oz) orange juice
1 tablespoon lemon juice
3 tablespoons chopped fresh flat-leaf
    parsley
1 teaspoon honey
1 teaspoon ground cumin

1 Bring the stock to the boil. Put the couscous and butter in a bowl, cover with the stock; leave for 10 minutes.
2 Heat 1 tablespoon of the oil in a large frying pan and cook the garlic and onion over low heat for 5 minutes, or until the onion is soft. Add the spices and cook for 1 minute, or until fragrant. Remove from the pan.
3 Add the remaining oil to the pan and cook the tomatoes, zucchini and corn over high heat until soft.
4 Line a 3 litre (96 fl oz) loaf tin with plastic wrap, letting it overhang the sides. Arrange the basil leaves in the shape of two flowers in the base of the tin. Drain the capsicums, reserving 2 tablespoons of the oil, then roughly chop. Add the onion mixture, tomato mixture, capsicum and chopped basil to the couscous and mix. Cool.
5 Press into the tin and fold the plastic wrap over to cover. Weigh down with cans of food to compress the loaf and refrigerate overnight.
6 To make the dressing, put the remaining ingredients and reserved capsicum oil in a screw-top jar and shake. Turn out the loaf, cut into slices and serve with the dressing.

NUTRITION PER SERVE
Protein 8.5 g; Fat 19 g; Carbohydrate 67 g;
Dietary Fibre 5 g; Cholesterol 13 mg;
1985 kJ (474 cal)

Cook the tomatoes, zucchini and corn over high heat until soft.

Arrange the basil leaves in the shape of two flowers in the base of the loaf tin.

Mix together the onion mixture, vegetables, capsicum, basil and couscous.

ASPARAGUS AND PISTACHIO RISOTTO

Preparation time: 10 minutes
Total cooking time: 30 minutes
Serves 4–6

1 litre (32 fl oz) vegetable stock
1 cup (250 ml/8 fl oz) white wine
1/3 cup (80 ml/2³/4 fl oz) extra virgin olive oil
1 red onion, finely chopped
2 cups (440 g/14 oz) arborio rice
310 g (10 oz) asparagus spears, trimmed and cut into short lengths
1/2 cup (125 ml/4 fl oz) cream

1 cup (100 g/3¹/2 oz) grated Parmesan
1/2 cup (40 g/1¹/4 oz) shelled pistachio nuts, toasted and roughly chopped

1 Heat the stock and wine in a large saucepan and keep at simmering point on the stove top.
2 Heat the oil in another large saucepan. Add the onion and cook over medium heat for 3 minutes, or until soft. Add the rice and stir for 1 minute, or until translucent.
3 Add 1/2 cup (125 ml/4 fl oz) hot stock, stirring constantly until the liquid is absorbed. Continue adding more stock, a little at a time, stirring constantly for 20–25 minutes, or until the rice is tender and creamy (you may not need to add all the stock, or you may not have quite enough and will need to add a little water as well—every risotto is different). Add the asparagus during the last 5 minutes of cooking.
4 Remove from the heat and leave for 2 minutes, then stir in the cream and Parmesan and season well. Serve sprinkled with pistachios.

NUTRITION PER SERVE (6)
Protein 15 g; Fat 30 g; Carbohydrate 60 g;
Dietary Fibre 3.5 g; Cholesterol 45 mg;
2425 kJ (580 cal)

Add the rice to the saucepan and stir until the grains are translucent.

Add the stock a little at a time, stirring until it is completely absorbed.

Leave the risotto to stand for 2 minutes, then stir in the cream and Parmesan.

171

LENTIL RISSOLES

Preparation time: 20 minutes +
    40 minutes cooling
Total cooking time: 45 minutes
Serves 4

1 tablespoon oil
1 onion, finely chopped
2 large cloves garlic, crushed
2 teaspoons ground cumin
1 teaspoon ground coriander
1 small carrot, finely diced
1 cup (250 g/8 oz) red lentils
1¹/2 cups (120 g/4 oz) fresh
    wholemeal breadcrumbs
²/3 cup (60 g/2 oz) walnuts, finely
    chopped
¹/2 cup (90 g/3 oz) frozen peas
3 tablespoons chopped fresh flat-leaf
    parsley
dry breadcrumbs, for coating
oil, for shallow-frying

1 Heat the oil in a large saucepan.
Cook the onion, garlic, cumin and
ground coriander over medium heat
for 2 minutes, or until the onion has
softened. Stir in the carrot, lentils and
2 cups (500 ml/16 fl oz) water. Slowly
bring to the boil, then reduce the heat
to low and simmer, covered, for
25–30 minutes, or until the lentils are
cooked and pulpy, stirring frequently
to stop them sticking and burning.
Remove the lid during the last
10 minutes to evaporate any
remaining liquid.
2 Transfer the mixture to a large bowl,
cover with plastic wrap and cool for
10 minutes. Stir in the fresh
breadcrumbs, walnuts, peas and
parsley. Form into eight 8 cm (3 inch)
round rissoles. Cover and refrigerate
for 30 minutes, or until they are firm.
3 Evenly coat the rissoles in dry
breadcrumbs, shaking off any excess.
Heat 1 cm (¹/2 inch) oil in a deep
frying pan, add the rissoles and cook
in two batches for 3 minutes each side,
or until golden brown. Drain on
crumpled paper towels, season with
salt and serve with a salad.

NUTRITION PER SERVE
Protein 24 g; Fat 20 g; Carbohydrate 50 g;
Dietary Fibre 14 g; Cholesterol 0 mg;
2014 kJ (480 cal)

Cover the pan and simmer the lentils until they are
cooked and pulpy.

With clean hands, form the mixture into eight
round rissoles.

FENNEL RISOTTO BALLS WITH CHEESY FILLING

Preparation time: 30 minutes +
  1 hour refrigeration
Total cooking time: 50 minutes
Serves 4–6

1.5 litres (48 fl oz) vegetable stock
1 tablespoon oil
30 g (1 oz) butter
2 cloves garlic, crushed
1 onion, finely chopped
2 fennel bulbs, finely sliced
1 tablespoon balsamic vinegar
1/2 cup (125 ml/4 fl oz) white wine
3 cups (650 g/1 lb 5 oz) arborio rice
1/2 cup (50 g/1 3/4 oz) grated
  Parmesan
1/2 cup (25 g/3/4 oz) snipped chives
1 egg, lightly beaten
150 g (5 oz) sun-dried tomatoes,
  chopped
100 g (3 1/2 oz) mozzarella, diced
1/2 cup (90 g/3 oz) frozen peas,
  thawed
flour, for dusting
3 eggs, lightly beaten, extra
2 cups (200 g/6 1/2 oz) dry
  breadcrumbs
oil, for deep-frying

1 Heat the stock in a saucepan and keep at simmering point.
2 Heat the oil and butter in a large saucepan and cook the garlic and onion for 3 minutes, or until soft. Add the fennel and cook for 10 minutes, or until it starts to caramelize. Add the vinegar and wine, increase the heat and boil until the liquid evaporates. Add the rice and stir for 1 minute, or until translucent.
3 Add 1/2 cup (125 ml/4 fl oz) hot stock, stirring constantly over medium heat until the liquid is absorbed. Continue adding the stock, a little at a time, stirring for 20–25 minutes, or until the rice is tender and creamy. Stir in the Parmesan, chives, egg and tomato. Tip into a bowl, cover and leave to cool.
4 Place the mozzarella and peas in a bowl and mash together. Season.
5 With wet hands, shape the risotto into 14 even balls. Flatten each ball out, slightly indenting the centre. Place

a heaped teaspoon of the pea mash into the indentation, then reform to make a ball. Roll each ball in seasoned flour, then dip in the extra egg and roll in breadcrumbs. Place on a foil-covered tray and chill for 30 minutes.
6 Fill a deep heavy-based saucepan one third full of oil and heat until a cube of bread dropped into the oil browns in 15 seconds. Cook the risotto balls in batches for 5 minutes, or until

golden and crisp and the cheese has melted inside. Drain on crumpled paper towels and season with salt. If the cheese has not melted, cook the balls on a tray in a moderate 180°C (350°F/Gas 4) oven for 5 minutes.

NUTRITION PER SERVE (6)
Protein 11 g; Fat 9.5 g; Carbohydrate 48 g; Dietary Fibre 2.5 g; Cholesterol 65 mg; 1377 kJ (329 cal)

Stir the Parmesan, chives, egg and sun-dried tomato into the risotto.

Place a heaped teaspoon of the cheesy pea mixture into the middle of each ball.

173

ASIAN BARLEY PILAU

Preparation time: 10 minutes +
  15 minutes standing
Total cooking time: 35 minutes
Serves 4

15 g (1/2 oz) dried sliced mushrooms
2 cups (500 ml/16 fl oz) vegetable
  stock
1/2 cup (125 ml/4 fl oz) dry sherry
1 tablespoon oil
3 large French shallots, thinly sliced
2 large cloves garlic, crushed
1 tablespoon grated fresh ginger
1 teaspoon Sichuan peppercorns,
  crushed (see NOTE)
11/2 cups (330 g/11 oz) pearl barley
500 g (1 lb) choy sum, cut into short
  lengths
3 teaspoons kecap manis
1 teaspoon sesame oil

1 Place the mushrooms in a bowl and cover with boiling water, then leave for 15 minutes. Strain, reserving 1/2 cup (125 ml/4 fl oz) of the liquid.
2 Bring the stock and sherry to the boil in a saucepan, then reduce the heat, cover and simmer until needed.
3 Heat the oil in a large saucepan and cook the shallots over medium heat for 2–3 minutes, or until soft. Add the garlic, ginger and peppercorns and cook for 1 minute. Add the barley and mushrooms and mix well. Stir in the stock and mushroom liquid, then reduce the heat and simmer, covered, for 25 minutes, or until the liquid evaporates.
4 Meanwhile, steam the choy sum until wilted. Add to the barley mixture. Stir in the kecap manis and sesame oil to serve.

NUTRITION PER SERVE
Protein 13 g; Fat 8.5 g; Carbohydrate 52 g;
Dietary Fibre 13 g; Cholesterol 0 mg;
1552 kJ (370 cal)

NOTE: You can buy Sichuan peppercorns at Asian food stores.

French shallots are like small onions. Peel them and then slice thinly.

Use a mortar and pestle to crush the Sichuan peppercorns.

Strain the mushrooms, reserving some of the liquid for flavouring the pilau.

Reduce the heat and simmer the pilau until the liquid has evaporated.

MISO TOFU STICKS WITH CUCUMBER AND WAKAME SALAD

Preparation time: 30 minutes +
  20 minutes standing
Total cooking time: 15 minutes
Serves 4

3 Lebanese cucumbers, thinly sliced
20 g (3/4 oz) dried wakame
500 g (1 lb) silken firm tofu, well
  drained
3 tablespoons shiro miso
1 tablespoon mirin
1 tablespoon sugar
1 tablespoon rice vinegar
1 egg yolk
100 g (3½ oz) bean sprouts,
  blanched
2 tablespoons sesame seeds, toasted

DRESSING
3 tablespoons rice vinegar
1/4 teaspoon soy sauce
1½ tablespoons sugar
1 tablespoon mirin

1 Sprinkle the cucumber generously with salt and leave for 20 minutes, or until very soft, then rinse and drain. To rehydrate the wakame, place it in a colander in the sink and leave it under cold running water for 10 minutes, then drain well.
2 Place the tofu in a colander, weigh down with a plate and leave to drain.
3 Place the shiro miso, mirin, sugar, rice vinegar and 2 tablespoons water in a saucepan and stir over low heat for 1 minute, or until the sugar dissolves. Remove from the heat, then add the egg yolk and whisk until glossy. Cool slightly.
4 Cut the tofu into thick sticks and place on a non-stick baking tray. Brush the miso mixture over the tofu and cook under a hot grill for 6 minutes each side, or until light golden on both sides.
5 To make the dressing, place all the ingredients and 1/2 teaspoon salt in a bowl and whisk together well.
6 To assemble, place the cucumber in the centre of a plate, top with the sprouts and wakame, drizzle with the dressing, top with tofu and serve sprinkled with the sesame seeds.

NUTRITION PER SERVE
Protein 10 g; Fat 7 g; Carbohydrate 8 g;
Dietary Fibre 2.5 g; Cholesterol 0 mg;
710 kJ (180 cal)

Once the cucumber is very soft, rinse the salt off under running water.

Place the wakame in a colander and leave it under cold running water.

Brush the miso mixture over the tofu sticks and grill under golden.

PUY LENTILS AND BEAN PUREE ON MUSHROOMS WITH RED WINE SAUCE

Preparation time: 30 minutes
Total cooking time: 35 minutes
Serves 4

4 large (10 cm/4 inch) field
    mushrooms
1 tablespoon olive oil
1 red onion, cut into thin wedges
1 clove garlic, crushed
1 cup (200 g/6^1/$_2$ oz) puy lentils
^{3}/$_4$ cup (185 ml/6 fl oz) red wine
1^3/$_4$ cups (440 ml/14 fl oz) vegetable
    stock
1 tablespoon finely chopped fresh flat-
    leaf parsley
30 g (1 oz) butter
2 cloves garlic, crushed, extra

BEAN PUREE
1 large potato, cut into chunks
2 tablespoons extra virgin olive oil
400 g (13 oz) can cannellini beans,
    drained and rinsed
2 large cloves garlic, crushed
1 tablespoon vegetable stock

RED WINE SAUCE
^{2}/$_3$ cup (170 ml/5^1/$_2$ fl oz) red wine
2 tablespoons tomato paste
1^1/$_2$ cups (375 ml/12 fl oz) vegetable
    stock
1 tablespoon soft brown sugar

1 Remove the stalks from the mushrooms and chop them. Heat the oil in a large saucepan and cook the onion over medium heat for 2–3 minutes, or until soft. Add the garlic and mushroom stalks and cook for a further 1 minute. Stir in the lentils, wine and stock and bring to the boil. Reduce the heat and simmer, covered, for 20–25 minutes, stirring occasionally, or until reduced and the lentils are cooked through. If the mixture is too wet, remove the lid and boil until slightly thick. Stir in the parsley and keep warm.

2 Meanwhile, to make the bean purée, bring a small saucepan of water to the boil over high heat and cook the potato for 10 minutes, or until tender. Drain and mash with a potato masher or fork until smooth. Stir in half the extra virgin olive oil. Combine the cannellini beans and garlic in a food processor bowl. Add the stock and the remaining oil and process until smooth. Transfer to a bowl and fold in the mashed potato. Keep warm.

3 Melt the butter in a deep frying pan. Add the mushrooms and extra garlic and cook in batches over medium heat for 4 minutes each side, or until tender. Remove and keep warm.

4 To make the red wine sauce, add the red wine to the same frying pan, then scrape the bottom to remove any sediment. Add the combined tomato paste, stock and sugar and bring to the boil. Cook for about 10 minutes, or until reduced and thickened.

5 To assemble, place the mushrooms onto serving plates and top with the bean purée. Spoon on the lentil mixture and drizzle with the red wine sauce. Season and serve immediately.

NUTRITION PER SERVE
Protein 23 g; Fat 23 g; Carbohydrate 42 g;
Dietary Fibre 17 g; Cholesterol 20 mg;
2198 kJ (525 cal)

NOTE: The mushrooms tend to shrivel if you keep them warm in the oven—either turn the oven off or find another warm place.

Remove the stalks from the field mushrooms and finely chop them.

Simmer the lentils until they are cooked through and the liquid is reduced.

Fold the mashed potato into the purée of cannellini beans and garlic.

Fry the mushrooms over medium heat until they are tender, turning once.

Scrape the bottom of the frying pan to stir in any sediment stuck to the pan.

Cook the red wine sauce for 10 minutes, until it is reduced and thickened.

RED LENTIL PILAU

Preparation time: 15 minutes
Total cooking time: 25 minutes
Serves 4–6

GARAM MASALA
1 tablespoon coriander seeds
1 tablespoon cardamom pods
1 tablespoon cumin seeds
1 teaspoon whole black peppercorns
1 teaspoon whole cloves
1 small cinnamon stick, crushed

3 tablespoons oil
1 onion, chopped

3 cloves garlic, chopped
1 cup (200 g/6$\frac{1}{2}$ oz) basmati rice
1 cup (250 g/8 oz) red lentils
3 cups (750 ml/24 fl oz) hot vegetable
    stock
spring onions, thinly sliced

1 To make the garam masala, place all the spices in a dry frying pan and shake over medium heat for 1 minute, or until fragrant. Blend in a spice grinder, blender or mortar and pestle to make a fine powder.
2 Heat the oil in a large saucepan. Add the onion, garlic and 3 teaspoons garam masala. Cook over medium heat for 3 minutes, or until soft.

3 Stir in the rice and lentils and cook for 2 minutes. Add the hot stock and stir well. Slowly bring to the boil, then reduce the heat and simmer, covered, for 15–20 minutes, or until the rice is cooked and all the stock has been absorbed. Gently fluff the rice with a fork. Garnish with spring onion.

NUTRITION PER SERVE (6)
Protein 13 g; Fat 11 g; Carbohydrate 42 g;
Dietary Fibre 7 g; Cholesterol 0 mg;
1333 kJ (318 cal)

NOTE: If time is short you can, of course, use ready-made garam masala instead of making your own.

Finely chop all the spices in a spice grinder until they make a fine powder.

Stir the rice and lentils into the onion and garlic mixture and cook for 2 minutes.

Simmer, covered, until the rice is cooked and all the stock has been absorbed.

MUSHROOM RISOTTO

Preparation time: 15 minutes
Total cooking time: 40 minutes
Serves 4

1.5 litres (48 fl oz) vegetable stock
2 cups (500 ml/16 fl oz) white wine
2 tablespoons olive oil
60 g (2 oz) butter
2 leeks, thinly sliced
1 kg (2 lb) flat mushrooms, sliced
500 g (1 lb) arborio rice
3/4 cup (75 g/2 1/2 oz) grated
    Parmesan, plus Parmesan
    shavings, to serve

3 tablespoons chopped fresh flat-leaf
    parsley
balsamic vinegar and fresh flat-leaf
    parsley, to serve

1 Place the stock and wine in a large saucepan and keep at simmering point on the stove top.
2 Heat the oil and butter in a large saucepan. Add the leek and cook over medium heat for 5 minutes, or until soft and golden. Add the mushrooms to the pan and cook for 5 minutes, or until tender. Add the rice and stir for 1 minute, or until translucent.
3 Add 1/2 cup (125 ml/4 fl oz) hot stock, stirring constantly over medium heat until the liquid is absorbed. Continue adding the stock, a little at a time, stirring constantly for 20–25 minutes, or until all the rice is tender and creamy (you may not need all the stock, or you may need to add a little water if you run out).
4 Stir in the Parmesan and chopped parsley and heat for 1 minute, or until all the cheese has melted. Serve drizzled with balsamic vinegar and topped with Parmesan shavings.

NUTRITION PER SERVE
Protein 26 g; Fat 30 g; Carbohydrate 105 g;
Dietary Fibre 11 g; Cholesterol 56 mg;
3299 kJ (788 cal)

Cook the leek and mushrooms in a large saucepan until tender.

Stir the rice constantly until most of the liquid has been absorbed.

Once the rice is tender, stir the grated Parmesan and parsley into the risotto.

SILVERBEET PARCELS

Preparation time: 40 minutes
Total cooking time: 1 hour
Serves 6

2 cups (500 ml/16 fl oz) vegetable
    stock
1 tablespoon olive oil
1 onion, chopped
2 cloves garlic, crushed
1 red capsicum, chopped
250 g (8 oz) mushrooms, chopped
1/2 cup (110 g/3 1/2 oz) arborio rice
60 g (2 oz) Cheddar, grated
1/4 cup (15 g/1/2 oz) shredded fresh
    basil
6 large silverbeet leaves
2 x 400 g (13 oz) cans chopped
    tomatoes
1 tablespoon balsamic vinegar
1 teaspoon soft brown sugar

1 Heat the vegetable stock in a pan and maintain at simmering point. Heat the oil in a large pan, add the onion and garlic and cook until the onion has softened. Add the capsicum, mushrooms and rice and stir until well combined. Gradually add 1/2 cup (125 ml/4 fl oz) hot stock, stirring until the liquid has been absorbed. Continue to add the stock, a little at a time, stirring constantly for 20–25 minutes, or until the rice is creamy and tender (you may not need all the stock, or you may need to add a little water if you run out). Remove from the heat, add the cheese and basil and season well.
2 Trim the stalks from the silverbeet and cook the leaves, a few at a time, in a large pan of boiling water for 30 seconds, or until wilted. Drain on a tea towel. Using a sharp knife, cut away any tough white veins from the centre of the leaves without cutting them in half. If necessary, overlap the two sides to make a flat surface. Place a portion of mushroom filling in the centre of each leaf, fold in the sides and roll up carefully. Tie with string.
3 Put the tomato, balsamic vinegar and sugar in a large, deep non-stick frying pan and stir to combine. Add the silverbeet parcels, cover and simmer for 10 minutes. Remove the string and serve with tomato sauce.

NUTRITION PER SERVE
Protein 7.5 g; Fat 6 g; Carbohydrate 20 g;
Dietary Fibre 4 g; Cholesterol 7 mg;
725 kJ (175 cal)

Add the stock, a little at a time, until the rice is tender and has absorbed the stock.

Using a sharp knife, cut away the white veins from the centre of the leaves.

Place the filling in the centre of each leaf, fold in the sides and roll up into parcels.

BAKED POLENTA WITH THREE CHEESES

Preparation time: 20 minutes
+ 2 hours chilling
Total cooking time: 45 minutes
Serves 4

POLENTA
2¹/₂ cups (600 ml/20 fl oz) vegetable stock
2 cups (300 g/10 oz) polenta (see NOTE)
¹/₂ cup (60 g/2 oz) grated Parmesan

CHEESE FILLING
100 g (3¹/₂ oz) havarti cheese, sliced
100 g (3¹/₂ oz) mascarpone cheese
100 g (3¹/₂ oz) blue cheese, crumbled
100 g (3¹/₂ oz) butter, sliced thinly
¹/₂ cup (60 g/2 oz) grated Parmesan

1 To make the polenta, brush a 7-cup (1.75 litre/56 fl oz) loaf tin with oil. Put the stock and 2 cups (500 ml/16 fl oz) water in a large pan and bring to the boil. Add the polenta and stir for 10 minutes until very thick.

2 Remove from the heat and stir in the Parmesan. Spread into the tin and smooth the surface. Refrigerate for 2 hours, then cut into about 30 thin slices. Preheat the oven to moderate 180°C (350°F/Gas 4).

3 Brush a large ovenproof dish with oil. Place a layer of polenta slices on the base. Top with a layer of half the combined havarti, mascarpone and blue cheeses and half the butter. Add another layer of polenta and top with the remainder of the three cheeses and butter. Add a final layer of polenta and sprinkle the Parmesan on top. Bake for 30 minutes, or until a golden crust forms. Serve immediately.

NUTRITION PER SERVE
Protein 20 g; Fat 38 g; Carbohydrate 35 g; Dietary Fibre 1.5 g; Cholesterol 113 mg; 2351 kJ (560 cal)

NOTE: Polenta is also known as cornmeal and is available from most supermarkets and delicatessens. Havarti is a Danish cheese with a full flavour.

Add the polenta to the stock and water and stir constantly until very thick.

Use the back of a spoon to spread the polenta in the tin.

Build up the layers of sliced polenta, butter and different cheeses.

Add the final layer of sliced polenta and then sprinkle with Parmesan cheese.

BARBECUE VEGETABLE AND TOFU KEBABS

Preparation time: 40 minutes +
    30 minutes marinating
Total cooking time: 30 minutes
Serves 4

500 g (1 lb) firm tofu, cubed
1 red capsicum, cubed
3 zucchini, thickly sliced
4 small onions, cut into quarters
300 g (10 oz) button mushrooms, cut
    into quarters
1/2 cup (125 ml/4 fl oz) tamari
1/2 cup (125 ml/4 fl oz) sesame oil
2.5 cm (1 inch) piece ginger, peeled
    and grated
1/2 cup (175 g/6 oz) honey

PEANUT SAUCE
1 tablespoon sesame oil
1 small onion, finely chopped
1 clove garlic, crushed
2 teaspoons chilli paste
1 cup (250 g/8 oz) smooth peanut
    butter
1 cup (250 ml/8 fl oz) coconut milk
1 tablespoon soft brown sugar
1 tablespoon tamari
1 tablespoon lemon juice
1/4 cup (40 g/11/4 oz) peanuts, roasted
    and chopped
1/4 cup (40 g/11/4 oz) sesame seeds,
    toasted

1 Soak 12 bamboo skewers in water for 2 hours. Thread the tofu, capsicum, zucchini, onions and mushrooms alternately onto the skewers. Lay out in a large flat dish.
2 Combine the tamari, oil, ginger and honey in a non-metallic bowl. Pour over the kebabs. Leave for 30 minutes. Cook on a hot barbecue or in a chargrill pan, basting and turning, for 10–15 minutes, or until tender. Remove and keep warm.
3 To make the peanut sauce, heat the oil in a large frying pan over medium heat and cook the onion, garlic and chilli paste for 1–2 minutes, or until the onion is soft. Reduce the heat, add the peanut butter, coconut milk, sugar, tamari and lemon juice and stir. Bring to the boil, then reduce the heat and simmer for 10 minutes, or until just thick. Stir in the peanuts. If the sauce is too thick, add water. Serve with the kebabs, sprinkled with sesame seeds.

NUTRITION PER SERVE
Protein 31.5 g; Fat 65 g; Carbohydrate 25.5 g; Dietary Fibre 15 g; Cholesterol 0 mg; 3334 kJ (795 cal)

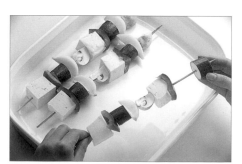

Thread alternating pieces of tofu and vegetables onto the skewers.

Cook the skewers on a barbecue, occasionally turning and basting them.

Simmer the peanut sauce for 10 minutes, or until just thickened.

THAI TEMPEH

Preparation time: 15 minutes +
  overnight marinating
Total cooking time: 20 minutes
Serves 4

THAI MARINADE
2 stems lemon grass,
  finely chopped
2 kaffir lime leaves, shredded
2 small red chillies, seeded and finely
  chopped
3 cloves garlic, crushed
2 teaspoons sesame oil
1/2 cup (125 ml/4 fl oz) lime juice
2 teaspoons shaved palm sugar
1/2 cup (125 ml/4 fl oz) soy sauce

600 g (1 1/4 lb) tofu tempeh, cut into
  twelve 5 mm (1/4 inch) slices
3 tablespoons peanut oil
1 tablespoon shaved palm sugar
100 g (3 1/2 oz) snow pea sprouts or
  watercress
kaffir lime leaves, finely shredded

1 To make the Thai marinade, mix the
lemon grass, lime leaves, chilli, garlic,
sesame oil, lime juice, sugar and soy
sauce in a non-metallic bowl. Add the
tempeh. Cover and marinate overnight
in the fridge, turning occasionally.
2 Drain the tempeh, reserving the
marinade. Heat half the peanut oil in a
frying pan over high heat. Cook the
tempeh in batches, turning once, for
5 minutes, or until crispy, adding more
oil when needed. Drain on paper
towels. Heat the reserved marinade
with the palm sugar in a saucepan
until syrupy.

3 Put a slice of tempeh on each
serving plate and top with some snow
pea sprouts. Continue the layers,
finishing with the tempeh on top.
Drizzle with the reserved marinade
and sprinkle with lime leaves.

NUTRITION PER SERVE
Protein 9.5 g; Fat 20 g; Carbohydrate 7 g;
Dietary Fibre 1.5 g; Cholesterol 0 mg;
1102 kJ (262 cal)

Cook the slices of tempeh in batches, turning
once, until they are crispy.

Heat the reserved marinade and palm sugar in a
saucepan until the mixture is syrupy.

CARROT AND PUMPKIN RISOTTO

Preparation time: 15 minutes
Total cooking time: 35 minutes
Serves 4

90 g (3 oz) butter
1 onion, finely chopped
250 g (8 oz) pumpkin, diced
2 carrots, diced
2 litres (64 fl oz) vegetable stock
2 cups (440 g/14 oz) arborio rice
90 g (3 oz) Romano cheese, grated
   (see NOTE)
1/4 teaspoon nutmeg

1 Heat 60 g (2 oz) of the butter in a large, heavy-based pan. Add the onion and fry for 1–2 minutes, or until soft. Add the pumpkin and carrot and cook for 6–8 minutes, or until tender. Mash slightly with a potato masher. In a separate saucepan keep the stock at simmering point.

2 Add the rice to the vegetables and cook for 1 minute, stirring constantly until the grains are translucent. Ladle in 1/2 cup (125 ml/4 fl oz) hot stock and stir well. Reduce the heat and add the stock little by little, stirring constantly for 20–25 minutes, or until the rice is tender and creamy. (You may not need to add all the stock, or

you may run out and need to use a little water. Every risotto is different.)

3 Remove from the heat, add the remaining butter, cheese, nutmeg and pepper and fork through. Cover and leave for 5 minutes before serving.

NUTRITION PER SERVE
Protein 27 g; Fat 34 g; Carbohydrate 95 g;
Dietary Fibre 5 g; Cholesterol 100 mg;
3318 kJ (793 cal)

NOTE: Romano is a hard, Italian grating cheese similar to Parmesan. Parmesan is a good substitute.

Heat the butter in a large pan and fry the onion until soft.

Cook the pumpkin and carrot until tender, then mash a little.

The secret to good risotto is to add the stock a little at a time and stir constantly.

GRILLED POLENTA WITH WILD MUSHROOMS

Preparation time: 30 minutes + chilling
Total cooking time: 1 hour 20 minutes
Serves 6–8

2¹/2 cups (600 ml/20 fl oz) vegetable
    stock
2 cups (300 g/10 oz) polenta
100 g (3¹/2 oz) Parmesan, grated

MUSHROOM SAUCE
1 kg (2 lb) mixed mushrooms (roman,
    oyster and flat)
¹/2 cup (125 ml/4 fl oz) olive oil

¹/2 cup (15 g/¹/2 oz) chopped parsley
4 cloves garlic, finely chopped
1 onion, chopped

1 Put the stock and 2 cups (500 ml/ 16 fl oz) water in a large pan and bring to the boil. Add the polenta and stir constantly for 10 minutes until very thick. Remove from the heat and stir in the Parmesan. Brush a 20 cm (8 inch) round springform tin with oil. Spread the polenta into the tin and smooth the surface. Refrigerate for 2 hours, turn out and cut into 6–8 wedges.
2 To make the sauce, wipe the mushrooms with a damp cloth and roughly chop the larger ones. Put the

mushrooms, oil, parsley, garlic and onion in a pan. Stir, cover and leave to simmer for 50 minutes, or until cooked through. Uncover and cook for 10 minutes, or until there is very little liquid left. Set aside.
3 Brush one side of the polenta with olive oil and cook under a preheated grill for 5 minutes, or until the edges are browned. Turn over and brown. Reheat the mushroom sauce and serve spooned over slices of polenta.

NUTRITION PER SERVE (6)
Protein 11 g; Fat 20 g; Carbohydrate 11 g;
Dietary Fibre 4 g; Cholesterol 12 mg;
1103 kJ (214 cal)

Stir the polenta until very thick, remove from the heat and add the Parmesan.

Refrigerate the tin of polenta for 2 hours, then turn out and cut into wedges.

Uncover the mushrooms and let them simmer for 10 minutes, until little liquid is left.

COUSCOUS PATTIES

Preparation time: 35 minutes +
   15 minutes refrigeration +
   10 minutes standing
Total cooking time: 30 minutes
Makes 4

1 cup (185 g/6 oz) couscous
4 tablespoons oil
1 eggplant, finely diced
1 onion, finely chopped
1 clove garlic, crushed
2 teaspoons ground cumin
2 teaspoons ground coriander
1 red capsicum, finely diced
2 tablespoons chopped fresh
   coriander
2 teaspoons grated lemon rind

2 teaspoons lemon juice
5 tablespoons natural yoghurt
1 egg, lightly beaten
oil, for shallow-frying

1 Place the couscous in a bowl. Add
1 cup (250 ml/8 fl oz) of boiling water
and leave for 10 minutes, or until all
the water has been absorbed. Fluff up
the grains with a fork.
2 Heat 2 tablespoons of the oil in a
large frying pan and fry the eggplant
until soft and golden, then place in
a bowl. Heat 1 tablespoon of the oil
in the pan. Add the onion, garlic,
cumin and ground coriander. Cook
over medium heat for 3–4 minutes,
or until soft, then add to the bowl.
Heat the remaining oil and cook the
capsicum for 5 minutes, or until soft.

Place in the bowl and stir well.
3 Add the vegetable mixture to the
couscous with the fresh coriander,
lemon rind, lemon juice, yoghurt and
egg. Season to taste and mix well.
4 Using damp hands, divide the
mixture into four portions and form
into large patties—they should be
about 2 cm (3/4 inch) thick. Cover and
refrigerate for 15 minutes. Shallow-fry
the patties over medium heat for
5 minutes on each side, or until
golden. Drain the patties well and
serve with yoghurt.

NUTRITION PER PATTY
Protein 9 g; Fat 25 g; Carbohydrate 35 g;
Dietary Fibre 4 g; Cholesterol 5 mg;
1760 kJ (420 cal)

When the couscous has absorbed the water, fluff
up the grains with a fork.

Season the patty mixture with salt and cracked
pepper and mix well.

With damp hands, form the mixture into four
large patties.

CARAWAY POLENTA WITH BRAISED LEEKS

Preparation time: 10 minutes
Total cooking time: 30 minutes
Serves 4

6 cups (1.5 litres/48 fl oz) vegetable
    stock
1¹/₂ cups (225 g/7¹/₂ oz) polenta
2 teaspoons caraway seeds
45 g (1¹/₂ oz) butter
2 large leeks, cut into thin strips
250 g (8 oz) Fontina cheese, cubed

1 Place the stock in a large heavy-based pan and bring to the boil. Pour in the polenta in a fine stream, stirring continuously. Add the caraway seeds and then reduce the heat and simmer for about 20–25 minutes, or until the polenta is very soft.
2 Melt the butter in a frying pan over medium heat and add the leeks. Cover and cook gently, stirring often, until wilted. Add the Fontina, stir a couple of times and remove from the heat.
3 Pour the polenta onto plates in nest shapes and spoon the leeks and cheese into the centre.

NUTRITION PER SERVE
Protein 17 g; Fat 25 g; Carbohydrate 40 g;
Dietary Fibre 3 g; Cholesterol 72 mg;
1908 kJ (456 cal)

HINT: Ready-made stock can be quite salty, so use half stock, half water.

NOTE: Polenta is also known as cornmeal and is available from most supermarkets and delicatessens.

Use a sharp knife to cut the leeks into very thin, long strips.

Bring the stock to the boil, then pour in the polenta, stirring continuously.

Cook the leeks in the butter until wilted, then stir in the cheese.

Casseroles, Curries & Bakes

EGGPLANT PARMIGIANA

Preparation time: 30 minutes
Total cooking time: 1 hour 15 minutes
Serves 6–8

3 tablespoons olive oil
1 onion, diced
2 cloves garlic, crushed
1.25 kg (2¹/₂ lb) tomatoes, peeled and
    chopped
1 kg (2 lb) eggplants
250 g (8 oz) bocconcini, sliced
185 g (6 oz) Cheddar cheese, finely
    grated
1 cup (50 g/1³/₄ oz) basil leaves
¹/₂ cup (50 g/1³/₄ oz) grated
    Parmesan

1 Heat the oil in a large frying pan; add the onion and cook over moderate heat until soft. Add the garlic and cook for 1 minute. Add the tomato and simmer for 15 minutes. Season with salt to taste. Preheat the oven to moderately hot 200°C (400°F/Gas 6).
2 Slice the eggplants very thinly and shallow-fry in oil in batches for 3–4 minutes, or until golden brown. Drain on paper towels.
3 Place one third of the eggplant in a 7-cup (1.75 litre) ovenproof dish. Top with half the bocconcini and Cheddar. Repeat the layers, finishing with a layer of eggplant.
4 Pour the tomato mixture over the eggplant. Scatter with torn basil leaves, then Parmesan. Bake for 40 minutes.

NUTRITION PER SERVE (6)
Protein 19 g; Fat 28 g; Carbohydrate 7 g;
Dietary Fibre 5 g; Cholesterol 60 mg;
1495 kJ (357 cal)

VARIATION: If you prefer not to fry the eggplant, brush it lightly with oil and brown lightly under a hot grill.

Shallow-fry the eggplant in batches, then drain on paper towels.

Arrange layers of eggplant, bocconcini and Cheddar in the dish.

MUSHROOM MOUSSAKA

Preparation time: 20 minutes
Total cooking time: 1 hour
Serves 4–6

1 eggplant (250 g/8 oz), cut into
    1 cm (¹/₂ inch) slices
1 large potato, cut into 1 cm (¹/₂ inch)
    slices
30 g (1 oz) butter
1 onion, finely chopped
2 cloves garlic, finely chopped
500 g (1 lb) flat mushrooms, sliced
400 g (13 oz) can chopped tomatoes
¹/₂ teaspoon sugar
40 g (1¹/₄ oz) butter, extra
¹/₃ cup (40 g/1¹/₄ oz) plain flour
2 cups (500 ml/16 fl oz) milk
1 egg, lightly beaten
40 g (1¹/₄ oz) grated Parmesan

1 Preheat the oven to hot 220°C (425°F/Gas 7). Line a large baking tray with foil and brush with oil. Put the eggplant and potato in a single layer on the tray and sprinkle with salt and pepper. Bake for 20 minutes.

2 Melt the butter in a large frying pan over medium heat. Add the onion and cook, stirring, for 3–4 minutes, or until soft. Add the garlic and cook for 1 minute, or until fragrant. Increase the heat to high, add the mushrooms and stir continuously for 2–3 minutes, or until soft. Add the tomato, reduce the heat and simmer rapidly for 8 minutes, or until reduced. Stir in the sugar.

3 Melt the extra butter in a large saucepan over low heat. Add the flour and cook for 1 minute, or until pale and foaming. Remove from the heat and gradually stir in the milk. Return to the heat and stir constantly until it boils and thickens. Reduce the heat

and simmer for 2 minutes. Remove from the heat and, when the bubbles subside, stir in the egg and Parmesan.

4 Reduce the oven to moderate 180°C (350°F/Gas 4). Grease a shallow 1.5 litre (48 fl oz) ovenproof dish. Spoon one third of the mushroom mixture into the dish. Cover with potato and top with half the remaining mushrooms, then the eggplant. Finish

with the remaining mushrooms, pour on the sauce and smooth the top. Bake for 30–35 minutes, or until the edges bubble. Leave for 10 minutes before serving.

NUTRITION PER SERVE (6)
Protein 12 g; Fat 16 g; Carbohydrate 18 g;
Dietary Fibre 5 g; Cholesterol 77 mg;
1125 kJ (268 cal)

A small amount of sugar added to the tomato mixture will bring out the flavours.

Remove the saucepan from the heat and stir in the egg and Parmesan.

Cover the tomato and mushroom mixture with the potato slices.

GREEN CURRY WITH SWEET POTATO AND EGGPLANT

Preparation time: 15 minutes
Total cooking time: 25 minutes
Serves 4–6

1 tablespoon oil
1 onion, chopped
1–2 tablespoons green curry paste
   (see NOTE)
1 eggplant, quartered and sliced
1½ cups (375 ml/12 fl oz) coconut
   milk
1 cup (250 ml/8 fl oz) vegetable stock
6 kaffir lime leaves

1 orange sweet potato, cubed
2 teaspoons soft brown sugar
2 tablespoons lime juice
2 teaspoons lime rind

1 Heat the oil in a large wok or frying pan. Add the onion and green curry paste and cook, stirring, over medium heat for 3 minutes. Add the eggplant and cook for a further 4–5 minutes, or until softened.
2 Pour in the coconut milk and vegetable stock, bring to the boil, then reduce the heat and simmer for 5 minutes. Add the kaffir lime leaves and sweet potato and cook for 10 minutes, or until the eggplant and sweet potato are very tender.

3 Mix in the sugar, lime juice and lime rind until well combined with the vegetables. Season to taste with salt and serve with steamed rice.

NUTRITION PER SERVE (6)
Protein 2.5 g; Fat 17 g; Carbohydrate 10 g; Dietary Fibre 3 g; Cholesterol 0.5 mg; 835 kJ (200 cal)

NOTE: Strict vegetarians should be sure to read the label and choose a green curry paste that doesn't contain shrimp paste. Alternatively, make your own curry pastes.

Eggplants are also known as aubergines. Use a sharp knife to quarter and slice the eggplant.

Stir-fry the onion and curry paste over medium heat for 3 minutes.

Cook, stirring occasionally, until the vegetables are tender.

SPICY VEGETABLE STEW WITH DHAL

Preparation time: 25 minutes +
    2 hours soaking
Total cooking time: 1 hour 35 minutes
Serves 4–6

DHAL
3/4 cup (165 g/5 1/2 oz) yellow split
    peas
5 cm (2 inch) piece of ginger, grated
2–3 cloves garlic, crushed
1 red chilli, seeded and chopped

3 tomatoes
2 tablespoons oil
1 teaspoon yellow mustard seeds
1 teaspoon cumin seeds
1 teaspoon ground cumin
1/2 teaspoon garam masala
1 red onion, cut into thin wedges
3 slender eggplants, thickly sliced
2 carrots, thickly sliced
1/4 cauliflower, cut into florets
1 1/2 cups (375 ml/12 fl oz) vegetable
    stock
2 small zucchini, thickly sliced
1/2 cup (90 g/3 oz) frozen peas
1/2 cup (15 g/1/2 oz) fresh coriander
    leaves

1 To make the dhal, put the split peas in a bowl, cover with water and soak for 2 hours. Drain. Place in a large saucepan with the ginger, garlic, chilli and 3 cups (750 ml/24 fl oz) water. Bring to the boil, reduce the heat and simmer for 45 minutes, or until soft.
2 Score a cross in the base of each tomato, soak in boiling water for 30 seconds, then plunge into cold water and peel the skin away from the cross. Deseed and roughly chop.

3 Heat the oil in a large saucepan. Cook the spices over medium heat for 30 seconds, or until fragrant. Add the onion and cook for 2 minutes, or until the onion is soft. Stir in the tomato, eggplant, carrot and cauliflower.
4 Add the dhal and stock, mix together well and simmer, covered, for 45 minutes, or until the vegetables are

tender. Stir occasionally. Add the zucchini and peas during the last 10 minutes of cooking. Stir in the coriander leaves and serve hot.

NUTRITION PER SERVE (6)
Protein 11 g; Fat 7 g; Carbohydrate 20 g;
Dietary Fibre 8.5 g; Cholesterol 17 mg;
780 kJ (186 cal)

Simmer the dhal for 45 minutes, or until the split peas are soft.

Score a cross in the top of each tomato, then soak in hot water to make the skin come away.

Add the dhal and stock to the stew and simmer for 45 minutes, or until the vegetables are tender.

SPICY BEANS ON BAKED SWEET POTATO

Preparation time: 20 minutes
Total cooking time: 1 hour 30 minutes
Serves 6

3 orange sweet potatoes
    (500 g/1 lb each)
1 tablespoon olive oil
1 large onion, chopped
3 cloves garlic, crushed
2 teaspoons ground cumin
1 teaspoon ground coriander
1/2 teaspoon chilli powder
400 g (13 oz) can chopped tomatoes
1 cup (250 ml/8 fl oz) vegetable
    stock
1 large zucchini, cubed
1 green capsicum, cubed
310 g (10 oz) can corn kernels,
    drained
2 x 400 g (13 oz) cans red kidney
    beans, rinsed and drained
3 tablespoons chopped fresh
    coriander leaves
sour cream and grated Cheddar, to
    serve

1 Preheat the oven to hot 210°C (415°F/Gas 6–7). Rinse the sweet potatoes, then pierce with a small sharp knife. Place them on a baking tray and bake for 1–1¹/₂ hours, or until soft when tested with a skewer or sharp knife.
2 Meanwhile, heat the oil in a large saucepan and cook the onion over medium heat for about 5 minutes, stirring occasionally, until very soft and golden. Add the garlic and spices, and cook, stirring, for 1 minute.
3 Add the tomato and stock, stir well, then add the vegetables and beans. Bring to the boil, then reduce the heat and simmer, partially covered, for

20 minutes. Uncover, increase the heat slightly, and cook for a further 10–15 minutes, or until the liquid has reduced and thickened. Stir in the coriander leaves just before serving.
4 To serve, cut the sweet potatoes in half lengthways. Spoon the vegetable mixture over the top. Add a dollop of sour cream and sprinkle with grated Cheddar cheese.

NUTRITION PER SERVE
Protein 15 g; Fat 5 g; Carbohydrate 72 g;
Dietary Fibre 17 g; Cholesterol 0 mg;
1665 kJ (397 cal)

Cook the spicy vegetable mixture until the liquid has reduced.

Cut the baked sweet potatoes in half lengthways and top with the spicy beans.

MUSHROOM NUT ROAST WITH TOMATO SAUCE

Preparation time: 25 minutes
Total cooking time: 50 minutes
Serves 6

2 tablespoons olive oil
1 large onion, diced
2 cloves garlic, crushed
300 g (10 oz) cap mushrooms, finely chopped
200 g (6½ oz) cashew nuts
200 g (6½ oz) brazil nuts
1 cup (125 g/4 oz) grated Cheddar
30 g (1 oz) Parmesan, grated
1 egg, lightly beaten
2 tablespoons chopped fresh chives
1 cup (80 g/2¾ oz) fresh wholemeal breadcrumbs

TOMATO SAUCE
1½ tablespoons olive oil
1 onion, finely chopped
1 clove garlic, crushed
400 g (13 oz) can chopped tomatoes
1 tablespoon tomato paste
1 teaspoon caster sugar

1 Preheat the oven to moderate 180°C (350°F/Gas 4). Grease a 15 x 20 cm (6 x 8 inch) tin and line with baking paper. Heat the oil in a frying pan and fry the onion, garlic and mushrooms over medium heat for 2–3 minutes, or until soft. Cool.
2 Finely chop the nuts in a food processor, but do not overprocess.
3 Combine the nuts, mushroom mixture, cheeses, egg, chives and breadcrumbs in a bowl. Press into the tin and bake for 45 minutes until firm. Leave for 5 minutes, then turn out.
4 Meanwhile, to make the sauce, heat the oil in a frying pan and add the onion and garlic. Cook over low heat for 5 minutes, or until soft. Add the tomato, tomato paste, sugar and ⅓ cup (80 ml) water. Simmer for 3–5 minutes, or until thick. Season. Serve with the sliced roast.

NUTRITION PER SERVE
Protein 18 g; Fat 44 g; Carbohydrate 16 g; Dietary Fibre 6.5 g; Cholesterol 55 mg; 2195 kJ (525 cal)

Finely chop the cashews and brazil nuts in a food processor but don't overprocess.

Press the nutty mushroom mixture into the prepared tin.

Simmer the tomato sauce for 3–5 minutes, or until thickened.

MOROCCAN TAGINE WITH COUSCOUS

Preparation time: 20 minutes
Total cooking time: 1 hour
Serves 4–6

2 tablespoons oil
2 onions, chopped
1 teaspoon ground ginger
2 teaspoons ground paprika
2 teaspoons ground cumin
1 cinnamon stick
pinch of saffron threads
1.5 kg (3 lb) vegetables, peeled
    and cut into large chunks (carrot,
    eggplant, orange sweet potato,
    parsnip, potato, pumpkin)
1/2 preserved lemon, rinsed, pith and
    flesh removed, thinly sliced
400 g (13 oz) can peeled tomatoes
1 cup (250 ml/8 fl oz) vegetable stock
100 g (31/2 oz) dried pears, halved
60 g (2 oz) pitted prunes
2 zucchini, cut into large chunks
300 g (10 oz) instant couscous
1 tablespoon olive oil
3 tablespoons chopped fresh flat-leaf
    parsley
1/3 cup (50 g/13/4 oz) almonds

1 Preheat the oven to moderate 180°C (350°F/Gas 4). Heat the oil in a large saucepan or ovenproof dish, add the onion and cook over medium heat for 5 minutes, or until soft. Add the spices and cook for 3 minutes.
2 Add the vegetables and cook, stirring, until coated with the spices and the outside begins to soften. Add the lemon, tomatoes, stock, pears and prunes. Cover, transfer to the oven and cook for 30 minutes. Add the zucchini and cook for 15–20 minutes, or until the vegetables are tender.

3 Cover the couscous with the olive oil and 2 cups (500 ml/16 fl oz) boiling water and leave until all the water has been absorbed. Flake with a fork.
4 Remove the cinnamon stick from the vegetables, then stir in the parsley. Serve on a large platter with the couscous formed into a ring and the

vegetable tagine in the centre, sprinkled with the almonds.

NUTRITION PER SERVE (6)
Protein 8 g; Fat 15 g; Carbohydrate 33 g;
Dietary Fibre 9 g; Cholesterol 0 mg;
1240 kJ (296 cal)

Cook the vegetables until they are coated in spices and the outside starts to soften.

Once all the water has been absorbed, flake the couscous with a fork.

Before serving, remove the cinnamon stick with a pair of tongs.

LENTIL AND CAULIFLOWER CURRY STACKS

Preparation time: 15 minutes
Total cooking time: 50 minutes
Serves 6

60 g (2 oz) ghee or butter
2 onions, thinly sliced
2 tablespoons Madras curry paste
2 cloves garlic, crushed
180 g (6 oz) button mushrooms, sliced
1 litre (32 fl oz) vegetable stock
300 g (10 oz) brown or green lentils
400 g (13 oz) can chopped tomatoes
2 cinnamon sticks
300 g (10 oz) cauliflower, cut into small
    florets
oil, for deep-frying
18 small (8 cm/3 inch) pappadums
plain yoghurt and coriander, to serve

1 Heat the ghee in a large pan over medium heat and cook the onion for 2–3 minutes, or until soft. Add the curry paste, garlic and mushrooms and cook for 2 minutes, or until soft.

2 Add the stock, lentils, tomato and cinnamon and mix well. Bring to the boil and cook for 40 minutes, or until the lentils are tender. Add the cauliflower in the last 10 minutes and cover. If the curry is too wet, continue to cook, uncovered, until the excess liquid has evaporated. Season to taste with salt and cracked black pepper. Remove the cinnamon.

3 Meanwhile, fill a deep heavy-based saucepan one third full of oil and heat until a cube of bread dropped into the oil browns in 15 seconds. Cook the pappadums in batches for 10 seconds, or until golden brown and puffed all over. Drain on crumpled paper towels

and season with salt.

4 To assemble, place a pappadum on each serving plate and spoon on a little of the curry. Place a second pappadum on top and spoon on some more curry. Cover with the remaining pappadum and top with a spoonful of yoghurt. Garnish with coriander sprigs and serve immediately (the pappadums will become soggy if left to stand for too long.)

NUTRITION PER SERVE
Protein 16 g; Fat 13 g; Carbohydrate 23 g;
Dietary Fibre 10 g; Cholesterol 24 mg;
1144 kJ (273 cal)

If the curry is too wet, continue cooking to evaporate the excess liquid.

Drop the pappadums into the oil and cook until puffed and golden.

CAULIFLOWER CHEESE

Preparation time: 15 minutes
Total cooking time: 20 minutes
Serves 4

500 g (1 lb) cauliflower, cut into pieces
30 g (1 oz) butter
30 g (1 oz) plain flour
1¼ cups (315 ml/10 fl oz) warm milk
1 teaspoon Dijon mustard
½ cup (60 g/2 oz) grated Cheddar
½ cup (60 g/2 oz) grated Parmesan
2 tablespoons fresh breadcrumbs
3 tablespoons grated Cheddar, extra

1 Brush a 1.5 litre (48 fl oz) heatproof dish with melted butter or oil. Cook the cauliflower in lightly salted boiling water until just tender. Drain. Place in the dish and keep warm.

2 Melt the butter in a pan. Stir in the flour and cook for 1 minute, or until golden and bubbling. Remove from the heat and whisk in the milk and mustard. Return to the heat and bring to the boil, stirring constantly. Cook, stirring, over low heat for 2 minutes, then remove from the heat. Add the cheeses and stir until melted. Season with salt and white pepper and pour over the cauliflower.

3 Mix together the breadcrumbs and extra Cheddar cheese and sprinkle over the sauce. Grill until the top is browned and bubbling and then serve immediately.

NUTRITION PER SERVE
Protein 22 g; Fat 33 g; Carbohydrate 15 g;
Dietary Fibre 2 g; Cholesterol 88 mg;
1840 kJ (440 cal)

Add the Cheddar and Parmesan and stir until the cheeses have melted.

POLENTA PIE

Preparation time: 20 minutes +
  15 minutes standing + refrigeration
Total cooking time: 50 minutes
Serves 6

2 eggplants, thickly sliced
1¹/₃ cups (350 ml/11 fl oz) vegetable
  stock
1 cup (150 g/5 oz) fine polenta
¹/₂ cup (60 g/2 oz) finely grated
  Parmesan
1 tablespoon olive oil
1 large onion, chopped
2 cloves garlic, crushed
1 large red capsicum, diced
2 zucchini, thickly sliced
150 g (5 oz) button mushrooms, cut
  into quarters
400 g (13 oz) can chopped tomatoes
3 teaspoons balsamic vinegar
olive oil, for brushing

1 Spread the eggplant in a single layer on a board, and sprinkle with salt. Leave for 15 minutes, then rinse, pat dry and cut into cubes.
2 Line a 22 cm (9 inch) round cake tin with foil. Pour the stock and 1¹/₃ cups (350 ml/11 fl oz) water into a saucepan and bring to the boil. Add the polenta in a thin stream and stir over low heat for 5 minutes, or until the liquid is absorbed and the mixture comes away from the side of the pan.
3 Remove from the heat and stir in the cheese until it melts through the polenta. Spread into the prepared tin, smoothing the surface as much as possible. Refrigerate until set.
4 Preheat the oven to moderately hot 200°C (400°F/Gas 6). Heat the oil in a large saucepan with a lid and add the onion. Cook over medium heat,

stirring occasionally, for 3 minutes, or until soft. Add the garlic and cook for a further 1 minute. Add the eggplant, capsicum, zucchini, mushrooms and tomato. Bring to the boil, then reduce the heat and simmer, covered, for 20 minutes, or until the vegetables are tender. Stir occasionally to prevent catching on the bottom of the pan. Stir in the vinegar and season.
5 Transfer the vegetable mixture to a 22 cm (9 inch) ovenproof pie dish, piling it up slightly in the centre.

6 Turn out the polenta, peel off the foil and cut into 12 wedges. Arrange smooth-side-down in a single layer, over the vegetables—don't worry about any gaps. Brush lightly with a little olive oil and bake for 20 minutes, or until lightly brown and crisp.

NUTRITION PER SERVE
Protein 8 g; Fat 8.5 g; Carbohydrate 23 g;
Dietary Fibre 4.5 g; Cholesterol 8 mg;
855 kJ (205 cal)

Cook the polenta, stirring, until all the liquid is absorbed and it is very thick.

Reduce the heat and simmer until the vegetables are tender.

Arrange the polenta wedges, smooth-side-down, over the vegetable mixture.

SOYA BEAN MOUSSAKA

Preparation time: 25 minutes
Total cooking time: 1 hour
Serves 4

2 eggplants
1 tablespoon oil
1 onion, finely chopped
2 cloves garlic, crushed
2 ripe tomatoes, peeled, seeded and
    chopped
2 teaspoons tomato paste
1/2 teaspoon dried oregano
1/2 cup (125 ml/4 fl oz) dry white wine
300 g (10 oz) can soya beans, rinsed
    and drained
3 tablespoons chopped fresh flat-leaf
    parsley
30 g (1 oz) butter
2 tablespoons plain flour
pinch of ground nutmeg
1 1/4 cups (315 ml/10 fl oz) milk
1/3 cup (40 g/1 1/4 oz) grated Cheddar

1 Preheat the oven to moderate 180°C
(350°F/Gas 4). Cut the eggplants in
half lengthways. Spoon out the flesh,
leaving a narrow border and place on
a large baking tray, cut-side-up. Use
crumpled foil around the sides of the
eggplant to help support it.
2 Heat the oil in a large frying pan.
Cook the onion and garlic over
medium heat for 3 minutes, or until
soft. Add the tomato, tomato paste,
oregano and wine. Boil for 3 minutes,
or until the liquid is reduced and the
tomato is soft. Stir in the soya beans
and parsley.
3 To make the sauce, melt the butter
in a saucepan. Stir in the flour and
cook over medium heat for 1 minute,
or until pale and foamy. Remove from
the heat and gradually stir in the
nutmeg and milk. Return to the heat
and stir constantly until the sauce boils
and thickens. Pour one third of the
white sauce into the tomato mixture
and stir well.
4 Spoon the mixture into the eggplant
shells. Smooth the surface before
spreading the remaining sauce evenly
over the top and sprinkling with
cheese. Bake for 50 minutes, or until
cooked through. Serve hot.

NUTRITION PER SERVE
Protein 35 g; Fat 33 g; Carbohydrate 20 g;
Dietary Fibre 20 g; Cholesterol 40 mg;
2192 kJ (524 cal)

Scoop out the eggplant flesh, leaving a narrow
border all the way around.

Add the soya beans and parsley to the tomato
mixture and stir well.

BEAN AND CAPSICUM STEW

Preparation time: 20 minutes +
  overnight soaking
Total cooking time: 1 hour 35 minutes
Serves 4–6

1 cup (200 g/6½ oz) dried haricot
  beans (see NOTE)
2 tablespoons olive oil
2 large cloves garlic, crushed
1 red onion, halved and cut into thin
  wedges
1 red capsicum, cubed
1 green capsicum, cubed
2 x 400 g (13 oz) cans chopped
  tomatoes
2 tablespoons tomato paste
2 cups (500 ml/16 fl oz) vegetable
  stock
2 tablespoons chopped fresh basil
2/3 cup (125 g/4 oz) Kalamata olives,
  pitted
1–2 teaspoons soft brown sugar

1 Put the beans in a large bowl, cover
with cold water and soak overnight.
Rinse well, then transfer to a saucepan,
cover with cold water and cook for
45 minutes, or until just tender. Drain.
2 Heat the oil in a large saucepan.
Cook the garlic and onion over
medium heat for 2–3 minutes, or until
the onion is soft. Add the red and
green capsicums and cook for a
further 5 minutes.
3 Stir in the tomato, tomato paste,
stock and beans. Simmer, covered, for
40 minutes, or until the beans are

cooked through. Stir in the basil, olives
and sugar. Season with salt and
pepper. Serve hot with crusty bread.

NUTRITION PER SERVE (6)
Protein 10 g; Fat 8 g; Carbohydrate 20 g;
Dietary Fibre 9.5 g; Cholesterol 0 mg;
825 kJ (197 cal)

NOTE: 1 cup of dried haricot beans
yields about 2½ cups cooked beans.
So use 2½ cups tinned haricot or
borlotti beans instead if you prefer.

Cook the garlic and onion until the garlic is soft,
then add the capsicum.

Simmer the stew for 40 minutes, or until the
beans are cooked through.

VEGETABLE CASSEROLE WITH HERB DUMPLINGS

Preparation time: 30 minutes
Total cooking time: 50 minutes
Serves 4

1 tablespoon olive oil
1 large onion, chopped
2 cloves garlic, crushed
2 teaspoons sweet paprika
1 large potato, chopped
1 large carrot, sliced
400 g (13 oz) can chopped tomatoes
1½ cups (375 ml/12 fl oz) vegetable
   stock
400 g (13 oz) orange sweet potato,
   cubed
150 g (5 oz) broccoli, cut into florets
2 zucchini, thickly sliced
1 cup (125 g/4 oz) self-raising flour
20 g (¾ oz) cold butter, cut into small
   cubes
2 teaspoons chopped fresh
   flat-leaf parsley
1 teaspoon fresh thyme
1 teaspoon chopped fresh rosemary
⅓ cup (80 ml/2¾ fl oz) milk
2 tablespoons sour cream

1 Heat the oil in a large saucepan and add the onion. Cook over low heat, stirring occasionally, for 5 minutes, or until soft. Add the garlic and paprika and cook, stirring, for 1 minute.
2 Add the potato, carrot, tomato and stock to the pan. Bring to the boil, then reduce the heat and simmer, covered, for 10 minutes. Add the sweet potato, broccoli and zucchini and simmer for 10 minutes, or until tender. Preheat the oven to moderately hot 200°C (400°F/Gas 6).
3 To make the dumplings, sift the flour and a pinch of salt into a bowl and add the butter. Rub the butter into the flour with your fingertips until it resembles fine breadcrumbs. Stir in the herbs and make a well in the centre. Add the milk, and mix with a flat-bladed knife, using a cutting action, until the mixture comes together in beads. Gather up the dough and lift onto a lightly floured surface, then divide into eight portions. Shape each portion into a ball.

4 Add the sour cream to the casserole. Pour into a 2 litre (64 fl oz) ovenproof dish and top with the dumplings. Bake for 20 minutes, or until the dumplings are golden and a skewer comes out clean when inserted in the centre.

NUTRITION PER SERVE
Protein 8 g; Fat 10 g; Carbohydrate 27 g; Dietary Fibre 7.5 g; Cholesterol 16 mg; 967 kJ (230 cal)

Add the remaining vegetables and simmer for 10 minutes, or until they are tender.

Rub the butter into the flour until the mixture resembles fine breadcrumbs.

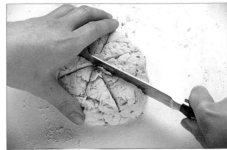
Divide the dough into eight equal portions and shape each portion into a dumpling.

201

ROMAN GNOCCHI

Preparation time: 15 minutes +
    1 hour refrigeration
Total cooking time: 40 minutes
Serves 4

3 cups (750 ml/24 fl oz) milk
1/2 teaspoon ground nutmeg
3/4 cup (90 g/3 oz) semolina
1 egg, beaten
11/2 cups (150 g/5 oz) grated
    Parmesan
60 g (2 oz) butter, melted
1/2 cup (125 ml/4 fl oz) cream
1/2 cup (60 g/2 oz) grated mozzarella

1 Line a deep 30 x 20 cm (12 x 8 inch) swiss roll tin with baking paper. Put the milk, half the nutmeg and some salt and pepper in a pan and bring to the boil. Reduce the heat and gradually stir in the semolina. Cook, stirring occasionally, for 5–10 minutes or until the semolina is very stiff.
2 Remove from the heat. Add the egg and 1 cup (100 g/3 1/2 oz) Parmesan and stir well. Spread into the tin and refrigerate for 1 hour or until firm.
3 Preheat the oven to moderate 180°C (350°F/Gas 4). Cut the semolina into rounds with a floured 4 cm (1 1/2 inch) cutter. Arrange in a greased shallow casserole dish.

4 Pour the butter over the top and then the cream. Sprinkle with the combined remaining Parmesan and mozzarella cheeses. Sprinkle with the remaining nutmeg. Bake for 20–25 minutes or until golden.

NUTRITION PER SERVE
Protein 33 g; Fat 53 g; Carbohydrate 24 g;
Dietary Fibre 0.5 g; Cholesterol 205 mg;
2918 kJ (697 cal)

NOTE: Roman gnocchi is also known as gnocchi alla semolina, to differentiate it from the small potato gnocchi that are boiled and served with pasta sauce.

Cook the semolina for 5–10 minutes, or until it is very stiff.

Use a floured biscuit cutter to cut the gnocchi into circles.

Mix together the grated Parmesan and mozzarella and sprinkle over the gnocchi.

MEDITERRANEAN VEGETABLE HOTPOT

Preparation time: 20 minutes
Total cooking time: 40 minutes
Serves 4

3 tablespoons olive oil
1 onion, chopped
2 cloves garlic, crushed
1 green capsicum, chopped
1 red capsicum, chopped
3 zucchini, sliced
3 slender eggplant, sliced
2 cups (440 g/14 oz) long-grain rice
1 cup (250 ml/8 fl oz) white wine

100 g (3½ oz) button mushrooms, sliced
3 cups (750 ml/24 fl oz) vegetable stock
400 g (13 oz) can crushed tomatoes
2 tablespoons tomato paste
150 g (5 oz) feta cheese

1 Heat the oil in a large heavy-based pan and cook the onion over medium heat for about 10 minutes, or until very soft but not browned. Add the garlic and cook for a further minute.
2 Add the green and red capsicums and cook, stirring, for 3 minutes, Add the zucchini and eggplant and sitr-fry for a further 5 minutes. Add the rice and stir-fry for 2 minutes.
3 Add the wine, mushrooms, stock, crushed tomatoes and tomato paste. Stir to combine. Bring to the boil, reduce the heat, cover and simmer for 20 minutes. The rice should be tender. Serve immediately, topped with the crumbled feta cheese.

NUTRITION PER SERVE
Protein 20 g; Fat 25 g; Carbohydrate 92 g;
Dietary Fibre 9 g; Cholesterol 25 mg;
2980 kJ (710 cal)

NOTE: Like most hotpots and casseroles, this is best made a day in advance to let the flavours develop.

Cook the onion for 10 minutes, until it is very soft but not browned.

Add the zucchini and eggplant to the pan and stir-fry for a little longer.

Add the wine, mushrooms, stock, crushed tomatoes and tomato paste.

POTATO GRATIN

Preparation time: 25 minutes
Total cooking time: 1 hour
Serves 4

30 g (1 oz) butter
1 onion, halved and thinly sliced
650 g (1 lb 5 oz) floury potatoes, thinly
    sliced
2/3 cup (90 g/3 oz) grated Cheddar
300 ml (10 fl oz) cream
100 ml (10 fl oz) milk

1 Heat the butter in a frying pan and cook the onion over low heat for 5 minutes, or until it is soft and translucent.

2 Preheat the oven to warm 160°C (315°F/Gas 3). Grease the base and sides of a deep 1 litre (32 fl oz) ovenproof dish. Layer the potato slices with the onion and cheese (reserving 2 tablespoons of cheese for the top). Whisk together the cream and milk, and season with salt and cracked black pepper. Slowly pour over the potato, then sprinkle with the remaining cheese.

3 Bake for 50–60 minutes, or until golden brown and the potato is very soft. Leave to rest for 10 minutes before serving.

NUTRITION PER SERVE
Protein 12 g; Fat 50 g; Carbohydrate 25 g;
Dietary Fibre 3 g; Cholesterol 155 mg;
2465 kJ (590 cal)

VARIATION: For something different, try combining potato and orange sweet potato, layering alternately. For extra flavour, add chopped fresh herbs to the cream and milk mixture.

Peel the onion and slice it in half before cutting into thin slices.

Use a large sharp knife to cut the potatoes into thin slices.

Add the onion to the butter and cook until soft and translucent.

TOMATO AND POTATO STEW

Preparation time: 30 minutes
Total cooking time: 1 hour 15 minutes
Serves 6

¹/₄ cup (60 ml/2 fl oz) olive oil
2 red capsicums, chopped
2 green capsicums, chopped
3 onions, thinly sliced
4 cloves garlic, crushed
2 x 400 g (13 oz) cans chopped
    tomatoes
3–4 sprigs thyme, plus extra to
    garnish
2 bay leaves
2 teaspoons caster sugar
1.2 kg (2 lb 7 oz) potatoes, cut into
    chunks
1 cup (125 g/4 oz) black olives, pitted
Parmesan shavings, to serve

1 Heat the oil in a large, heavy-based pan. When the oil is hot, cook the capsicum, onion and garlic over medium heat for 10 minutes, or until softened. Add the chopped tomatoes, 125 ml (4 fl oz) water, thyme sprigs, bay leaves and sugar. Season with salt and pepper to taste and leave to simmer gently for 15 minutes.
2 Add the potato chunks, cover and cook very gently for about an hour, or until tender. Stir in the olives. Garnish with Parmesan shavings and thyme.

NUTRITION PER SERVE
Protein 10 g; Fat 12 g; Carbohydrate 40 g;
Dietary Fibre 9 g; Cholesterol 3 mg;
1330 kJ (320 cal)

When the oil is hot, fry the capsicum, onion and garlic until soft.

Add the chunks of potato to the tomato mixture and cook very gently until tender.

The easiest way to make Parmesan shavings is to run a vegetable peeler over the block.

STUFFED ZUCCHINI

Preparation time: 20 minutes
Total cooking time: 45 minutes
Serves 4

8 zucchini
35 g (1¼ oz) white bread, crusts
    removed
milk, for soaking
125 g (4 oz) ricotta cheese
3 tablespoons grated Cheddar cheese
¹/₃ cup (35 g/1¼ oz) grated
    Parmesan

2 teaspoons chopped fresh oregano
2 teaspoons chopped fresh thyme
1 clove garlic, crushed
1 egg yolk

1 Preheat the oven to moderately hot 190°C (375°F/Gas 5). Cook the zucchini in boiling salted water for 5 minutes, then drain. Meanwhile, soak the bread in milk until soft, then squeeze dry. Cut the zucchini in half and scoop out the flesh with a spoon.
2 Chop the zucchini flesh finely. Place in a bowl and add the bread, cheeses, herbs, garlic, egg yolk and season with

salt and pepper. Mix together, adding a little milk to make it bind if necessary.
3 Fill the zucchini shells with the stuffing. Brush an ovenproof baking dish with oil and arrange the zucchini close together. Bake in the oven for 35–40 minutes, until golden on top. Serve immediately.

NUTRITION PER SERVE
Protein 12 g; Fat 10 g; Carbohydrate 10 g;
Dietary Fibre 4.5 g; Cholesterol 73 mg;
758 kJ (180 cal)

Cut the zucchini in half and scoop out the flesh with a teaspoon.

Combine the zucchini, cheeses, herbs, garlic and egg yolk in a bowl.

Arrange the stuffed zucchini close together in the oiled baking dish.

CHEESE AND SPINACH PANCAKES

Preparation time: 40 minutes
Total cooking time: 50 minutes
Serves 4

250 g (8 oz) cooked, drained
   English spinach, chopped
1/2 cup (125 g/4 oz) ricotta cheese
1/4 cup (30 g/1 oz) grated Cheddar
freshly grated nutmeg
1/4 cup (25 g/3/4 oz) grated Parmesan
1/2 teaspoon paprika
1/2 cup (40 g/11/4 oz) fresh breadcrumbs

BATTER
1 cup (125 g/4 oz) plain flour
11/4 cups (315 ml/10 fl oz) milk
1 egg
butter, for cooking

CHEESE SAUCE
2 tablespoons butter
1/4 cup (30 g/1 oz) plain flour
13/4 cups (440 ml/14 fl oz) milk
1 cup (125 g/4 oz) grated Cheddar

1 Put the spinach, cheeses and nutmeg in a bowl and mix well.
2 To make batter, sift the flour and a pinch of salt into a bowl. Add half the milk and the egg. Whisk until smooth; add the remaining milk. Heat a teaspoon of butter in a frying pan and pour in a thin layer of batter. Cook the base until golden, then flip. The batter should make 8 pancakes.
3 To make the cheese sauce, melt the butter over low heat, stir in the flour until smooth and cook for 1 minute. Remove from the heat and slowly stir in the milk. Bring to the boil, stirring constantly. Remove from the heat and add salt and pepper and the grated cheese.
4 Preheat the oven to 180°C (350°F/Gas 4). Divide the filling among the pancakes, roll up and put in a greased ovenproof dish. Pour cheese sauce over the pancakes. Mix the Parmesan, paprika and breadcrumbs together and sprinkle over the sauce. Bake for 30 minutes, or until golden brown.

NUTRITION PER SERVE
Protein 18 g; Fat 17 g; Carbohydrate 34 g;
Dietary Fibre 3 g; Cholesterol 96 mg;
1511 kJ (360 cal)

Put the spinach, cheese, pepper and nutmeg in a bowl and mix well.

Cook until both sides of the pancake are golden, then remove with a spatula.

Remove the sauce from the heat and add salt and pepper, to taste, and grated cheese.

Divide the filling among the pancakes, roll up and put in the greased dish.

OVEN-BAKED POTATO, LEEK AND OLIVES

Preparation time: 20 minutes
Total cooking time: 1 hour
Serves 4–6

2 tablespoons extra virgin olive oil
1 leek, finely sliced
1½ cups (375 ml/12 fl oz) vegetable
    stock
2 teaspoons chopped fresh thyme
1 kg (2 lb) potatoes, unpeeled, cut into
    thin slices
6–8 pitted black olives, sliced
½ cup (60 g/2 oz) grated Parmesan
30 g (1 oz) butter, chopped

1 Preheat the oven to moderate 180°C (350°F/Gas 4). Brush a shallow 1.25 litre (40 fl oz) ovenproof dish with a little olive oil. Heat the remaining oil in a large pan and cook the leek over moderate heat until soft. Add the stock, thyme and potato. Cover and leave to simmer for 5 minutes.
2 Using tongs, lift out half the potato and put in the ovenproof dish. Sprinkle with olives and Parmesan and season with salt and pepper.
3 Layer with the remaining potato, then spoon the leek and stock mixture in at the side of the dish, keeping the top dry.
4 Scatter chopped butter over the potato and then bake, uncovered, for 50 minutes, or until cooked and golden brown. Leave in a warm place for about 10 minutes before serving.

NUTRITION PER SERVE (6)
Protein 7.5 g; Fat 13 g; Carbohydrate 23 g;
Dietary Fibre 3 g; Cholesterol 20 mg;
1019 kJ (243 cal)

NOTE: Keeping the top layer of potato dry as you pour in the stock mixture will give the dish a crisp finish.

Cook the leek until soft, then add the stock, thyme and potato.

Lift out half the potato with tongs and put into an ovenproof dish.

Spoon the leek and stock mixture around the side, trying to keep the top dry.

Bake, uncovered, until the potatoes on top are golden brown.

POTATO PORCINI BAKE

Preparation time: 30 minutes
Total cooking time: 45 minutes
Serves 4–6

20 g (³/₄ oz) dried porcini mushrooms
³/₄ cup (185 ml/6 fl oz) hot milk
¹/₂ cup (125 ml/4 fl oz) cream
1 kg (2 lb) waxy potatoes, unpeeled
30 g (1 oz) butter
1 clove garlic, crushed
60 g (2 oz) spring onions, sliced
1 cup (120 g/4 oz) grated Fontina or
    Gruyère cheese

1 Lightly brush a large shallow ovenproof dish with oil. Make sure the porcini are free of dirt or grit and put them in a bowl with the hot milk. Cover the bowl and set aside for 15 minutes. Remove the porcini, finely chop them and then return to the milk. Add the cream.
2 Meanwhile, slice the potatoes fairly thinly and cook in boiling salted water until just tender, then drain well. Melt the butter in a small pan and cook the garlic and onion until soft.
3 Preheat the oven to moderate 180°C (350°F/Gas 4). Layer the potato in the

dish with the spring onion and cheese, spooning the porcini mixture over each layer and seasoning with salt and pepper. Bake for 35 minutes, or until golden and tender. Serve hot.

NUTRITION PER SERVE (6)
Protein 10 g; Fat 20 g; Carbohydrate 25 g;
Dietary Fibre 3 g; Cholesterol 65 mg;
1375 kJ (330 cal)

Put the dried mushrooms in a bowl and leave to soak in the hot milk.

Cut the unpeeled potatoes into slices, then boil until tender.

Layer the potato, spring onion and cheese in the dish, spooning the porcini over each layer.

RED VEGETABLE CURRY

Preparation time: 25 minutes
Total cooking time: 20 minutes
Serves 4

225 g (7 oz) bamboo shoots or tips,
    drained
2 cups (500 ml/16 fl oz) coconut milk
2 tablespoons Thai red curry paste
1 onion, finely chopped
4 kaffir lime leaves
2 potatoes, roughly chopped
200 g (6¹/₂ oz) pumpkin, chopped
150 g (5 oz) green beans, chopped

1 red capsicum, chopped
3 small zucchini, chopped
2 tablespoons chopped fresh basil
    leaves
2 tablespoons lime juice
3 teaspoons soft brown sugar

1 Cut the bamboo shoots in half, discard the tough ends and set the shoots aside. Combine the coconut milk and curry paste in a large wok or pan with ¹/₂ cup (125 ml/4 fl oz) water. Bring to the boil, stirring occasionally.
2 Add the onion and kaffir lime leaves and allow to boil for 3 minutes.

3 Add the potato and pumpkin to the wok and cook over medium heat for 8 minutes, or until the pumpkin is nearly cooked. Add the beans, capsicum and zucchini and simmer for another 5 minutes. Add ¹/₂ cup (125 ml/4 fl oz) of water if the curry is too thick. Add the bamboo shoots and basil. Add the lime juice and sugar and taste for seasoning. Serve with steamed rice.

NUTRITION PER SERVE
Protein 7 g; Fat 26 g; Carbohydrate 22 g;
Dietary Fibre 6.5 g; Cholesterol 0 mg;
1443 kJ (345 cal)

Cut the bamboo shoots in half and discard the tough ends.

Stir in the onion and kaffir lime leaves and boil for 3 minutes.

Add the potato and pumpkin to the curry and simmer until the pumpkin is almost cooked.

CURRIED LENTILS

Preparation time: 15 minutes
Total cooking time: 30 minutes
Serves 4

1 cup (250 g/8 oz) red lentils
2 cups (500 ml/16 fl oz) vegetable
    stock
1/2 teaspoon ground turmeric
50 g (1 3/4 oz) ghee
1 onion, chopped
2 cloves garlic, finely chopped
1 large green chilli, seeded and finely
    chopped

2 teaspoons ground cumin
2 teaspoons ground coriander
2 tomatoes, chopped
1/2 cup (125 ml/4 fl oz) coconut milk

1 Rinse the lentils and drain well.
Place the lentils, stock and turmeric in
a large heavy-based pan. Bring to the
boil, reduce the heat and simmer,
covered, for 10 minutes, or until just
tender. Stir occasionally and check the
mixture is not catching on the bottom
of the pan.
2 Meanwhile, heat the ghee in a small
frying pan and add the onion. Cook
until soft and golden and add the

garlic, chilli, cumin and coriander.
Cook, stirring, for 2–3 minutes until
fragrant. Stir the onions and spices into
the lentil mixture and then add the
tomato. Simmer over very low heat for
5 minutes, stirring frequently.
3 Season to taste and add the coconut
milk. Stir until heated through. Serve
with naan bread or rice.

NUTRITION PER SERVE
Protein 15 g; Fat 20 g; Carbohydrate 25 g;
Dietary Fibre 10 g; Cholesterol 35 mg;
1500 kJ (355 cal)

Stir the lentil mixture occasionally so that it does
not stick to the bottom of the pan.

Add the chopped tomato and simmer over very
low heat for 5 minutes.

Season the lentils and add the coconut milk. Stir
until heated through.

PEANUT AND POTATO CURRY

Preparation time: 30 minutes
Total cooking time: 1 hour 30 minutes
Serves 4–6

3 tablespoons oil
3 cloves garlic, finely chopped
2 red chillies, finely chopped
2 teaspoons ground coriander
1 teaspoon ground cumin
1/2 teaspoon ground fenugreek seeds
pinch each of ground cinnamon and
    nutmeg

2 onions, chopped
1.5 kg (3 lb) potatoes, cubed
3/4 cup (125 g/4 oz) dry roasted
    peanuts, chopped
500 g (1 lb) ripe tomatoes, chopped
1 teaspoon soft brown sugar
2 teaspoons finely grated lime rind
2 tablespoons lime juice
coriander leaves and roughly chopped
    peanuts, to garnish

1 Heat the oil in a large, deep pan or wok and stir-fry the garlic, chilli and spices over low heat for 3 minutes, or until very fragrant. Add the onion and cook for another 3 minutes.

2 Add the potato to the pan, tossing to coat with the spice mixture. Add 1/2 cup (125 ml/4 fl oz) water, cover and cook over low heat for 10 minutes, stirring regularly.

3 Add the peanuts and tomato, uncover and simmer for 1 hour 10 minutes, stirring occasionally. Season with the sugar, rind, juice and salt and pepper. Garnish with coriander and peanuts. Serve with rice.

NUTRITION PER SERVE (6)
Protein 15 g; Fat 20 g; Carbohydrate 40 g;
Dietary Fibre 7 g; Cholesterol 0 mg;
1720 kJ (410 cal)

Stir the garlic, chilli and spices in the hot oil until very fragrant.

Use two wooden spoons to toss the potato and thoroughly coat with the spices.

Use very ripe tomatoes to give the best flavour. Add to the curry with the peanuts.

HOT VEGETABLE CURRY WITH SPICED NOODLES

Preparation time: 40 minutes
Total cooking time: 35 minutes
Serves 4–6

CURRY PASTE
5 red chillies, seeded and chopped
1 stem lemon grass, sliced
1 tablespoon chopped galangal
2 garlic cloves, crushed
1 small onion, chopped
1 tablespoon chopped fresh coriander
10 black peppercorns
2 tablespoons lime juice
2 teaspoons oil

2 tablespoons oil
1¹/₂ cups (375 ml/12 fl oz) coconut milk
200 g (6¹/₂ oz) green beans, cut into short lengths
2 small zucchini, thickly sliced
1 eggplant, cubed
200 g (6¹/₂ oz) pumpkin, cubed
5 kaffir lime leaves
2 tablespoons lime juice
¹/₄ cup (15 g/¹/₂ oz) chopped fresh coriander
¹/₂ cup (30 g/1 oz) chopped fresh basil

SPICED NOODLES
2 tablespoons oil
1 small onion, chopped
1 clove garlic, crushed
¹/₂–1 teaspoon dried chilli flakes
¹/₂ teaspoon garam masala
200 g (6¹/₂ oz) thin egg noodles

1 To make the curry paste, blend all the ingredients in a food processor or blender to make a smooth paste.
2 Heat the oil in a pan and stir-fry the curry paste for 2 minutes. Add the coconut milk and ¹/₂ cup (125 ml/4 fl oz) water and bring to the boil. Reduce the heat and add the vegetables, kaffir lime leaves and lime juice. Cook, covered, until tender. Add the coriander and basil.
3 To make the spiced noodles, heat the oil in a pan. Cook the onion and garlic over low heat for 5 minutes. Add the chilli flakes and garam masala and cook for 2 minutes. Meanwhile, cook the noodles in boiling water until tender and drain. Add to the onion mixture and toss well. Serve with the vegetable curry.

NUTRITION PER SERVE (6)
Protein 5 g; Fat 25 g; Carbohydrate 15 g;
Dietary Fibre 5 g; Cholesterol 0 mg;
1415 kJ (335 cal)

Lemon grass and galangal are both available from Asian food stores.

Heat the oil in a pan and stir-fry the curry paste for 2 minutes.

Add the noodles to a large pan of boiling water and cook until tender.

DRY POTATO AND PEA CURRY

Preparation time: 15 minutes
Total cooking time: 20–25 minutes
Serves 4

2 teaspoons brown mustard seeds
2 tablespoons ghee or oil
2 onions, sliced
2 cloves garlic, crushed
2 teaspoons grated fresh ginger
1 teaspoon ground turmeric
1/2 teaspoon chilli powder

1 teaspoon ground cumin
1 teaspoon garam masala
750 g (1 1/2 lb) potatoes, cubed
2/3 cup (100 g/3 1/2 oz) peas
2 tablespoons chopped mint

1 Heat the mustard seeds in a dry pan until they start to pop. Add the ghee or oil, onion, garlic and ginger and cook, stirring, until the onion is soft.
2 Add the turmeric, chilli powder, cumin, garam marsala and potato, and season with salt and pepper. Stir until the potato is coated with the spice mixture. Add 125 ml (4 fl oz) water

and simmer, covered, for about 15–20 minutes, or until the potato is just tender. Stir occasionally to stop the curry sticking to the bottom of the pan.
3 Add the peas and stir until well combined. Simmer, covered, for 3–5 minutes, or until the potato is cooked and all the liquid is absorbed. Stir in the mint and season well.

NUTRITION PER SERVE
Protein 5 g; Fat 10 g; Carbohydrate 30 g;
Dietary Fibre 5 g; Cholesterol 25 mg;
985 kJ (235 cal)

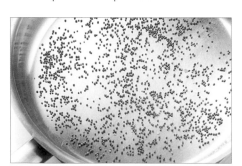
Fry the mustard seeds in a dry pan until they begin to pop.

Add the potato cubes and stir until they are well coated in the spice mixture.

Stir in the chopped mint before seasoning with salt and pepper, to taste.

CHICKPEA CURRY

Preparation time: 10 minutes
Cooking time: 40 minutes
Serves 4

1 tablespoon ghee or oil
2 onions, sliced
4 cloves garlic, crushed
1 teaspoon chilli powder
1 teaspoon salt
1 teaspoon ground turmeric
1 teaspoon paprika

1 tablespoon ground cumin
1 tablespoon ground coriander
880 g (1 lb 13 oz) can chickpeas,
  rinsed and drained
440 g (14 oz) can chopped tomatoes
1 teaspoon garam masala

1 Heat the ghee or oil in a pan. Add the onion and garlic and cook, stirring, until the onion is soft. Add the chilli powder, salt, turmeric, paprika, cumin and coriander. Cook, stirring, for 2–3 minutes.
2 Stir in the chickpeas and tomato.

Simmer, covered, over low heat for 20 minutes, stirring occasionally.
3 Stir in the garam masala. Simmer, covered, for a further 10 minutes. Serve with paratha or naan bread.

NUTRITION PER SERVE
Protein 45 g; Fat 20 g; Carbohydrate 120 g;
Dietary Fibre 35 g; Cholesterol 15 mg;
3315 kJ (790 cal)

Add the chilli powder, salt, turmeric, paprika, cumin and coriander to the pan.

Add the rinsed and drained chickpeas, and chopped tomatoes.

Stir in 1 teaspoon of garam masala and then simmer, covered, for 10 minutes.

215

CURRIED SUMMER FRUITS

Preparation time: 25 minutes
Total cooking time: 15 minutes
Serves 4

2 Granny Smith apples
1 small rockmelon
1/2 large pineapple
1/2 pawpaw
1 mango
2 large bananas
70 g (2 1/4 oz) dried dates, pitted

50 g (1 3/4 oz) ghee
3 cm (1 1/4 inches) fresh ginger, finely grated
1 1/2 tablespoons curry powder
4 spring onions, chopped
2 tablespoons lemon juice
50 g (1 3/4 oz) cashews, toasted
plain yoghurt, to serve

1 Peel all the fruits and cut into bite-size pieces. Roughly chop the dates.
2 Melt the ghee over low heat in a heavy-based pan. Gently cook the ginger, curry powder and spring onion for 3 minutes. Add the fruit and gently

toss to coat in the mixture.
3 Cook gently for 7 minutes, or until the fruit just starts to soften. Add the lemon juice and stir gently. Serve with steamed rice, garnished with the cashews and yoghurt. Serve either as a main meal, or as an accompaniment to a hot vegetable curry.

NUTRITION PER SERVE
Protein 10 g; Fat 20 g; Carbohydrate 80 g;
Dietary Fibre 15 g; Cholesterol 35 mg;
2185 kJ (520 cal)

Cut the pawpaw, rockmelon, pineapple and mango into bite-size chunks.

Cook the ginger, curry powder and spring onion over low heat for 3 minutes.

Add the lemon juice to the pan and gently stir through the fruit.

THREE BEAN CHILLI

Preparation time: 20 minutes +
    2 hours standing
Total cooking time: 1 hour 35 minutes
Serves 4

1 cup (220 g/7 oz) dried black beans
    (see NOTE)
2 tablespoons oil
1 large onion, finely chopped
3 cloves garlic, crushed
2 tablespoons ground cumin
1 tablespoon ground coriander
1 teaspoon ground cinnamon
1 teaspoon chilli powder
400 g (13 oz) can crushed tomatoes
1½ cups (375 ml/12 fl oz) vegetable
    stock
400 g (13 oz) can chickpeas, rinsed
    and drained
400 g (13 oz) can red kidney beans,
    rinsed and drained
2 tablespoons tomato paste
1 tablespoon sugar
sour cream and corn chips, to serve

1 Place the black beans in a large pan, cover with water and bring to the boil. Turn off the heat and set aside for 2 hours. Drain the beans, cover with fresh water and boil for 1 hour, until the beans are tender but not mushy. Drain well.

2 Heat the oil in a large pan and cook the onion over medium-low heat for 5 minutes, until golden, stirring frequently. Reduce the heat, add the garlic and spices; stir for 1 minute.

3 Add the tomatoes, stock, chickpeas, kidney beans and black beans and combine with the onion mixture. Bring to the boil, then simmer for 20 minutes, stirring occasionally.

4 Add the tomato paste, sugar and salt and pepper, to taste. Simmer for a further 5 minutes. Serve with sour cream and corn chips on the side.

NUTRITION PER SERVE
Protein 40 g; Fat 55 g; Carbohydrate 125 g;
Dietary Fibre 36 g; Cholesterol 40 mg;
4775 kJ (1140 cal)

NOTE: If black beans are unavailable, double the quantity of kidney beans and chickpeas.

Do not confuse black beans with Asian black beans, which are fermented soy.

Cook the chopped onion, stirring frequently, until it turns golden.

Add the tomatoes, stock, chickpeas, kidney beans and black beans to the pan.

Add salt and pepper to taste and simmer the chilli for a further 5 minutes.

217

Parties, Picnics & Snacks

VEGETABLE SHAPES WITH CREME FRAICHE AND FRIED LEEK

Preparation time: 25 minutes
Total cooking time: 45 minutes
Makes 35

2 x 425 g (14 oz) long thin orange
    sweet potatoes
5 beetroot
1/2 cup (125 g/4 oz) crème fraîche
1 clove garlic, crushed
1/4 teaspoon grated lime rind
oil, for deep-frying
2 leeks, cut lengthways into very fine
    slices

1 Bring two large saucepans of water to the boil over high heat and place the sweet potatoes in one saucepan and the beetroot in the other. Boil, covered, for 30–40 minutes, or until tender, adding more boiling water if it starts to evaporate. Drain separately and set aside until cool enough to touch. Remove the skins from the beetroot. Trim the ends from the beetroot and sweet potatoes and cut both into 1 cm (1/2 inch) slices. Using a biscuit cutter, cut the slices into shapes. Drain on paper towels.
2 Place the crème fraîche, garlic and lime rind in a bowl and mix together well. Refrigerate until ready to use.
3 Fill a deep heavy-based saucepan one third full of oil and heat until a cube of bread dropped into the oil browns in 10 seconds. Cook the leek in four batches for 30 seconds, or until golden brown and crisp. Drain on paper towels and season with salt.
4 Place a teaspoon of crème fraîche mixture on top of each vegetable shape and top with some fried leek.

NUTRITION PER VEGETABLE SHAPE
Protein 1 g; Fat 2 g; Carbohydrate 5.5 g;
Dietary Fibre 1 g; Cholesterol 2.5 mg;
180 kJ (43 cal)

HINT: You can make the crème fraîche mixture and deep-fry the leek the day before and keep them in separate airtight containers. If the leek softens, place on a baking tray and crisp in a hot oven for 5 minutes.

Using a biscuit cutter, cut the beetroot and sweet potato into shapes.

Deep-fry the leek in batches until golden brown and crisp.

TAMARI NUT MIX

Preparation time: 15 minutes
Total cooking time: 25 minutes
Serves 10–12

250 g (8 oz) mixed nuts
    (almonds, brazil nuts,
    peanuts, walnuts)
125 g (4 oz) pepitas (see NOTE)
125 g (4 oz) sunflower seeds
125 g (4 oz) cashew nuts
125 g (4 oz) macadamia nuts
1/2 cup (125 ml/4 fl oz) tamari

1 Preheat the oven to very slow 140°C (275°F/Gas 1). Lightly grease two large baking trays.
2 Place the mixed nuts, pepitas, sunflower seeds, cashew nuts and macadamia nuts in a large bowl. Pour the tamari over the nuts and seeds and toss together well, coating them evenly in the tamari. Leave for 10 minutes.
3 Spread the nut and seed mixture evenly over the baking trays and bake for 20–25 minutes, or until dry roasted. Cool completely and store in an airtight container for up to 2 weeks.

NUTRITION PER SERVE (12)
Protein 11.5 g; Fat 36 g; Carbohydrate 4 g;
Dietary Fibre 5 g; Cholesterol 0 mg;
1604 kJ (383 cal)

NOTE: Pepitas are peeled pumpkin seeds—they are available at most supermarkets and health-food stores.

STORAGE: Once stored, the nuts may become soft. If they do, spread them out flat on a baking tray and bake in a slow (150°C/300°F/Gas 2) oven for 5–10 minutes.

Stir the tamari through the nuts, pepitas and sunflower seeds.

Spread the nut mixture evenly over two lightly greased baking trays.

Dry-roast the tamari-coated nuts in the oven for 20–25 minutes.

VEGETABLE CHIPS

Preparation time: 20 minutes
Total cooking time: 15 minutes
Serves 6–8

250 g (8 oz) orange sweet potato
250 g (8 oz) beetroot, peeled
250 g (8 oz) potato
oil, for deep-frying

1 Preheat the oven to moderate 180°C (350°F/Gas 4). Run a sharp vegetable peeler along the length of the sweet potato to create ribbons. Cut the beetroot into paper-thin slices with a sharp vegetable peeler or knife. Cut the potato into thin slices, using a mandolin slicer or knife with a crinkle-cut blade (see NOTE).

2 Fill a deep heavy-based saucepan one third full of oil and heat until a cube of bread dropped into the oil browns in 10 seconds. Cook the vegetables in batches for about 30 seconds, or until golden and crispy. You may need to turn them with tongs or a long-handled metal spoon. Drain on paper towels and season with salt.

3 Place all the vegetable chips on a baking tray and keep warm in the oven while cooking the remaining vegetables. Serve with drinks.

NUTRITION PER SERVE (8)
Protein 2 g; Fat 5 g; Carbohydrate 12 g;
Dietary Fibre 2 g; Cholesterol 0 mg;
413 kJ (99 cal)

NOTE: If you don't have a mandolin or crinkle-cut knife at home, simply use a sharp knife to cut fine slices. The cooking time for the chips will remain the same.

Use a sharp vegetable peeler to peel thin strips of sweet potato.

If you have a mandolin, use it for slicing the potatoes very finely.

Deep-fry the vegetables in batches until they are golden and crispy.

221

BAKED HERBED FETA

Preparation time: 10 minutes
Total cooking time: 15 minutes
Serves 6

300 g (10 oz) piece of feta cheese
1 tablespoon chopped fresh rosemary
1 tablespoon chopped fresh oregano
1 tablespoon chopped fresh thyme
2 tablespoons olive oil

1 Preheat the oven to moderate 180°C (350°F/Gas 4). Put the feta on a piece of foil about 30 cm (12 inches) square. Mix together the rosemary, oregano and thyme, and press onto the sides of the feta. Drizzle with the oil and season to taste with cracked black pepper. Gently fold the sides and ends of the foil over to make a parcel.

2 Place on a baking tray and bake for 10–15 minutes, or until the feta is soft.

Drain off any excess liquid before serving. Serve hot or cold, with bread or as part of a cheese platter or salad.

NUTRITION PER SERVE
Protein 9 g; Fat 20 g; Carbohydrate 0 g; Dietary Fibre 0 g; Cholesterol 35 mg; 820 kJ (195 cal)

NOTE: If the piece of feta is thick, it may need an extra 5 minutes in the oven to heat through.

Press the combined herbs onto the sides of the piece of feta.

Fold the foil firmly over the feta to make a secure parcel and then bake until the cheese is soft.

Using a sharp knife, finely chop the rosemary, oregano and thyme.

BLUE CHEESE AND PORT PATE

Preparation time: 10 minutes + refrigeration
Total cooking time: Nil
Serves 8

350 g (11 oz) cream cheese, at room temperature
60 g (2 oz) unsalted butter, softened
1/3 cup (80 ml/2³/4 fl oz) port
300 g (10 oz) blue cheese, at room temperature, mashed
1 tablespoon snipped fresh chives
45 g (1¹/2 oz) walnut halves

1 Using electric beaters, beat the cream cheese and butter until smooth, then stir in the port. Add the blue cheese and chives and stir until just combined. Season to taste.
2 Spoon the mixture into a serving bowl and smooth the surface. Cover the paté with plastic wrap and refrigerate until firm.
3 Arrange the walnuts over the top of the paté, pressing down lightly. Serve at room temperature with crusty bread, crackers and celery sticks.

NUTRITION PER SERVE
Protein 12 g; Fat 37 g; Carbohydrate 2.5 g;
Dietary Fibre 0.5 g; Cholesterol 100 mg;
1650 kJ (395 cal)

Stir the blue cheese and chives into the cream cheese and butter mixture.

Arrange the walnut halves over the surface, pressing down lightly.

TEMPURA VEGETABLES WITH WASABI MAYONNAISE

Preparation time: 20 minutes
Total cooking time: 20 minutes
Serves 4–6

WASABI MAYONNAISE
2 tablespoons mayonnaise
3 teaspoons wasabi paste
1/2 teaspoon grated lime rind

2 egg yolks
1 cup (250 ml/8 fl oz) chilled soda
    water
1/4 cup (30 g/1 oz) cornflour
110 g (31/2 oz) plain flour
1/4 cup (40 g/11/4 oz) sesame seeds,
    toasted
oil, for deep-frying
1 small (250 g/8 oz) eggplant, sliced
    5 mm (1/4 inch) thick
1 large onion, sliced 5 mm (1/4 inch)
    thick, with rings intact
300 g (10 oz) orange sweet potato,
    sliced 5 mm (1/4 inch) thick

1 To make the wasabi mayonnaise, mix together all the ingredients. Cover with plastic wrap and refrigerate until ready to use.
2 Place the egg yolks and soda water in a jug and mix lightly with a whisk. Sift the cornflour and flour into a bowl. Add the sesame seeds and a good sprinkling of salt and mix well. Pour the soda water and egg yolk mixture into the flour and stir lightly with chopsticks or a fork until just combined but still lumpy.
3 Fill a deep heavy-based saucepan or wok one-third full of oil and heat until a cube of bread dropped into the oil browns in 15 seconds. Using tongs, pick up two pieces of vegetable together—eggplant and onion or sweet potato and onion or eggplant and sweet potato—and dip into the batter. Deep-fry for 3–4 minutes, or until golden brown and cooked through. Drain on crumpled paper towels and season well with salt. Keep warm, but do not cover or the batter will go soggy. Serve as soon as possible with the wasabi mayonnaise.

NUTRITION PER SERVE (6)
Protein 6 g; Fat 14 g; Carbohydrate 30 g; Dietary Fibre 3.5 g; Cholesterol 62 mg; 1112 kJ (266 cal)

Gently stir the combined soda water and egg yolk into the flour mixture.

Pick up two different pieces of vegetable with tongs and dip into the batter.

Deep-fry the battered vegetables until they are golden brown and cooked through.

SALT AND PEPPER TOFU PUFFS

Preparation time: 15 minutes
Total cooking time: 10 minutes
Serves 4–6

2 x 190 g (6¹/₂ oz) packets fried tofu
    puffs
2 cups (250 g/8 oz) cornflour
2 tablespoons salt
1 tablespoon ground white pepper
2 teaspoons caster sugar
4 egg whites, lightly beaten
oil, for deep-frying (see NOTE)
¹/₂ cup (125 ml/4 fl oz) sweet chilli
    sauce
2 tablespoons lemon juice
lemon wedges, to serve

1 Cut the tofu puffs in half and pat dry
with paper towels.
2 Mix the cornflour, salt, pepper and
caster sugar in a large bowl.
3 Dip the tofu into the egg white in
batches, then toss in the cornflour
mixture, shaking off any excess.
4 Fill a deep heavy-based saucepan or
wok one-third full of oil and heat until
a cube of bread dropped into the oil
browns in 15 seconds. Cook the tofu
in batches for 1–2 minutes, or until
crisp. Drain well on paper towels.
5 Place the sweet chilli sauce and
lemon juice in a bowl and mix
together well. Serve immediately with
the tofu puffs and lemon wedges.

NUTRITION PER SERVE (6)
Protein 55 g; Fat 10 g; Carbohydrate 44 g;
Dietary Fibre 1 g; Cholesterol 0 mg;
1135 kJ (270 cal)

NOTE: It is best to use a good-quality
peanut oil to deep-fry the tofu puffs—
the flavour will be slightly nutty.

Dip the tofu puffs in the egg white, then in the
cornflour, shaking off any excess.

Deep-fry the tofu in batches until crisp, then
remove with a slotted spoon.

BEAN NACHOS

Preparation time: 20 minutes
Total cooking time: 10 minutes
Serves 4

4 large ripe tomatoes
2 ripe avocados, mashed
1 tablespoon lime juice
1 tablespoon sweet chilli sauce
1 tablespoon oil
2 small red onions, diced
1 small red chilli, chopped
2 teaspoons ground oregano
2 teaspoons ground cumin
1/4 teaspoon chilli powder
1 tablespoon tomato paste

1 cup (250 ml/8 fl oz) white wine
2 x 440 g (14 oz) cans red kidney
    beans, rinsed and drained
3 tablespoons chopped fresh
    coriander leaves
200 g (6¹/2 oz) packet corn chips
²/3 cup (90 g/3 oz) grated Cheddar
sour cream, to serve

1 Score a cross in the base of each
tomato. Put them in a bowl of boiling
water for 30 seconds, then plunge into
cold water and peel the skin away
from the cross. Cut in half and scoop
out the seeds with a teaspoon. Chop
the tomato flesh.
2 Mix together the avocado, lime juice
and sweet chilli sauce.

3 Heat the oil in a large frying pan.
Cook the onion, chilli, oregano, cumin
and chilli powder over medium heat
for 2 minutes. Add the tomato, tomato
paste and wine and cook for
5 minutes, or until the liquid reduces.
Add the beans and coriander.
4 Divide the corn chips into four
portions on heatproof plates. Top with
the bean mixture and sprinkle with
cheese. Flash under a hot grill until the
cheese melts. Serve with the avocado
mixture and sour cream.

NUTRITION PER SERVE
Protein 26 g; Fat 35 g; Carbohydrate 53 g;
Dietary Fibre 20 g; Cholesterol 20 mg;
2845 kJ (680 cal)

Scoop out the seeds of the tomatoes and roughly
chop the flesh.

Cook the onion, chilli, oregano and spices in a
large frying pan.

Cook the mixture until the liquid is reduced and
the tomato is soft.

FELAFEL WITH TOMATO SALSA

Preparation time: 40 minutes + 4 hours
 soaking + 30 minutes standing
Total cooking time: 20 minutes
Serves 8

2 cups (440 g/14 oz) dried chickpeas
1 small onion, finely chopped
2 cloves garlic, crushed
4 tablespoons chopped fresh flat-leaf
 parsley
2 tablespoons chopped fresh
 coriander leaves
2 teaspoons ground cumin
1/2 teaspoon baking powder
oil, for deep-frying

TOMATO SALSA
2 tomatoes
1/4 Lebanese cucumber, finely
 chopped
1/2 green capsicum, diced
2 tablespoons chopped fresh flat-leaf
 parsley
1 teaspoon sugar
2 teaspoons chilli sauce
1/2 teaspoon grated lemon rind
2 tablespoons lemon juice

1 Soak the chickpeas in 1 litre (32 fl oz) water for 4 hours or overnight. Drain. Place in a food processor and blend for 30 seconds, or until finely ground. Add the onion, garlic, parsley, coriander, cumin, baking powder and 1 tablespoon water, then process for 10 seconds to make a rough paste. Leave, covered, for 30 minutes.

2 To make the salsa, score a cross in the base of each tomato. Put them in a bowl of boiling water for 30 seconds, then plunge into cold water and peel the skin away from the cross. Finely chop, then place in a bowl with all the other ingredients and mix well.

3 Using your hands, shape heaped tablespoons of the felafel mixture into even-sized balls. If there is any excess liquid, squeeze it out. Fill a large heavy-based saucepan one-third full of oil and heat until a cube of bread dropped into the oil browns in 15 seconds.

4 Lower the felafel balls into the oil and cook in batches of five for 3–4 minutes, or until well browned all over. Remove the felafel with a slotted spoon and drain on paper towels. Serve hot or cold on a bed of the tomato salsa, with pitta bread.

NUTRITION PER SERVE
Protein 10.5 g; Fat 8 g; Carbohydrate 22.5 g;
Dietary Fibre 8 g; Cholesterol 0 mg;
855 kJ (204 cal)

Grind the drained chickpeas in a food processor until finely chopped.

Shape heaped tablespoons of the felafel mixture into even-sized balls.

Cook until well browned, then remove them with a slotted spoon and drain.

MEDITERRANEAN LAYERED COB

Preparation time: 45 minutes +
   30 minutes standing + overnight
   refrigeration
Total cooking time: 30 minutes
Serves 6

2 eggplants
500 g (1 lb) orange sweet potato
2 large red capsicums
4 zucchini, sliced lengthways
1/3 cup (80 ml/2³/4 fl oz) olive oil
23 cm (9 inch) round cob loaf
165 g (5¹/2 oz) pesto
200 g (6¹/2 oz) ricotta cheese
1/3 cup (30 g/1 oz) grated Parmesan

1 Slice the eggplants lengthways and
put in a colander. Sprinkle with salt
and leave for 30 minutes, then rinse
well and pat dry with paper towels.
2 Thinly slice the sweet potato.
Quarter the capsicums and remove the
seeds and membranes. Cook under a
hot grill, skin-side-up, until the skins
have blistered and blackened. Cool in
a plastic bag, then peel. Brush the
eggplant, sweet potato and zucchini
with oil and chargrill or grill in batches
until well browned.
3 Slice off the top of the loaf. Scoop
out the soft bread from inside, leaving
a thin shell. Brush the inside of the loaf
and top with the pesto. Layer the
zucchini and capsicum inside the loaf,
then spread with the combined ricotta
and Parmesan. Layer the sweet potato
and eggplant, lightly pressing down.
Replace the top of the loaf.
4 Cover the loaf with plastic wrap and
place on a baking tray. Put a tray on
top of the loaf and weigh down with
food cans. Refrigerate overnight.
5 Preheat the oven to very hot 250°C
(500°F/Gas 10). Remove the plastic
wrap, return the loaf to the baking tray
and bake for about 10 minutes, or until
crispy. Cut into wedges to serve.

NUTRITION PER SERVE
Protein 15 g; Fat 23 g; Carbohydrate 44 g;
Dietary Fibre 7 g; Cholesterol 22 mg;
1870 kJ (447 cal)

Quarter the capsicums, then remove the seeds
and membranes.

Chargrill the eggplant, sweet potato and zucchini
in batches until well browned.

Remove the soft bread from inside the loaf,
leaving a thin shell.

Layer the sweet potato and eggplant inside the
loaf over the other ingredients.

VEGETABLE FRITTATA WITH HUMMUS AND BLACK OLIVES

Preparation time: 35 minutes
Total cooking time: 40 minutes
Makes 30 pieces

2 large red capsicums
600 g (1¼ lb) orange sweet potato,
    cut into 1 cm (½ inch) slices
¼ cup (60 ml/2 fl oz) olive oil
2 leeks, finely sliced
2 cloves garlic, crushed
250 g (8 oz) zucchini, thinly sliced
500 g (1 lb) eggplant, cut into 1 cm
    (½ inch) slices
8 eggs, lightly beaten
2 tablespoons finely chopped fresh
    basil
1¼ cups (125 g/4 oz) grated
    Parmesan
200 g (6½ oz) hummus
black olives, pitted and halved, to
    garnish

1 Cut the capsicums into large pieces, removing the seeds and membrane. Place, skin-side-up, under a hot grill until the skin blackens and blisters. Cool in a plastic bag, then peel.
2 Cook the sweet potato in a saucepan of boiling water for 4–5 minutes, or until just tender. Drain.
3 Heat 1 tablespoon of the oil in a deep round 23 cm (9 inch) frying pan and stir the leek and garlic over medium heat for 1 minute, or until soft. Add the zucchini and cook for 2 minutes, then remove from the pan.
4 Heat the remaining oil in the same pan and cook the eggplant in batches for 2 minutes each side, or until golden. Line the base of the pan with half the eggplant and spread with the leek mixture. Cover with the roasted capsicum, then with the remaining eggplant and finally the sweet potato.
5 Put the eggs, basil, Parmesan and pepper in a jug, mix well and pour over the vegetables. Cook over low heat for 15 minutes, or until almost cooked. Place the pan under a hot grill for 2–3 minutes, or until golden and cooked. Cool before inverting onto a board. Trim the edges and cut into 30 squares. Top each square with a dollop of hummus and half an olive.

NUTRITION PER PIECE
Protein 4.5 g; Fat 6 g; Carbohydrate 5 g;
Dietary Fibre 2 g; Cholesterol 52 mg;
387 kJ (92 cal)

Lay the roasted capsicum pieces over the leek and zucchini mixture.

Pour the egg mixture over the vegetables so that they are covered.

Cook the frittata under a hot grill until it is golden brown on top.

CALIFORNIA ROLLS

Preparation time: 35 minutes +
   15 minutes standing
Total cooking time: 15 minutes
Makes 30

500 g (1 lb) short-grain white rice
¼ cup (60 ml/2 fl oz) rice vinegar
1 tablespoon caster sugar
5 nori sheets
1 large Lebanese cucumber, cut
   lengthways into long batons
1 avocado, thinly sliced
1 tablespoon black sesame seeds,
   toasted
30 g (1 oz) pickled ginger slices
½ cup (125 g/4 oz) mayonnaise
3 teaspoons wasabi paste
2 teaspoons soy sauce

1 Wash the rice under cold running water, tossing, until the water runs clear. Put the rice and 3 cups (750 ml/24 fl oz) water in a saucepan. Bring to the boil over low heat and cook for 5 minutes, or until tunnels form in the rice. Remove from the heat, cover and leave for 15 minutes.
2 Place the vinegar, sugar and 1 teaspoon salt in a small saucepan and stir over low heat until the sugar and salt dissolve.
3 Transfer the rice to a non-metallic bowl and use a wooden spoon to separate the grains. Make a slight well in the centre, slowly stir in the vinegar dressing, then cool a little.
4 Lay a nori sheet, shiny-side-down, on a bamboo mat or flat surface and spread out one-fifth of the rice, leaving a narrow clear border at one end. Arrange one-fifth of the cucumber, avocado, sesame seeds and ginger lengthways over the rice, keeping away from the border. Spread on some of the combined mayonnaise, wasabi and soy sauce and roll to cover the filling. Continue rolling tightly to join the edge, then hold in place for a few seconds. Trim the ends and cut into slices. Serve with wasabi mayonnaise.

NUTRITION PER PIECE
Protein 1.5 g; Fat 3 g; Carbohydrate 15 g;
Dietary Fibre 1 g; Cholesterol 1.5 mg;
380 kJ (90 cal)

Cook the rice until tunnels appear, then cover and leave for 15 minutes.

Slowly pour the vinegar dressing into the rice and stir it through.

Spread the wasabi mayonnaise mixture over the vegetables and start rolling.

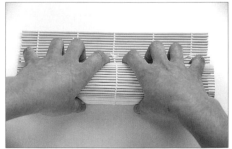
Roll the mat tightly to join the edge, then hold in place for a few seconds.

VIETNAMESE SPRING ROLLS

Preparation time: 30 minutes +
   10 minutes standing
Total cooking time: 10 minutes
Serves 4

75 g (2¹/₂ oz) dried rice vermicelli
200 g (6¹/₂ oz) firm tofu
1 teaspoon sesame oil
1 tablespoon peanut oil
1 packet 15 cm (6 inch) square rice-
   paper wrappers
¹/₂ small Lebanese cucumber, cut into
   julienne strips
¹/₂ carrot, cut into julienne strips

¹/₂ cup (10 g/¹/₄ oz) fresh mint
¹/₃ cup (50 g/1³/₄ oz) roasted salted
   cashews, roughly chopped
3 tablespoons hoisin sauce
2 tablespoons kecap manis
1 tablespoon lime juice

1 Place the vermicelli in a bowl, cover with boiling water and leave for 10 minutes. Drain well.
2 Pat the tofu dry and cut into four slices. Heat the oils in a large frying pan and cook the tofu over medium heat for 3 minutes each side, or until golden. Drain on paper towels. Cut each slice into four widthways.
3 Fill a bowl with warm water. Dip one wrapper at a time into the water for about 15 seconds, or until pliable.
4 Place the wrapper on a work surface, top with some vermicelli, tofu, cucumber, carrot, mint and cashews. Roll tightly, folding in the sides and put on a plate, seam-side-down. Cover with a damp cloth and repeat.
5 To make the dipping sauce, place the hoisin sauce, kecap manis and lime juice in a bowl and mix. Serve immediately with the spring rolls.

NUTRITION PER SERVE
Protein 6 g; Fat 12 g; Carbohydrate 16 g;
Dietary Fibre 2 g; Cholesterol 0 mg;
580 kJ (136 cal)

Cook the tofu over medium heat, turning once, until golden brown on both sides.

Dip one wrapper at a time into the water until soft and pliable.

Fold the sides of the wrappers in and roll up tightly, enclosing the filling.

231

MUSHROOM PATE WITH TOASTS

Preparation time: 15 minutes +
    5 hours refrigeration +
    10 minutes cooling
Total cooking time: 20 minutes
Makes 24

60 g (2 oz) butter
1 small onion, chopped
3 cloves garlic, crushed
375 g (12 oz) button mushrooms,
    quartered
1 cup (125 g/4 oz) slivered almonds,
    toasted
2 tablespoons cream
2 tablespoons finely chopped fresh
    thyme
3 tablespoons finely chopped fresh
    flat-leaf parsley
6 thick slices wholegrain or wholemeal
    bread

1 Heat the butter in a large frying pan. Cook the onion and garlic over medium heat for 2 minutes, or until soft. Increase the heat, add the mushrooms and cook for 5 minutes, or until the mushrooms are soft and most of the liquid has evaporated. Leave to cool for 10 minutes.

2 Roughly chop the almonds in a food processor. Add the mushroom mixture and process until smooth. With the motor running, gradually pour in the cream. Stir in the herbs and season with salt and cracked black pepper. Spoon into two 1 cup (250 ml/ 8 fl oz) ramekins and smooth the surface. Cover and refrigerate for 4–5 hours to let the flavours develop.

3 To make the toasts, preheat the oven to moderate 180°C (350°F/Gas 4). Toast one side of the bread under a hot grill until golden. Remove the crusts and cut each slice into four triangles. Place on a large oven tray in a single layer, toasted-side-down, and cook for 5–10 minutes, or until crisp. Serve immediately with the paté.

NUTRITION PER TOAST WITH PATE
Protein 2.5 g; Fat 5.5 g; Carbohydrate 3.5 g; Dietary Fibre 1.5 g; Cholesterol 7.5 mg; 310 kJ (75 cal)

Cook the onion, garlic and mushrooms until the mushrooms are soft.

Blend the almonds and mushroom mixture in a food processor until smooth.

Spoon the paté into the ramekins and smooth the surface.

BEETROOT HUMMUS

Preparation time: 15 minutes
Total cooking time: 40 minutes
Serves 8

500 g (1 lb) beetroot, trimmed
4 tablespoons olive oil
1 large onion, chopped
1 tablespoon ground cumin
400 g (13 oz) can chickpeas, drained
1 tablespoon tahini
1/3 cup (90 g/3 oz) plain yoghurt
3 cloves garlic, crushed
1/4 cup (60 ml/2 fl oz) lemon juice
1/2 cup (125 ml/4 fl oz) vegetable
    stock

1 Scrub the beetroot well. Bring a large saucepan of water to the boil over high heat and cook the beetroot for 35–40 minutes, or until soft and cooked through. Drain and cool slightly before peeling.
2 Meanwhile, heat 1 tablespoon of the oil in a frying pan over medium heat and cook the onion for 2–3 minutes, or until soft. Add the cumin and cook for a further 1 minute, or until fragrant.
3 Chop the beetroot and place in a food processor or blender with the onion mixture, chickpeas, tahini, yoghurt, garlic, lemon juice and stock and process until smooth. With the motor running, add the remaining oil

in a thin steady stream. Process until the mixture is thoroughly combined. Serve with Lebanese or Turkish bread.

NUTRITION PER SERVE
Protein 5.5 g; Fat 13 g; Carbohydrate 13 g; Dietary Fibre 5 g; Cholesterol 1.5 mg; 792 kJ (190 cal)

NOTE: Beetroot hummus can be a great accompaniment to a main meal or is delicious as part of a meze platter with bruschetta or crusty bread. Its vivid colour sparks up any table.

VARIATION: You can use 500 g (1 lb) of any vegetable to make the hummus. Try carrot or pumpkin.

Cook the beetroot until soft, then drain and cool slightly before peeling off the skins.

Cook the onion until soft, then add the cumin and cook until fragrant.

Put all the hummus ingredients in a food processor and blend until smooth.

233

ONION BHAJIS WITH SPICY TOMATO SAUCE

Preparation time: 30 minutes
Total cooking time: 35 minutes
Makes about 25

SPICY TOMATO SAUCE
2–3 red chillies, chopped
1 red capsicum, diced
425 g (14 oz) can chopped tomatoes
2 cloves garlic, finely chopped
2 tablespoons soft brown sugar
1¹/₂ tablespoons cider vinegar

1 cup (125 g/4 oz) plain flour
2 teaspoons baking powder
¹/₂ teaspoon chilli powder
¹/₂ teaspoon ground turmeric
1 teaspoon ground cumin
2 eggs, beaten
1 cup (60 g/2 oz) chopped fresh
    coriander leaves
4 onions, very thinly sliced
oil, for deep-frying

1 To make the sauce, combine all the ingredients with 3 tablespoons water in a saucepan. Bring to the boil, then reduce the heat and simmer for 20 minutes, or until the mixture thickens. Remove from the heat.
2 To make the bhajis, sift the flour, baking powder, spices and 1 teaspoon salt into a bowl and make a well in the centre. Gradually add the combined egg and 3 tablespoons water, whisking to make a smooth batter. Stir in the coriander and onion.
3 Fill a deep heavy-based saucepan one-third full of oil and heat until a cube of bread dropped into the oil browns in 15 seconds. Drop dessertspoons of the mixture into the oil and cook in batches for 90 seconds each side, or until golden. Drain on paper towels. Serve with the spicy tomato sauce.

NUTRITION PER BHAJI
Protein 1.5 g; Fat 2 g; Carbohydrate 7 g;
Dietary Fibre 1 g; Cholesterol 14 mg;
218 kJ (52 cal)

Peel the four onions and use a sharp knife to slice them very thinly.

Simmer the spicy tomato sauce for 20 minutes, or until it thickens.

Whisk together a smooth batter, then add the sliced onion and coriander and stir to coat.

Drop spoonfuls of the onion batter into the oil and cook in batches until golden.

EGGPLANT AND SPINACH TERRINE

Preparation time: 1 hour + overnight refrigeration
Total cooking time: 55 minutes
Serves 6

3 large red capsicums
1 large potato, halved
40 g (1¼ oz) butter
2 cloves garlic, crushed
800 g (1 lb 10 oz) English spinach leaves, shredded
¼ cup (60 ml/2 fl oz) cream
1 egg yolk
⅓ cup (80 ml/2¾ fl oz) olive oil
2 eggplants, cut into 5 mm (¼ inch) slices lengthways
1 cup (30 g/1 oz) fresh basil
350 g (11 oz) ricotta cheese
2 cloves garlic, crushed, extra

1 Cut the capsicums into large pieces, removing the seeds and membranes. Cook, skin-side-up, under a hot grill until the skin blisters. Cool, then peel.
2 Preheat the oven to moderate 180°C (350°F/Gas 4). Grease a 1.5 litre (48 fl oz) terrine and line with baking paper. Bring a saucepan of salted water to the boil and cook the potato for 10 minutes. Drain and cool. Cut into 5 mm (¼ inch) slices.
3 Melt the butter in a large saucepan and cook the garlic for 30 seconds. Add the spinach and toss. Steam, covered, over low heat for 2–3 minutes, or until wilted. Cool slightly and place in a food processor or blender and process until smooth. Squeeze out any excess liquid, put in a bowl and stir in the cream and egg.
4 Heat a chargrill plate over high heat and brush with some of the oil. Cook the eggplant for 2–3 minutes each side, or until golden, brushing with the remaining oil while cooking.
5 To assemble, arrange one third of the eggplant neatly in the base of the terrine, cutting to fit. Top with a layer of half the capsicum, spinach mixture, basil, all the potato, and all the combined ricotta and garlic. Repeat with the remaining ingredients, finishing with eggplant. Oil a piece of foil and cover the terrine, sealing well.

Place in a baking dish and half-fill with water. Bake for 25–30 minutes. Remove from the oven, put a piece of cardboard on top and weigh the terrine down with weights or small food cans. Refrigerate overnight, then turn out and cut into slices.

NUTRITION PER SERVE
Protein 12 g; Fat 30 g; Carbohydrate 8 g; Dietary Fibre 5 g; Cholesterol 88 mg; 1457 kJ (348 cal)

Grill the capsicum pieces until the skin blackens, cool in a plastic bag, then peel.

Blend the spinach mixture in a food processor until smooth.

Spread a layer of the spinach mixture over the second layer of capsicum.

235

GRISSINI

Preparation time: 30 minutes +
  1 hour 10 minutes standing
Total cooking time: 20 minutes
Makes 24

7 g (¹/₄ oz) sachet dried yeast
1 teaspoon sugar
4 cups (500 g/1 lb) plain flour
¹/₄ cup (60 ml/2 fl oz) olive oil
¹/₄ cup (15 g/¹/₂ oz) chopped basil
4 cloves garlic, crushed
50 g (1³/₄ oz) Parmesan, grated
2 teaspoons sea salt flakes
2 tablespoons grated Parmesan, extra

1 Put the yeast, sugar and 1¹/₄ cups (315 ml/10 fl oz) warm water in a small bowl and leave in a warm place for about 5–10 minutes, or until frothy. Sift the flour and 1 teaspoon salt into a bowl and stir in the yeast and oil. Add more water if the dough is dry.
2 Gather the dough into a ball and turn out onto a lightly floured surface. Knead for 10 minutes, or until soft and elastic. Divide into two portions and flatten into rectangles. Put the basil and garlic on one portion and the Parmesan on the other. Fold the dough to enclose the fillings, then knead for a few minutes to incorporate evenly.
3 Place the doughs into two lightly oiled bowls and cover with plastic wrap. Leave in a warm place for about 1 hour, or until doubled in volume. Preheat the oven to very hot 230°C (450°F/Gas 8) and lightly grease two large baking trays.
4 Punch down the doughs and knead each again for 1 minute. Divide each piece of dough into 12 portions, and roll each portion into a stick 30 cm (12 inches) long. Place on the baking trays and brush with water. Sprinkle the basil and garlic dough with the sea salt, and the cheese dough with the extra Parmesan. Bake for 15 minutes, or until crisp and golden brown. These can be kept in an airtight container for up to a week.

NUTRITION PER GRISSINI
Protein 3.5 g; Fat 3.5 g; Carbohydrate 16 g;
Dietary Fibre 1 g; Cholesterol 3 mg;
457 kJ (109 cal)

Stir the frothy yeast and oil into the flour and salt until well combined.

Flatten one portion of dough into a rectangle and put the basil and garlic on top.

Punch down the dough with your fist to expel the air and then knead for a minute.

Divide the dough into 12 portions and roll each one into a long stick.

MARINATED CHILLI MUSHROOMS

Preparation time: 20 minutes + overnight refrigeration
Total cooking time: Nil
Serves 8 (as part of an antipasto platter, see HINT)

750 g (1 1/2 lb) button mushrooms
2 cups (500 ml/16 fl oz) light olive oil
2 tablespoons lemon juice
1 clove garlic, finely chopped
1/4 teaspoon caster sugar
1 red chilli, finely chopped
1 green chilli, finely chopped
1 tablespoon chopped fresh coriander
1 tablespoon chopped fresh flat-leaf parsley

1 Wipe the mushrooms clean with a damp paper towel and put in a bowl.
2 Mix together the oil, lemon juice, garlic, sugar and chilli. Pour over the mushrooms and mix well. Cover with plastic wrap and marinate in the refrigerator overnight.
3 Just before serving, add the herbs, season and mix well.

NUTRITION PER SERVE
Protein 3.5 g; Fat 1.5 g; Carbohydrate 2 g; Dietary Fibre 2.5 g; Cholesterol 0 mg; 150 kJ (35 cal)

NOTE: The coriander and parsley are added just before serving so that they keep their colour. If you prefer a stronger flavour, add them before marinating.

HINT: Serve as part of an antipasto platter, with a selection of sun-dried vegetables, marinated artichokes, caperberries and toasted bruschetta.

Wipe the mushrooms with a damp paper towel to remove any dirt.

Pour the combined oil, lemon juice, garlic, sugar and chilli over the mushrooms.

Chop the coriander and parsley and add to the mushrooms just before serving.

Marinated Olives

Marinated olives are delicious on their own or as part of an antipasto platter, and will generally keep in the fridge for up to 6 months. To successfully store the olives, it is important to sterilise the storage jar first by rinsing it with boiling water and putting it in a warm oven to dry (don't use a tea towel).

CITRUS HERBED OLIVES

Combine the julienned zest and juice of 1 orange and 1 lemon in a wide-necked, 750 ml (24 fl oz) sterilised jar. Add 1 tablespoon fresh thyme leaves, 2 tablespoons fresh oregano leaves, 1 crushed clove garlic and 1 tablespoon extra virgin olive oil. Seal and shake. Add 2 cups (370 g/ 12 oz) rinsed Kalamata olives and turn the jar to coat the olives, then add more oil to fully cover the olives. Marinate for 1–2 weeks in the refrigerator. Store in the refrigerator but bring back to room temperature before serving.

LEMON AND CHILLI GREEN OLIVES

Place 2 teaspoons chopped red chilli, the julienned zest and juice of 1 lemon, 2 teaspoons sugar, 1 crushed clove garlic and 2 tablespoons extra virgin olive oil in a wide-necked, 750 ml (24 fl oz) sterilised jar. Seal and shake well to combine the ingredients. Add 2 cups (450 g/14 oz) rinsed large green olives and turn the jar to coat the olives, adding more oil to fully cover. Seal and marinate in the refrigerator for 1–2 weeks. Store in the refrigerator but serve at room temperature.

DILL AND LEMON OLIVES

Finely slice half a lemon and cut the slices into wedges. Rinse and drain 500 g (1 lb) Riviera or Ligurian olives. Layer the olives in a wide-necked, 750 ml (24 fl oz) sterilised jar with 3–4 sprigs fresh dill, 1 teaspoon fennel seeds, 3 finely sliced cloves garlic and the lemon wedges. Pour in the juice of half a lemon and 1 3/4 cups (440 ml/ 14 fl oz) oil, or enough to cover the olives. Seal and marinate in the refrigerator for 1–2 weeks before using. Store in the refrigerator. Return to room temperature before serving.

SUN-DRIED TOMATO OLIVES

Rinse and drain 500 g (1 lb) black olives. Cut two slits into each olive. Layer in a wide-necked, 750 ml (24 fl oz) sterilised jar with 100 g (3½ oz) drained and chopped sun-dried tomatoes in oil (reserve the oil), 2 crushed cloves garlic, 2 bay leaves and 3 teaspoons fresh thyme leaves. Add 1 tablespoon red wine vinegar and 1 cup (250 ml/8 fl oz) oil (use the reserved sun-dried tomato oil) or enough to cover the olives. Shake well, seal and leave to marinate in the refrigerator for 1–2 weeks. Store in the refrigerator and return to room temperature before serving.

OLIVES WITH HERBS DE PROVENCE

Rinse and drain 500 g (1 lb) Niçoise or Ligurian olives. Put 1 crushed clove garlic, 2 teaspoons chopped fresh basil, 1 teaspoon each chopped fresh thyme, rosemary, marjoram, oregano and mint, 1 teaspoon fennel seeds, 2 tablespoons lemon juice and ½ cup (125 ml/4 fl oz) olive oil in a bowl and mix together. Put the olives and marinade in a wide-necked, 750 ml (24 fl oz) sterilised jar, adding extra olive oil to cover the olives. Seal and shake. Marinate in the refrigerator for 1–2 weeks. Store in the refrigerator but serve at room temperature.

HONEY CITRUS OLIVES

Mix together the zest of 1 lemon, lime and orange, 2 tablespoons lime juice, 4 tablespoons lemon juice, 1 tablespoon orange juice, 1 tablespoon honey, 2 teaspoons wholegrain mustard, ½ cup (125 ml/4 fl oz) extra virgin olive oil, 2 thinly sliced cloves garlic, ¼ teaspoon dried oregano or 1 tablespoon chopped fresh oregano leaves and 6 thin slices of lemon and lime. Add 1½ cups (265 g/8½ oz) drained unpitted black olives, 1½ cups (265 g/8½ oz) drained unpitted green olives, 2 tablespoons chopped fresh parsley, salt and pepper. Place in a wide-necked, 750 ml (24 fl oz) sterilised jar and seal. Shake, then marinate in the refrigerator for 1–2 weeks. Store in the refrigerator but serve at room temperature.

LEMON OLIVES WITH VERMOUTH

Rinse and drain 340 g (11 oz) whole green or stuffed olives. Layer in a wide-necked, 750 ml (24 fl oz) sterilised jar with ½ cup (125 ml/4 fl oz) dry vermouth, 2 tablespoons lemon juice, 1 tablespoon shredded lemon rind and ⅓ cup (80 ml/2¾ fl oz) extra virgin olive oil. Shake well, seal and marinate in the refrigerator overnight. Store in the refrigerator but return to room temperature before serving.

From left to right: Citrus herbed olives; Lemon and chilli green olives; Sun-dried tomato olives; Dill and lemon olives; Olives with herbs de Provence; Honey citrus olives; Lemon olives with vermouth.

DOLMADES

Preparation time: 1 hour +
  1 hour soaking
Total cooking time: 1 hour
Makes 42

275 g (9 oz) vine leaves in brine
3/4 cup (185 ml/6 fl oz) olive oil
2 onions, finely chopped
3/4 cup (165 g/51/2 oz) short-grain rice
6 spring onions, finely chopped
1/3 cup (20 g/3/4 oz) chopped fresh dill
1 tablespoon chopped fresh mint
1 tablespoon lemon juice

1 Rinse the vine leaves in cold water, soak in warm water for 1 hour and then drain.
2 Heat 1/2 cup (125 ml/4 fl oz) oil in a heavy-based pan. Add the onion and cook over low heat for 5 minutes. Remove from the heat, cover and leave for 5 minutes. Mix in the rice, spring onion, herbs and lemon juice.
3 Lay out a vine leaf, vein-side-up, on a plate. Place 3 teaspoons of filling on the centre. Fold the sides over the mixture, then roll up towards the tip of the leaf. Repeat to make 42 dolmades.
4 Use five or six vine leaves to line the base of a large heavy-based pan. Pack the dolmades in the lined pan in two layers and drizzle with the remaining oil. Put a plate on top of the dolmades, to keep them in place, and cover with 11/2 cups (375 ml/12 fl oz) water. Bring to the boil, reduce the heat and simmer, covered, for 45 minutes. Remove the plate, lift out the dolmades with a slotted spoon and drizzle with lemon juice. Serve either warm or cold.

NUTRITION PER DOLMADE
Protein 2 g; Fat 4.5 g; Carbohydrate 3 g;
Dietary Fibre 0 g; Cholesterol 0 mg;
220 kJ (50 cal)

Put the vine leaves in a colander and rinse thoroughly under cold water.

Fold the sides of the vine leaf over the filling and roll up towards the tip of the leaf.

Cover the dolmades with a plate to keep them in place, then pour in the water.

LABNEH (YOGHURT CHEESE)

Preparation time: 20 minutes +
  4 days refrigeration
Total cooking time: Nil
Makes 24

1 kg (2 lb) thick Greek yoghurt
1¹/₂ cups (375 ml/12 fl oz) extra virgin
  olive oil
2 cloves garlic, chopped
2 tablespoons fresh
  rosemary leaves
6–8 sprigs fresh thyme

1 Put the yoghurt in a bowl and season with 2 teaspoons salt and 1 teaspoon ground pepper. Line a bowl with a piece of muslin folded in half to make a 45 cm (18 inch) square. Spoon the yoghurt mixture into the centre. Bring the corners together and, using a long piece of kitchen string, tie as closely as possible to the yoghurt, leaving a loop at the end.

2 Thread the loop through the handle of a wooden spoon and hang the yoghurt over a bowl to drain in the fridge for 3 days.

3 Mix the oil, garlic, rosemary and thyme together. Untie the muslin and

roll tablespoons of drained yoghurt into balls (they won't be completely smooth). Make sure your hands are cool, and wash them often. Rinse a large wide-necked jar with boiling water and dry in a warm oven. Put the labneh in the jar and cover with the herbed olive oil. Cover and refrigerate for 24 hours. Return to room temperature and serve with bread. Store in the fridge for up to 1 week.

NUTRITION PER PIECE
Protein 2 g; Fat 6.5 g; Carbohydrate 2 g;
Dietary Fibre 0 g; Cholesterol 6.5 mg;
312 kJ (75 cal)

Spoon the seasoned yoghurt into the centre of the muslin square.

Thread the loop through the handle of a wooden spoon to hang the yoghurt.

With cool hands, roll the drained yoghurt into balls. Wash your hands after making a few.

241

ROASTED BALSAMIC ONIONS

Preparation time: 15 minutes +
  overnight refrigeration
Total cooking time: 1 hour 30 minutes
Serves 8 (as part of an antipasto
  platter)

1 kg (2 lb) pickling onions, unpeeled
  (see NOTE)
3/4 cup (185 ml/6 fl oz) balsamic
  vinegar
2 tablespoons soft brown sugar
3/4 cup (185 ml/6 fl oz) olive oil

1 Preheat the oven to warm 160°C
(315°F/Gas 2–3). Place the unpeeled
onions in a baking dish and roast for
1 1/2 hours. Leave until cool enough to
handle. Trim the stems from the
onions and peel away the skin (the
outer part of the root should come
away but the onions will remain
intact). Rinse a 1 litre (32 fl oz) wide-
necked jar with boiling water and dry
in a warm oven (do not dry with a tea
towel). Add the onions to the jar.
2 Put the vinegar and sugar in a small
screw-top jar and stir to dissolve the
sugar. Add the oil, seal the jar and
shake vigorously—the mixture will be
paler and may separate on standing.
3 Pour the vinegar mixture over the
onions, seal, and turn upside down
to coat. Marinate overnight in the
fridge, turning occasionally. Return to
room temperature and shake to
combine the dressing before serving.

NUTRITION PER SERVE
Protein 0.5 g; Fat 7.5 g; Carbohydrate 20 g;
Dietary Fibre 2 g; Cholesterol 0 mg;
677 kJ (162 cal)

NOTE: Pickling onions are very small
and usually packed in 1 kg (2 lb) bags.
The ideal size is around 35 g (1 1/4 oz)
each. The sizes in the bag will
probably range from 20 g (3/4 oz) up
to 40 g (1 1/4 oz). The cooking time
given is suitable for this range and
there is no need to cook the larger
ones for any longer. The marinating
time given is a minimum—the onions
may be marinated for up to 3 days in
the refrigerator. The marinade may
separate after a few hours, which is
fine—simply stir occasionally.

When cool, trim the stems from the onions and
peel away the skin.

Add the oil to the vinegar and sugar and shake
vigorously to combine.

Pour the vinegar mixture over the onions, turning
the jar to coat thoroughly.

CHARGRILLED VEGETABLE TERRINE

Preparation time: 30 minutes +
   overnight refrigeration
Total cooking time: Nil
Serves 8

350 g (11 oz) ricotta cheese
2 cloves garlic, crushed
8 large slices chargrilled eggplant,
   drained (see NOTE)
10 slices chargrilled red capsicum,
   drained (see NOTE)
8 slices chargrilled zucchini, drained
   (see NOTE)
45 g (1¹/2 oz) rocket leaves
3 marinated artichokes, drained and
   sliced (page 247)
85 g (3 oz) semi-dried tomatoes,
   drained and chopped (page 245)
100 g (3¹/2 oz) marinated mushrooms,
   drained and halved (page 237)

1 Beat together the ricotta and garlic until smooth. Season well and set aside. Line a 23¹/2 x 13 x 6¹/2 cm (9 x 5 x 2¹/2 inch) loaf tin with plastic wrap, leaving a generous amount hanging over the sides.
2 Line the base of the tin with half the eggplant, cutting and fitting to cover the base. Top with a layer of half the capsicum, then all the zucchini slices. Spread evenly with the ricotta mixture and press down firmly. Place the rocket leaves on top of the ricotta. Arrange the artichoke, tomato and mushrooms in three rows lengthways on top of the ricotta.
3 Top with another layer of capsicum and finish with the eggplant. Cover securely with the overhanging plastic wrap. Put a piece of cardboard on top and weigh it down with weights or

small food cans. Refrigerate overnight.
4 To serve, peel back the plastic wrap and turn the terrine out onto a plate. Remove the plastic wrap and cut into thick slices to serve.

NUTRITION PER SERVE
Protein 6 g; Fat 5 g; Carbohydrate 3 g;
Dietary Fibre 2 g; Cholesterol 20 mg;
350 kJ (85 cal)

NOTE: You will find chargrilled vegetables at your local delicatessen. Alternatively, make your own by slicing the vegetables, brushing with oil and cooking on a barbecue or chargrill pan until lightly browned. Remove the skin from the capsicum first, by blackening it under a hot grill, then leaving in a plastic bag until the skin will peel away easily.

Put the ricotta and crushed garlic in a bowl and beat until smooth.

Arrange the mushrooms, tomato and artichoke in three rows over the rocket.

Cover the terrine with cardboard and weigh down with small food cans.

ASHED HERBED GOAT'S CHEESE

Preparation time: 15 minutes +
 overnight refrigeration
Total cooking time: 20 minutes
Serves 8

4 sprigs fresh sage
4 sprigs fresh rosemary
4 sprigs fresh thyme

4 sprigs fresh marjoram
4 x 100 g (3½ oz) goat's cheese
 rounds or logs

1 Place the sage, rosemary, thyme and marjoram in a small pan. Cover and dry-cook over medium heat for 20 minutes without removing the lid. Remove from the heat and leave, covered, for 5 minutes. The herbs will be blackened. Transfer to a food processor and finely chop.

2 Pat the goat's cheese dry with paper towels. Spread the ash out on a large plate. Roll the goat's cheese in the ashed herbs to coat evenly. Cover with plastic wrap and refrigerate overnight. Serve as part of a cheese or antipasto platter, or toss through a salad.

NUTRITION PER SERVE
Protein 10 g; Fat 16 g; Carbohydrate 0 g;
Dietary Fibre 0 g; Cholesterol 50 mg;
775 kJ (185 cal)

After the herbs have been dry-cooked they will be blackened.

Put the goat's cheese on paper towels and pat dry so that the ash will stick to it.

Roll the goat's cheeses in the blackened herbs before refrigerating overnight.

SEMI-DRIED TOMATOES

Preparation time: 10 minutes +
    24 hours refrigeration
Total cooking time: 2 hours 30 minutes
Fills a 500 ml (16 fl oz) jar

16 Roma (egg or plum) tomatoes
3 tablespoons fresh thyme,
    chopped
2 tablespoons olive oil

1 Preheat the oven to warm 160°C (315°F/Gas 2–3). Cut the tomatoes into quarters lengthways and lay them skin-side-down on a wire rack in a baking tray.
2 Sprinkle with 1 teaspoon of salt, 1 teaspoon of cracked black pepper and the thyme and cook in the oven for 2^1/$_2$ hours. Check occasionally to make sure the tomatoes don't burn.
3 Toss the tomatoes in the olive oil and leave to cool before packing into

sterilised jars and sealing. Store in the refrigerator for 24 hours before using. Semi-dried tomatoes should be eaten within 3–4 days.

It is not possible to make a nutritional analysis for this recipe.

NOTE: To sterilise a storage jar, rinse with boiling water then place in a warm oven until completely dry. Do not dry with a tea towel.

Cut the tomatoes into quarters and lay them skin-side-down on a wire rack.

Season the tomatoes with salt, cracked pepper and fresh thyme.

Cover the tomatoes with olive oil and toss until well coated.

245

MARINATED FETA

Preparation time: 10 minutes +
  1 week refrigeration
Total cooking time: Nil
Serves 6 (as part of an antipasto
  platter)

350 g (11 oz) feta cheese
1 tablespoon dried oregano
1 teaspoon coriander seeds
1 tablespoon cracked black pepper
125 g (4 oz) sun-dried tomatoes in oil
4 small fresh red chillies
3–4 sprigs fresh rosemary
olive oil

1 Pat the feta dry with paper towels, and cut into 2 cm (3/4 inch) cubes. Place in a bowl and sprinkle the oregano, coriander seeds and pepper over the cheese.
2 Drain the sun-dried tomatoes over a bowl so that you catch all of the oil. Arrange the feta, chillies, rosemary and sun-dried tomatoes in a sterilised 3-cup (750 ml/24 fl oz) wide-necked jar with a clip-top lid. Cover with the reserved sun-dried tomato oil—you should have about 3 tablespoons— and top up with olive oil. Seal and refrigerate for 1 week (it will keep for 1–2 months in the fridge). Serve at room temperature.

NUTRITION PER SERVE
Protein 10 g; Fat 15 g; Carbohydrate 1 g;
Dietary Fibre 0.5 g; Cholesterol 40 mg;
698 kJ (167 cal)

NOTE: To sterilise a storage jar, rinse with boiling water then place in a warm oven until completely dry.

Sprinkle the oregano, coriander seeds and pepper over the cubes of feta.

Drain the sun-dried tomatoes over a small bowl to catch all the oil.

Arrange the ingredients in the jar and pour in the sun-dried tomato oil. Top up with olive oil.

GARLIC AND HERB MARINATED ARTICHOKES

Preparation time: 20 minutes +
  overnight refrigeration
Total cooking time: Nil
Serves 8 (as part of an antipasto
  platter)

2 cloves garlic, chopped
1/2 cup (125 ml/4 fl oz) olive oil
2 tablespoons finely chopped
  fresh dill

3 tablespoons finely chopped fresh
  parsley
2 tablespoons finely chopped fresh
  basil
2 tablespoons lemon juice
2 x 400 g (13 oz) canned artichokes
1/4 cup (40 g/1 1/4 oz) finely diced
  red capsicum

1 To make the marinade, whisk together the garlic, oil, herbs and lemon juice in a bowl. Season with salt and cracked black pepper.
2 Drain the artichokes and add to the bowl with the capsicum. Mix well to coat. Cover and marinate in the refrigerator overnight. Serve as part of an antipasto platter or use in salads.

NUTRITION PER SERVE
Protein 1 g; Fat 7.5 g; Carbohydrate 1 g;
Dietary Fibre 1.5 g; Cholesterol 0 mg;
320 kJ (75 cal)

STORAGE TIME: The artichokes will keep in an airtight container in the refrigerator for up to 1 week.

Finely chop the fresh herbs. You will need dill, parsley and basil.

Combine the garlic, oil, herbs and lemon juice to make the marinade.

Drain the artichokes well before adding to the marinade. Marinate in the fridge overnight.

247

MARINATED BOCCONCINI

Preparation time: 15 minutes +
  3 days refrigeration
Total cooking time: 5 minutes
Serves 8

400 g (13 oz) bocconcini, sliced
150 g (5 oz) sun-dried capsicums in oil
1 cup (50 g/1¾ oz) small fresh basil
  leaves
1¼ cups (315 ml/10 fl oz) extra virgin
  olive oil
¼ cup (60 ml/2 fl oz) lemon juice

1 Dry the bocconcini with paper towels. Drain the capsicums, retaining the oil in a pan, and cut into strips. Gently crush the basil leaves. Pour 1 cup (250 ml/8 fl oz) of the olive oil into the pan with the capsicum oil and gently heat for 5 minutes. Stir the lemon juice into the warmed oil.
2 Put a layer of bocconcini slices in a wide-necked 3-cup (750 ml/24 fl oz) sterilised clip-top jar. Sprinkle with cracked pepper. Put a thin layer of basil leaves on top of the cheese and cover with some of the capsicum. Continue layering, then cover with the warmed oil, using the remaining olive oil if necessary. Seal the jar and marinate in the refrigerator for 3 days. Return to room temperature and drain before serving.

NUTRITION PER SERVE
Protein 13 g; Fat 25 g; Carbohydrate 1 g;
Dietary Fibre 0 g; Cholesterol 30 mg;
1194 kJ (285 cal)

NOTE: To sterilise a storage jar, rinse with boiling water then place in a warm oven until completely dry. Don't dry with a tea towel.

Drain the oil from the sun-dried capsicums into a small pan.

Gently crush the basil leaves with a knife to release more of the flavour.

Layer the bocconcini, basil and capsicum and then cover with the warmed oil.

SPICED PEARS

Preparation time: 10 minutes
Total cooking time: 1 hour
Serves 8

1/3 cup (80 ml/2³/₄ fl oz)
   kecap manis (see NOTE)
3 tablespoons soy sauce
2 teaspoons sesame oil
1 teaspoon five-spice powder
6 ripe beurre bosc pears,
   unpeeled and quartered

1 Preheat the oven to slow 150°C (300°F/Gas 2). Line two shallow baking trays with foil and place a wire rack in each tray. In a large bowl, mix the kecap manis, soy sauce, sesame oil and five-spice powder.
2 Brush the pears all over with the soy mixture. Place apart, skin-side-down, in a single layer on the racks. Bake for 30 minutes. Brush the pears again with the marinade and continue baking for a further 30 minutes, or until tender and caramelized around the edges.
3 Serve the pears warm or at room temperature with cheese and biscuits.

NUTRITION PER SERVE
Protein 1 g; Fat 1 g; Carbohydrate 15 g; Dietary Fibre 2.5 g; Cholesterol 0 mg; 280 kJ (65 cal)

HINT: The foil will catch any excess drops of the soy mixture. If the mixture scorches or burns during cooking, replace the foil lining halfway through the cooking time.

NOTE: Kecap manis is an Indonesian sauce similar to—but sweeter than—soy sauce. It is generally flavoured with garlic and star anise.

Wash but don't peel the pears, then cut them into quarters. Be sure to use ripe pears.

Mix together the kecap manis, soy sauce, sesame oil and five-spice powder.

Arrange the pears, skin-side-down, in a single layer on the wire rack.

CAMEMBERT AND POTATO TERRINE

Preparation time: 1 hour + overnight refrigeration
Total cooking time: 50 minutes
Serves 8

1 kg (2 lb) new potatoes, unpeeled
3 Granny Smith apples
125 g (4 oz) butter
3 tablespoons olive oil
200 g (6¹/2 oz) Camembert, chilled and very thinly sliced
2 tablespoons chopped fresh parsley

1 Boil the potatoes in a large saucepan of salted water for about 15 minutes, or until soft. Drain and cool, then peel and cut into slices 1 cm (¹/2 inch) thick. Core and slice the apples into 5 mm (¹/4 inch) thick rounds. Heat half the butter and half the oil in a pan and cook the potato until just golden. Drain on paper towels. Heat the remaining butter and oil. Lightly fry the apple until golden. Drain on paper towels.
2 Line a 25 x 11 cm (10 x 4¹/2 inch) terrine with baking paper. Preheat the oven to moderate 180°C (350°F/Gas 4).
3 Arrange a layer of potato in the base of the terrine. Add a layer of apple and then Camembert. Sprinkle with the

parsley and season well. Build up the layers, finishing with potato.
4 Lightly oil a piece of foil and cover the terrine, sealing well. Put the terrine in a baking dish and half-fill the dish with water. Bake for 20 minutes. Remove from the oven and cover the terrine with a piece of cardboard. Put weights or food cans on top of the cardboard to compress the terrine. Refrigerate overnight. Turn out and cut into slices to serve.

NUTRITION PER SERVE
Protein 8 g; Fat 25 g; Carbohydrate 20 g;
Dietary Fibre 3 g; Cholesterol 65 mg;
1456 kJ (350 cal)

Slice the apples into thick rounds and fry in the butter and oil until golden.

Arrange the potato, apple and Camembert in layers in the terrine.

Cover the terrine with cardboard and put heavy tins on top to compress it overnight.

POTATO NOODLE NIBBLES

Preparation time: 30 minutes + cooling
Total cooking time: 40 minutes
Serves 4–6

450 g (14 oz) floury potatoes, chopped
40 g (1¼ oz) butter, softened
2 tablespoons grated Parmesan or Pecorino cheese
100 g (3½ oz) besan (chickpea) flour
2 teaspoons ground cumin
2 teaspoons garam masala
1 teaspoon ground coriander
1 teaspoon chilli powder
1 teaspoon cayenne pepper
1½ teaspoons ground turmeric
vegetable oil, for frying

1 Boil the potato until tender. Drain and cool for 15–20 minutes, then mash with the butter and cheese. Add the besan, cumin, garam masala, coriander, chilli powder, cayenne, turmeric and ¾ teaspoon of salt. Mix with a wooden spoon until a soft, light dough forms. Turn out and knead lightly 10–12 times, until smooth.
2 Fill a large pan with vegetable oil to a depth of at least 10 cm (4 inches) and heat to 190°C (375°F). Test the temperature by dropping a small ball of dough into the oil. It is ready if the dough rises straight to the surface.
3 Using a piping bag with a 1 cm (½ inch) star nozzle, pipe short lengths of dough into the oil, in manageable batches. They will rise to the surface and turn golden quickly. Remove them with a slotted spoon and drain on paper towels. Serve within 2 hours, as a snack or to accompany drinks.

NUTRITION PER SERVE (6)
Protein 7 g; Fat 15 g; Carbohydrate 20 g; Dietary Fibre 4 g; Cholesterol 20 mg; 1050 kJ (250 cal)

Boil the potato until tender and then mash with the butter and cheese.

Turn out the dough and knead lightly to give a smooth texture.

Pipe short lengths of the dough into the hot oil. They will rise to the surface immediately.

Index

USEFUL INFORMATION

The recipes in this book were developed using the Australian tablespoon measure of 20 ml. In the United States the tablespoon is 15 ml. Likewise, the Australian cup measures 250 ml and in the United States the cup is 240 ml. For most recipes this difference will not be noticeable but, for recipes using baking powder, gelatin, baking soda, small amounts of flour and cornstarch, we suggest that, if you are using the smaller tablespoon, you add an extra teaspoon for each tablespoon.

Liquid cup measures

1/4 cup	60 ml	2 fluid oz
1/3 cup	80 ml	2 3/4 fluid oz
1/2 cup	125 ml	4 fluid oz
3/4 cup	180 ml	6 fluid oz
1 cup	250 ml	8 fluid oz

Spoon measures

1/4 teaspoon	1.25 ml
1/2 teaspoon	2.5 ml
1 teaspoon	5 ml
1 tablespoon	20 ml

Nutritional Information

The nutritional information given for each recipe does not include any garnishes or accompaniments, such as rice or pasta, unless they are included in specific quantities in the ingredients list. The nutritional values are approximations and can be affected by biological and seasonal variations in foods, the unknown composition of some manufactured foods, and uncertainty in the dietary database. Nutrient data given are derived primarily from the NUTTAB95 database produced by the Australian New Zealand Food Authority.

Oven Temperatures

You may find cooking times vary depending on the oven you are using. For convection ovens, as a general rule, set oven temperature to 70°F lower than indicated in the recipe.

Note: Those who might be at risk from the effects of salmonella food poisoning (the elderly, pregnant women, young children, and those suffering from immune deficiency diseases) should not eat recipes containing raw eggs.

Weight

10 g	1/4 oz	220 g	7 oz	425 g	14 oz
30 g	1 oz	250 g	8 oz	475 g	15 oz
60 g	2 oz	275 g	9 oz	500 g	1 lb
90 g	3 oz	300 g	10 oz	600 g	1 1/4 lb
125 g	4 oz	330 g	11 oz	650 g	1 lb 5 oz
150 g	5 oz	375 g	12 oz	750 g	1 1/2 lb
185 g	6 oz	400 g	13 oz	1 kg	2 lb

British names		American names
bicarbonate of soda	—	baking soda
besan flour	—	chickpea flour
capsicum	—	red or green bell pepper
chickpeas	—	garbanzo beans
cornflour	—	cornstarch
fresh coriander	—	cilantro
single cream	—	cream
aubergine	—	eggplant
flat-leaf parsley	—	Italian parsley
hazelnut	—	filbert
minced beef	—	ground beef
plain flour	—	all-purpose flour
polenta	—	cornmeal
prawn	—	shrimp
Roma tomato		plum tomato
sambal oelek	—	chili paste
mangetout	—	snow pea
spring onion	—	scallion
thick cream	—	heavy cream
tomato purée	—	tomato paste
courgette	—	zucchini

THUNDER BAY
P · R · E · S · S

This edition published by **Thunder Bay Press**, an imprint of the Advantage Publishers Group, 5880 Oberlin Drive, San Diego, CA 92121-4794 www.advantagebooksonline.com

First published in 2001 by Murdoch Books, a division of Murdoch Magazines, GPO Box 1203, Sydney NSW 2001, Australia

Editor: Jane Price **Designer:** Annette Fitzgerald **Chief Executive:** Mark Smith

Copyright © Murdoch Books 2000 Printed in HONG KONG